D1187334

Upper Circle

The names of H. M. Tennent and 'Binkie' Beaumont conjure up an era when an apparently endless succession of star-studded plays with lavish sets and costumes dominated the West End stage, and names such as Edith Evans, Emlyn Williams, Vivien Leigh, Noël Coward, Margaret Rutherford and John Gielgud shared the bills with young 'discoveries' like Richard Burton, Mai Zetterling, Alan Badel, Brenda Bruce and Stanley Baker. For thirty years, from 1936 onwards, Binkie virtually controlled the London theatre, producing over 400 plays with, at one point, fifteen productions running simultaneously in London and the provinces. And yet, though the name is familiar, Binkie's story has never been told. He has remained a legendary figure known only to the upper circle of the theatrical profession – and to those who worked closely with him.

This is Kitty Black's unique vantage point. She joined Tennent's as a junior shorthand typist in 1937 and remained intimately involved with the organisation in increasingly influential posts until her departure to become a leading play agent in 1953. Here, then, is literally the inside story of that period: the end of the thirties with theatrical elegance at its peak; the war years, which brought their own special drama to the theatre; and the post-war launching of the famous Company of Four at the Lyric Hammersmith and its prestigious premieres of work by Arthur Miller, Peter Ustinov, Christopher Fry and the French playwrights Sartre and Anouilh, in translations by Kitty Black herself.

With twenty-four pages of photos, Kitty Black's chronicle of some of the most ebullient years in the life of the British theatre will provide instant nostalgia for those who saw these productions 'from the front' and will be an eye-opener to those for whom modern theatre begins with *Waiting for Godot*.

KITTY BLACK

UPPER CIRCLE

A Theatrical Chronicle

METHUEN · LONDON

For my friends pictured within –

and all the pussycats.

First published in Great Britain in 1984
by Methuen London Ltd
11 New Fetter Lane, London EC4P 4EE
Copyright © 1984 Kitty Black

Filmset, printed and bound in Great Britain

British Library Cataloguing in Publication Data

Black, Kitty
  Upper circle: a theatrical chronicle.
  1. Beaumont, Binkie   2. Theatrical producers
  and directors—Great Britain—Biography
  I. Title
  792'.092'4.   PN2598.B44/

  ISBN 0-413-51040-9

Contents

Illustrations

12 *The Seagull*: (*a*) Isabel Jeans and Ian Hunter (*b*) Mai Zetterling and Paul Scofield. (*c*) *Tuppence Coloured*: Max Adrian, John Heawood and the Emett front cloth (photo: Angus McBean).

13 (*a*) *The Reluctant Debutante*: Anna Massey finds happiness with Jack Merivale (*b*) the Lunts (*c*) *Troilus and Cressida* at the Memorial Theatre, Stratford-upon-Avon: Laurence Harvey, Anthony Quayle and Muriel Pavlow (photo: Angus McBean).

14 (*a*) *Captain Brassbound's Conversion*: Flora Robson, Malcolm Russell, with Michael Cacoyannis on the ground (*b*) *Heartbreak House*: Robert Donat and Deborah Kerr in a modern 'North West Passage' (*c*) *The Eagle Has Two Heads*: Eileen Herlie and James Donald (photo: Angus McBean).

15 (*a*) *Point of Departure*: Mai Zetterling and Dirk Bogarde (*b*) 'The Only Orpheus': Dirk Bogarde and Hugh Griffith (*c*) *Legend of Lovers*: Dorothy Maguire and Richard Burton. (Photos: Angus McBean and John Swope.)

16 Advertisement page from the *New York Herald Tribune* 23.12.51: one flop amid the successes.

17 Two designs: (*a*) Vivien Leigh's first act costume by Roger Furse for *The Skin of Our Teeth* (*b*) front cloth by Roland Pym for *Oranges and Lemons*. (Photos: Fatimah Namder (*a*) reproduced by kind permission of Allan Davis (*b*) from KB's collection.

18 (*a*) Alec Clunes in *The Lady's Not for Burning* (*b*) Yvonne Arnaud in *The Circle* (*c*) *Men Without Shadows*: Alan Rilbern, Sidney James, Philip Leaver, Hector MacGregor, Lyn Evans, Mary Morris – Aubrey Woods on the floor (photos: (*a*) Angus McBean (*b*) Cecil Beaton, reproduced courtesy of Southerly Publications Ltd).

19 Jeannetta Cochrane's everlasting costumes: (*a*) *Love for Love* (Rosalie Crutchley far right) (*b*) *The Relapse*: Cyril Ritchard surrounded; Jessie Evans and Paul Scofield are amused (*c*) *The Rehearsal*: Walter Plinge, Lockwood West, Diana Churchill, Maggie Smith, Robert Hardy, Alan Badel, Phyllis Calvert (photo: Angus McBean).

20 *The Soldier's Tale*. Libretto by C. F. Ramuz, translation by Michael Flanders and Kitty Black (photo: Scottish Tourist Board).

21 *Venice Preserv'd*: (*a*) John Gielgud and Eileen Herlie, 'Oh Mercy' (*b*) Paul Scofield and Pamela Brown (*c*) David Garrick and Mrs Cibber (photos: Angus McBean; E.T. Archive Ltd; Zoffany, reproduced courtesy of the Garrick Club).

22 (*a*) *Ring Round the Moon*: Daphne Newton, Mona Washbourne, Marie Löhr, William Mervyn, Paul Scofield, Claire Bloom and assorted flunkeys (*b*) *Irma La Douce*: Elizabeth Seal on the table hailed by Denis Quilley and pals (photo: Angus McBean).

23 (*a*) Lunch at the Villa Mauresque: Somerset Maugham, Vivienne Byerley, Alan Searle's back and KB. Picasso 'Harlequin gisant' on the wall. (*b*) J. B. Priestley at the BBC (photos: Illustrated; Jack Esten; BBC).

24 Four H. M. Tennent posters: (*a*) *George and Margaret* (*b*) the Gielgud season at the Haymarket (*c*) the Sartre plays at the Lyric, Hammersmith (*d*) *The Rehearsal* at the Globe.

The costume design for Puss in Boots on page 161 is reproduced by kind permission of Joan Jefferson Farjeon.

Acknowledgements

So many friends have helped in the compiling of this book that it would be impossible to list them all. However, particular thanks are due to Ray Mander, Joe Mitchenson and their incomparable theatre collection, Vivienne Byerley, Allan Davis, the *Daily Telegraph* information desk, and Sheila Formoy of H. M. Tennent Ltd. Also to the Shakespeare Birthplace Trust for supplying the photograph of Muriel Pavlow, Fatimah Namder for taking the pictures of the designs in Illustration 17, and the executors of the late Enid Bagnold for permission to quote the obituary of Hugh Beaumont on page 244. Special thanks go to the Managing Trustees of the Phoenix Trust for the grant which helped to meet the costs of research and even more special thanks to Angus McBean whose contributions to the photographic record decorates the whole chronicle.

Chapter **I**

Behind the box office of the Globe Theatre in Shaftesbury Avenue is probably the smallest lift in London. It holds two people if they squash up very tightly together, and leads directly up to the anteroom of what since 1936 has been the office of H. M. Tennent Ltd., the most prestigious English impresarios for over three decades. There on an afternoon of June, 1937, I attended in search of a job as junior shorthand typist at £3 a week. I shared the lift with an extremely handsome, dark-haired young man of about my own age and thought: "If this is the kind of thing that lies around this office, I'd better get this job." Well, I did, and he and I have been friends ever since. His name was and is Allan Davis – the director, among other successes, of the record-breaking *No Sex Please, We're British*, but at that time he was a mere stage manager and part of the great organisation I was aspiring to join.

My interview was with a small fair woman of about 40 – just old enough to be my mother, but there was never anything maternal about Elsie Beyer. Easily the most feared dragon in the business she had the usual reputation of being able to squeeze blood out of a stone, and in years to come was reputedly seen standing on the roof of the Globe Theatre, picking up the fire bombs as they fell and tossing them on to the roofs of the adjoining theatres. However, this again was to look far into the future and for the day in question she was merely concerned with my shorthand and typing speeds.

"Two hundred and ten words a minute, and eighty," I replied. "But I can do about one hunded and seventy words a minute in French and I'm virtually bilingual."

Impassively Elsie made a note. She wore blue tinted glasses, but even without them she would have given nothing away. Later she admitted that she had quite simply not believed me.

"Business experience?"

"Three weeks in an advertising office in Cape Town."

"You will be required to do the filing, take my letters and do any other general office work. The firm consists of Mr Tennent, whose secretary I am, Miss Gibbs, who works for Mr Beaumont, one of our directors, and myself. We can't offer you £3 a week, I'm afraid, but we'll start you at £2.10s and then after a month on approval, if you're satisfactory, we will raise your salary to £2.15s. The hours are ten to six, Saturdays ten to one, and you'll have a fortnight's paid holiday a year. Is that acceptable?"

Acceptable? I couldn't believe it. I had come prepared to offer all kinds of additional qualifications – music diplomas, years of theatre-going on both sides of the Atlantic and all over Europe, to say nothing of seeing *Peter Pan* at His Majesty's Theatre in Johannesburg at the age of six, an experience that had left me stage-struck for life, but that was it. In due course I received a letter typed on the famous embossed H. M. Tennent paper with the logo created by Gladys Calthrop, who designed all the settings for Noël Coward's plays – the initials stamped in the four spaces of the X formed by crossing a fool's bauble with the torch of drama – telling me to start on 19 July. Although I have kept the letter, I don't need it to remind me of the date, for it was my youngest brother's birthday and oddly enough it was to become a memorable day throughout my theatrical career. (My own birthday, April 30th, coincided with various famous openings, thus giving me a cast iron argument for being allocated first night seats.)

On 19 July I duly presented myself at the office, paying my respects to Miss Gibbs (with whom I was to share the outer office), the telephonist, Margaret Morris (known to everyone as Morrie, who presided over the plug-and-cord switchboard in an inner area totally devoid of fresh air and sunlight), the office boy, Banks (an ebullient youth of about fifteen, in the truly Dickensian tradition of the bouncy Cockney, who proved to have an uncanny talent for copying newspaper photographs in very dark pencil), and the large desk which was to become my second home for the next eight years.

The Tennent office is, as I have said, at the top of the Globe Theatre, on the same level as the back of the Upper Circle,

and the lay-out was simple, if forbidding. The lift opened directly on to a small landing, where stood a row of filing cabinets, a mahogany settee and a table with theatrical magazines. This was divided from the switchboard area by a glass door through which only a privileged few were allowed to pass unannounced, and beyond that were two adjacent doors, one to Elsie Beyer's office and the other to Hugh Beaumont's. Both doors always stood open for easy communication between those two, but if either door was closed, it meant they were busy and no one – but no one – was allowed to enter without first ascertaining the nature of the business. Mr Tennent presided over everything on an upper floor, which again had a small anteroom, where briefly, years later, for some unhappy weeks I was banished.

There was an old-fashioned bell display panel in the outer office, like in a Victorian house – I have one in the kitchen of my own home, though it hasn't worked since I have lived there – and a glance showed who was ringing for attention. One ring meant Miss Gibbs was wanted, two were for Banks, so naturally my signal became three bells, at which I would pick up my stenotype machine, a notebook and pencil, and report to whichever room needed my services.

That first morning it was Elsie Beyer who pressed the button. When I sat down to take her dictation she looked at my little gadget in amazement.

"What's that?"

"A stenotype machine. A French invention, but it's being used more and more in England."

She looked at me suspiciously.

"Can't you do Pitman shorthand?"

"Yes," I replied. "But I can only do about 100 words a minute. With this I can do verbatim reporting speed . . ."

"Very well," she said. "Now, write to . . ."

And we were off. She dictated perhaps half a dozen letters, handed me the correspondence, and then said: "I don't think Mr Tennent will like the noise that machine makes."

I returned to my desk and was reflecting miserably that I had probably been written off as unsatisfactory when the bell pealed three times. Mr Tennent. Very startled I picked up 'Axel', my machine, and climbed the stairs.

3

"I hear you use a very interesting gadget," said Mr Tennent. "How does it work?"

I showed him. The principle is very simple. Unlike a typewriter, a stenotype's 21 keys strike straight forward just like a piano, with the result that the letters are spaced out on the ribbon of paper that is fed automatically from a lower spool to an upper. As capital letters are used, after a little practice anyone can read back the imprint and even use the machine once they grasp the principle. Words are broken up into syllables, and as all the keys can be pressed simultaneously, these syllables are "struck" like so many chords on the piano. Mr Tennent, an accomplished musician, had no difficulty in picking up the idea and was absolutely delighted with his own skill and the new invention. In no time at all, far from being told to confine myself to Pitman's, my stenotype became the latest talking point in the office and every new V.I.P. had to be given a demonstration, the pianists among them, like Noël Coward, immediately demanding to be allowed to use it, to their infinite satisfaction.

Harry Moncrieff Tennent, who had given his name to the firm, was in his late fifties at that time. A tall, grey-haired figure, with horn-rimmed glasses, he held himself extremely erect and strode about like an ex-guardsman. He had worked for Broadwood's when he came down from Oxford and was an excellent musician. Indeed, with Christopher Hassall as lyricist, he had written several standards, among them Rudy Vallee's theme song, 'Your Time Is My Time', and the popular 'When You and I Were 17'. After the first world war Tennent became booking manager for Moss' Empires, Ltd., and worked for them until 1931, when he switched to the equally prestigious firm of Howard & Wyndham in a similar capacity. In 1933 he joined the new firm of Moss' Empires Tours and Howard & Wyndham, a producing company created to supply starring attractions for the two major touring circuits in England, or rather, Great Britain, for Howard & Wyndham owned the King's Theatres in Edinburgh and Glasgow, as well as the Theatre Royal in Newcastle and many others. The Empires referred to were obviously the theatres in Birmingham, Sunderland, and elsewhere, all enormous, and all needing quality productions to see them through the year.

The firm with the unwieldy name had been tremendously successful, producing among other things *Call It A Day* by Dodie Smith – for which my friend Allan Davis had been stage manager – *Jill Darling*, a musical starring Arthur Riscoe and Frances Day with John Mills as juvenile lead, as well as *The Wind and The Rain* by Merton Hodge, the play about medical students that had predated the *Doctor In The House* series.

Hugh Beaumont had been invited to join the firm by the managing director, 'old' Mr Cruickshank, who had spotted his talent and declared that he would rather have him on his own side than against him. Elsie Beyer had been Harry Tennent's secretary, and when he moved from Piccadilly House to the Globe to set up his own organisation, she had followed him, together with Hugh Beaumont, whom everybody in the theatre always referred to as Binkie. Elsie adored them both – Harry as the great man he was, but Binkie with a fierce possessiveness which at times was very frightening. Eventually, when her nose had been put out of joint – as mine was to be – by new arrivals in the office, she was loaned out to Laurence Olivier's first tour of Australia, but as her job was filled during her absence she stayed on in Australia and became the general manager of the Elizabethan Theatre Trust.

When I met him, Binkie was in his mid-twenties and had a curious background. Born Hughes Griffiths Morgan, in 1908, the illegitimate son of a respectable Welsh timber merchant, he was one of the most beautiful young men I ever saw. Medium height, with pale blue eyes and a startlingly white skin of magnolia petal quality, he dressed impeccably, mostly in dark blue or light grey, with white shirts and pale blue or grey ties – I never saw him wear stripes or a pattern – and was always immaculate. His mother took in theatrical lodgers and gave him the pet name which stuck for the rest of his life. Always stagestruck Binkie gravitated to the theatre at an early age, beginning as a call-boy at the Prince of Wales Theatre, Cardiff, reputedly at the age of twelve. A friend of his elder half-brother Jack remembers the good looking little boy, wearing an Eton collar, helping in the box office when he could barely see over the counter, and Ivor Novello, who lived in the same street in Cardiff, always gave him help and encouragement. By the time he was twenty, Binkie was business manager for

Aubrey Smith's touring company and the following year worked for Philip Ridgeway at the Little Theatre in Barnes, where the young John Gielgud played Baron Tusenbach in a production of *Three Sisters* by Komisarjevsky. He moved on to the Duke of York's Theatre before joining Harry and the production company.

Binkie had a passion for very weak China tea and as often as not the bell summons would be for another pot of the wishy-washy stuff which he continued to pour out long after it appeared to be stone cold.

By this time his mother had married again, a portly charac-ter called Schwerzee whom Binkie hated, though he seemed pleasant enough. Mrs Schwerzee was a frequent visitor to the office but showed no sign of having provided her son with his good looks and studied elegance.

Once, a few years later, when we were trying out a play in Cardiff I returned ahead of the party to the Angel Hotel (known to its theatrical clientele as the Devil Hotel), and was informed by the receptionist that a man was enquiring for Mr Beaumont. Addressing myself to the caller I enquired if I could help him.

"I'm his secretary," I announced.

"I don't think so," was his reply. "I'm his brother."

And that was the only time I met one of Binkie's Morgan relations. There seemed very little physical resemblance, and I don't remember any other contact between them, though there was some legal correspondence in connection with a block of brewery shares, which made Binkie grin appreci-atively. As a bastard of course he wouldn't have been entitled to any part of the inheritance but nobody had established that fact officially so, as he put it, "there was I kicking on the coverlet and nobody said a word." He got his brewery shares.

When he furnished his first flat it was in the school of Sibyl Colefax and pickled everything – a horrible fashion which resulted in the destruction of a good many priceless antiques. Years later, when he had learnt a good deal more about furniture, he showed me a Chippendale mirror that had suffered at the hands of the ubiquitous strippers which he was now having restored to its original colour. By the time he died he had collected a fortune in antiques, each piece more beauti-

ful than the next.

His current boy friend when I first met him was a certain Donald . . . an extremely personable and charming young man, very much upper-class, who eventually joined the army and went overseas with the B.E.F. Sadly he was reported missing after Dunkirk and months of agony went by before the news came that he had been taken prisoner. Communication with the P.O.W.s was by special Red Cross forms, one a month being allowed to each prisoner. Donald's mother sent one of these precious documents to Binkie, but by that time he had fallen in love with someone else and the form remained tucked into a corner of his blotter for the rest of the war. Finally Donald's camp was liberated but the column of prisoners was bombed and he was killed. When the news came through, Binkie took the Red Cross form, tore it across and dropped it in his waste paper basket. He never mentioned the matter again.

Tennent's had been launched after three years of highly profitable productions, but in the first eight months of trading under the new name they lost their entire capital with a succession of flops. Then when the lowest ebb seemed to have been reached, Elise Beyer attended a Sunday night performance of *George and Margaret* by an actor, Gerald Savory, a domestic comedy which nobody had thought much of, and which had been given to the Repertory Players to try out. Elsie immediately bought the rights, the play transferred to Wyndham's Theatre, became a smash-hit and the tide in the firm's fortunes was turned. One of my first bonuses was to be told I could have free seats for the firm's plays whenever I liked. It made a nice change to be sitting in the stalls instead of queuing for the pit or gallery.

The first month went by, the five shillings were duly added to my salary (the first week's pay had had to be handed over to the agency who had found me the job) and I realised that I had at last found the thing I most wanted to do in life. Not only was the theatre my abiding passion, but I was actually going to be allowed to earn my living by working in it. The square peg had found the square hole and I was supremely happy.

Chapter **II**

The path to the theatre lift could perhaps be said to have started on the sands at Muizenberg, a seaside resort outside Cape Town, immortalised in Kipling's poem about the national flowers of the British Empire. Here my father, newly arrived from England, fell in love at first sight with my mother, not surprising as she was on horseback, tall and slim, riding side-saddle of course, her skirt draped becomingly below a nineteen-inch waist.

My father was one of thirteen – only, to use his own expression, "luckily five died", in one of those Victorian diphtheria epidemics that emptied the nursery, though this didn't seem to have inhibited the parents who set to work immediately to provide replacements. They even used two of the original names again.

As my mother was one of nine, it was perhaps surprising that their own offspring numbered a mere half-dozen. Five in as many years and then a four-year gap. So when I popped out, the news was duly flashed to the grandparents in England. I have the copy of the cable still – a silky buff-coloured sheet of opaque paper. "The second little daughter so much wanted arrived last night. A fine little girl exactly like her father." For personal reasons this was regrettable, for my father, though a fine-looking man with sandy hair, was no kind of model for a girl, whereas my mother was a ravishing brunette with huge velvety brown eyes and such charm that she bowled over anyone who met her.

The Black family originally hailed from Tullynessle in Perthshire, so when my grandfather moved to London he somewhat pretentiously called his Wandsworth Common villa 'Dhu House', and, like Harry Tennent later, went to work for Broadwood's. As his wife, Elizabeth, was busy producing babies, his eldest daughter Elizabeth (known to us as Auntie Duckie) accompanied him to concerts and operatic

8

performances, including all the original Wagner first nights conducted by Hans Richter. Auntie Duckie was supposed to have visited Germany as a music student and stayed with Clara Schumann, who one day entertained Brahms to tea, but this is probably a family *canard* or, as it took place in Darmstadt, should perhaps more properly be called an *Ente*. However, one family legend is incontrovertible, and that was the presence of Auntie Duckie at the Crystal Palace among the altos to give the first performance of 'Land of Hope and Glory' with Clara Butt as soloist – the ink on the hand-written parts scarcely dry.

Another sister, Gertrude, was one of the first women to graduate from Girton and possessed a formidable intellect. A younger brother became a doctor and ended as head of the College of Surgeons in Singapore, while a cousin, Trixie Philip, whose father had sculpted part of the Albert Memorial, married first Godwin, the father of Ellen Terry's children, and then, when he died, James McNeill Whistler. So with all this cultural background the parental rage can be imagined when my father, the eldest son, apprenticed himself to a carpenter for three years at a salary of six shillings a week for the first year, eight shillings the second and ten shillings the third. 'Carpenter' seems to have been an understatement, for Mr Johnson, his boss, taught him the building craft so thoroughly that once out of his indentures my father was able to find immediate employment with, among others, Mr Bovis, founder of the firm that still bears his name. All of which meant that when he decided to go out to South Africa in 1896 to seek his fortune (his younger brother hinted that he had had to fly the country as a result of too-ardent amorous activities) he went armed with a sheaf of testimonials covering his proficiency in matters ranging from road-paving to the installation of domestic hot water.

Having picked "the dearest wife of his heart" as he called her in one of his letters (her name was Elizabeth, wouldn't you know), he proceeded to build her a very attractive bungalow – with a Dutch gable to remind her of her native Cape Province – in Yeovil, an outlying suburb of Johannesburg (another wing had to be added to accommodate the growing family) with a big back garden, laundry, stabling, servants' quarters,

and some extra land on the other side of the road intended for a tennis court but where, in the meantime, the horses and a cow were comfortably installed. He set up as a quantity surveyor, an occupation then considered fairly humble compared to the gentlemanly pursuit of architecture, but, by force of personality and tremendous efficiency, he rapidly gained recognition for his profession and ended as the first chairman of the newly formed association of quantity surveyors.

Business flourished, social events abounded, and in addition to everything else he became the first secretary of the new Johannesburg Golf Club, while my mother became a very useful medium-length handicap player.

Two years after their marriage, he brought his bride and eldest son to England to meet his parents, with the result that my sister was born at Sandown in the Isle of Wight – I used to think her delicate constitution resulted from the debilitating effects of the English climate. Whatever the reason, she was tiny and anaemic, with a mane of dark red auburn hair, my mother's pride and joy; but wiseacres shook their heads and said the glorious stuff was taking all the child's strength. As a teenager she could actually sit on it, but my mother couldn't bear to have it cut until just before her death soon after her twentieth birthday.

In 1910 the family moved to Pretoria, where the Union Buildings were being constructed, as my father was working for M.C.A. Meischke, one of the sub-contractors employed by Herbert Baker on this £700,000 project. Such was his reputation that my father was appointed General Manager for the entire scheme, and soon afterwards was given the same job in connection with the construction of the new City Hall in Johannesburg, at a cost of some £340,000, so that simultaneously he was responsible for the two largest building contracts undertaken in South Africa up to that time.

His fees amounted to the satisfactory sum of £10,000, and, with this in hand, after four years the family returned to Johannesburg where the following April I was born. As the birth of each child had always been marked by the gift of a diamond, this time my mother received a large uncut gem (known as a "virgin" stone) from the Premier mine in Pretoria, which was subsequently cut and set as a $3\frac{1}{2}$ carat

pendant in Amsterdam. Later I too was to acquire a "virgin" stone, and they do have a rather special aura for their owners as compared to your over-the-counter stuff.

The First World War didn't affect our family particularly; apart from the requisitioning of the carriage horses – the boys were too young and my father too old to be called up – but in any case by 1917 he had contracted Hodgkin's disease. My mother, and the family doctor, Paul Pettavel, who had brought all of us (except my sister) into the world, had to face an agonising period of twelve months while they watched him being destroyed.

Eventually he died on my fourth birthday, an event which has clouded that anniversary ever since, and my mother set up as a single parent to raise her six children, the hand that had rocked the cradle occasionally having to wield the sjambok. In turn, the boys went away to boarding school at Grahamstown in Natal, the third son even leaving for Dartmouth to join the Navy at the age of thirteen, and my sister went as a boarder to the branch of Roedean that had been set up in a neighbouring suburb to introduce South African girls to the joys of a classic English education. The resulting loneliness made my mother keep me at home with a governess, so from the age of six I became the sole object of the attentions of a Miss Good, sister to King George V's racing expert, and the epitome of the Victorian/Edwardian maiden lady. She taught the usual subjects, including music, French and needlework, and had hay fever which made her sneeze exactly thirteen times whenever she suffered an attack – I used to count in absolute fascination, especially if, as occasionally happened, we would get up to twelve, followed by a long pause, but the thirteenth invariably followed. Memories of the schoolroom include rows of sopping wet handkerchiefs draped over the fireguard while Goodie punctuated her spasms with the only rude expression she allowed herself, "Dash it." "Dash it." "Atishoo – atishoo – dash it – atishoo – dash it –" and so on. When I was about nine, a faith healer set up in Johannesburg and everyone flocked to his miraculous seances. Believe it or not, he 'cured' Goodie, who never sneezed again. I only wish he had been able to cure my chilblains.

From the moment she was engaged, Goodie became the

object of my childish affection, for my mother was by then completely wrapped up in my ailing sister, and I embarked on the joyous business of learning under the guidance of someone for whom teaching was the natural extension of her daily life. No one who has not experienced the full-time attention of an adult can imagine how much can be crammed into any given twenty four hours, and in an era before television and wireless, the reading of books aloud was part of every evening's enjoyment.

Soon my piano playing began to expand beyond Goodie's modest talents and I moved on to lessons with a formidable lady, Miss Hyams, under whose guidance I passed an annual grade of the Trinity College of Music exams which were held in July (the depth of winter for us, ensuring that my chilblains would be at their very worst), each success rewarded with a feast of oysters and Guinness at the Trocadero Restaurant in downtown Johannesburg. By the time I was twelve, Mother felt I needed competition and I followed my sister as a boarder to Roedean, where my classmate and dormitory neighbour, Nora Coaton, became my "best friend" and academic rival. Later, when she qualified as an architect, Nora asked her first Clerk of Works if he remembered my father. "Oh yes, indeed," replied the expert. "Francis Black was the only man who could convince me $11\frac{1}{2}$ inches made a foot." I always felt I would have liked my father.

Although everyone complained of the lack of theatrical entertainment in South Africa we were always taken to the annual pantomime at His Majesty's Theatre (now, alas, a supermarket), but I absolutely hated the inconsistencies in the story, and was once scared out of my wits at finding Dick Whittington's cat perched on the balustrade beside me. To the disgusted embarrassment of my brothers, my screams necessitated my immediate removal, and I didn't change my dislike of the theatre until I was taken to see *Peter Pan*. From then on I was hooked and, with anyone who was available, would act out scenes from the Never-never Land by the hour, or dramatise all the incidents from whatever book I happened to be reading.

I was taken to see Sybil Thorndike and Lewis Casson in the repertoire they presented in 1926 – *Jane Clegg*, *The Lie*, *Medea*,

Macbeth and *The Trojan Women*, as well as Arthur Bouchier in *Treasure Island* just before his death, Irene Vanbrugh in *Miss Nell of New Orleans*, and Angela Baddeley and Glen Byam Shaw in a series of popular successes. At Roedean, a play was improvised every Saturday night – you would be given the assignment in the morning, must choose the story, collect your cast and rehearse them during the afternoon, picking out costumes from the dressing-up box, and then entertain your colleagues after supper. Each term one of the three houses put on a properly rehearsed play, and once a year we did an open-air Shakespeare in the main courtyard – yelling our lungs out against a background of screening trees. After giving my all as Sir Andrew Aguecheek it was a little disconcerting to be asked by one of my brothers, "Everyone else wore cushions on their fronts to look like stomachs. Why did you wear yours on your behind?"

Sadly, after only two years it all came to an end – my mother decided to come to London to be with the rest of the family who by now were involved in University life and I was dumped in a private school near St. Albans which was supposed to turn me into a lady but which instead turned out to be a total nightmare. Still, there were consolations – my new piano teacher was a genius, my first London show was *Funny Face* with Fred and Adele Astaire, and, as soon as I could, I passed my University entrance exams and escaped to a finishing school in Paris where the diction teacher who came on Monday afternoons was Georges Leroy, a sociétaire of the Comédie Française and the eventual professor of the medal-winning lady who changed her name to Edwige Feuillière.

The finishing school, which took seven pupils, was situated in Auteuil, in the Rue Poussin, and run by a dynamic blonde called Marguerite Vincent, known to all as Guégué, and physically rather like Elsie Beyer. Her two passions were history and the theatre, she was an ardent Royalist, and took us to a play or opera at least once a week with visits to the Louvre and other museums on Tuesdays and Fridays. Her most illustrious ex-pupil was Daphne du Maurier, and she had a passion for England and things English that was a little unusual among French intellectuals of that time. So outspoken was she on the subject that during the war, when she was able

to cross into the unoccupied zone for a short holiday, she sat down to write to all her ex-pupils (including me) to explain that France must not be held responsible for the weaknesses of the Pétain government, but as a fellow holidaymaker betrayed her correspondence, on her return to Paris she was arrested and sentenced to six months imprisonment. She found the whole experience enthralling because she was sent to La Force, the women's prison where Marie Antoinette was first held before being transferred to the Conciergerie and nearly all her fellow prisoners were prostitutes, who were able to have intercourse with the men in the adjoining block through an iron grille separating the lavatories in the two sections.

Her first words to me, in June 1945 when I was able to cross to Paris, were not in any way connected with the terrible experiences through which we had both lived, but a violent diatribe against the pretentiousness of Jean-Louis Barrault's production of *Antony and Cleopatra*, though she added I must on no account miss it; his performance as Eros was my first introduction to that remarkable and controversial young man.

Those Paris school days covered the period when international singers such as Frieda Leider, Lotte Lehmann, Lauritz Melchior, Herbert Janssen and Jussi Björling were the stars of the operatic scene, with native talent including the exquisite Eida Noréna, Georges Thil and André Baugé demonstrating French technique to perfection (no one I have heard since has come within a mile of Baugé's Figaro). My music teacher by this time was one Marthe Rennesson, who had been a friend of Debussy; she talked me out of going up to Oxford, persuading me instead to persevere with my piano, with the result that, after acquiring my *premier prix à l'unanimité*, gave my first public recital when I was seventeen in the tiny hall of the Maison Pleyel where, in the Grande Salle on a stiflingly hot June night, Guégué and I had been present at the fairwell concert of the piano trio formed by Cortot, Thiébault and Casals.

The theatre offered Sacha Guitry, then married to Yvonne Printemps, in a series of his own plays, Pierre Fresnay in the Marcel Pagnol trio of *Marius, Fanny* and *César*, while the Comédie Française was led by Cécile Sorel and Albert Lambert *fils* (both over seventy) with Marie Bell and Madeleine Renaud

among the juveniles. By the rules of the Société (laid down by Napoleon in collaboration with Talma in the Emperor's tent outside Moscow), the senior members of the company played the leading roles by right, so one evening we were treated to a memorable experience when the two septuagenarians played the young lovers in Victor Hugo's *Marion de Lorme*. Even the long-suffering Parisians appreciated the absurdity; soon after-wards Gaston Baty took over the theatre direction and blew fresh air through the dusty crevices of the Maison de Molière.

The Johannesburg house was sold, and Mother and I travelled for the next four years, with stops to hear Mengelberg and the Concertgebouw in Amsterdam, *Tann-häuser* at the Vienna Opera House, conducted by Weingartner, and trips to Canada and America, with the Lunts in *Idiot's Delight*, Helen Hayes in *Victoria Regina*, and on Good Friday *Parsifal* at the Met. (no applause allowed). I made my curtsey to Queen Mary in white satin and ostrich feather fan, enjoyed the racing from the Royal Enclosure at Ascot, and attended the Jubilee Ball at Buckingham Palace in 1935 together with the crowned heads of Europe, the Diplomatic Corps and every dignitary from the British Empire wearing a dazzling assort-ment of jewels and decorations.

In addition there was a long cruise to the West Indies and South America, a year in South Africa to visit my aunts, and at last a London home.

Sober reflection had proved the impossibility of earning a living as a concert pianist, so the invention of Stenotyping provided the ideal answer. Armed with a certificate of profi-ciency I signed on with the only agency in London that was prepared to find me a secretarial job. The way to the Globe was open.

One evening, many years later, I was holidaying in the South of France with my usual companions, Dorothy Mather and Vivienne Byerley. We were staying at a small hotel in St. Raphael and one excursion included lunch with Somerset Maugham at the Villa Mauresque, after which we drove over the Italian border to San Remo to eat pasta and fill the boot with duty-free gin. It was well after midnight when we started the drive back (my car) and the other two realised I was in grave danger of falling asleep. In self-defence they hit on the

idea of asking me to tell them the story of my life as the best means of keeping me awake and I embarked on the gist of the above. It certainly got us back in one piece.

Chapter III

Arriving at the Globe as a stage-struck theatregoer, I soon
discovered how little of the organisation behind a production
is known to the public, and that the office was merely the
epicentre, or perhaps the spider at the heart of the web,
directing a multiplicity of operations fanning out in all directions and involving every possible branch of the theatrical
discipline.

First there were the authors or literary agents who submitted scripts, introduced the writers and eventually negotiated a
contract by which they would receive royalties based on the
box office takings, and an advance – usually £100, a sum that
remained the same over the next twenty years. This gave the
management a six months' option on the play which could be
renewed; what the author was supposed to live on in the
meantime was never discussed. These documents were always
printed and ran to some dozen or fifteen pages – just as well, I
thought, with all those forasmuchases and heretofores – but all
the other contracts were typed in the office. Mr Parker, a
plump little man with glasses, would arrive from Howard &
Wyndham with the investors' details, and I would be set to
work typing on very thick legal paper with red lined margins,
eventually tied up with pink or green string, listing the
amount each individual or firm would subscribe towards the
cost of production, giving the capitalisation of each play and
the percentage the investment represented. Once the production costs were recovered, 60 per cent of the profits would be
allocated to the investors and 40 per cent to the management.
Production costs varied between £2,000 and £5,000, and the
'nut' – to use the American term – was supposed to be
recovered in ten weeks at the most. Successful plays could pay
off their production costs during a preliminary tour, and a run
of six months in London was considered highly satisfactory. If
a play lasted for a year the rejoicings were tremendous –

extravagant parties would celebrate the event at the Savoy Hotel, and everyone would give and receive anniversary presents.

As far as the actors were concerned, the firm had a special arrangement with Equity whereby they wrote their own elegantly phrased contracts instead of using the official printed forms, beginning with "We have pleasure in engaging you . . ." and ending with "all other terms and conditions shall be according to the Equity contract", which saved me an awful lot of additional typing. Signatures were over a sixpenny stamp, which turned a piece of paper into a legal document, and the stamp book, kept by Banks, faithfully recorded these and all other items of expenditure down to the ultimate halfpenny.

All the firm's scenery was built by Brunskill & Loveday, an expert organisation that managed to make the Tennent sets seem more solid than any turned out by rival contractors. A special feature was always the mahogany doors, which could be used singly or in pairs and became almost the firm's hallmark in the fashionable drawing-room settings that practically every play seemed to require. The flats would then go to Alick Johnstone's studios for painting – work which was carried out by a team of brilliant artists. When they had finished, the three-dimensional effect was perfect – look at any of the Cecil Beaton photographs of John Gielgud's *Love For Love* at the Haymarket and see if you can separate the mouldings from the painted sections. Even watered and damask wallpapers could be copied with incredible perfection, the leading expert in this line being a young Japanese.

Costumes, period and modern, were supplied by B. J. Simmons, Nathan's, Fox's and later Berman's. Apart from one or two favourites, none of the stars wore couture clothes, the firm preferring to use stage designers after one disastrous episode. A lovely minor actress in a party scene had worn a Schiaparelli creation which had cost £300 (an enormous sum in those days) and was guaranteed to be unique, but Marlene Dietrich appeared in the audience on the first night wearing a duplicate, and the rage and fury on both sides of the curtain can be easily imagined.

London theatres only possessed skeleton lighting – some of

the touring houses seemed to have even less than that – so extra equipment was hired from the Strand Electric, and their tiny managing director, Stanley Earnshaw, was a frequent visitor to the office.

Publicity was handled by 'Popie' (W. Macqueen-Pope), whose large imposing figure was usually to be seen leaning against Morrie's counter as he waited to be given instructions, or to show a set of the latest photographs which needed the bosses' approval before being sent out to the press or framed for the front of house. His assistant, another tall man, was Harold Conway, later a dramatic critic on the *Evening News*, and Popie became the historian of Drury Lane and wrote several theatrical memoirs and volumes of reminiscences.

Harry Tennent was also managing director of Drury Lane and had been responsible for launching Ivor Novello on his incredible string of successes there. In one book, Popie relates how Harry invited Ivor to lunch at the Ivy and told him the Board were desperate for a new production, whereupon Ivor launched into an impromptu description of a show which was eventually staged as *Glamorous Night*. It was an immediate hit and ran from May to November, when it had to give way to the annual pantomime. Ivor's second production, *Careless Rapture*, had just finished its run when I joined the firm, but *Crest of the Wave* went into rehearsal soon afterwards, and we all attended the dress rehearsal at the end of August. Christopher Hassall was the lyricist, and the scenic effects were tremendous – a pleasure cruiser turned into a battleship, and a train rushed by with 'real' steam pouring from its engine and 'crashed' spectacularly. Splendid stuff and far more exciting than anything the movies could offer. Think how many scenes in the early talkies were supposed to take place in a theatre – the Hollywood moguls were obviously as stage-struck as any of us theatre fans at the time.

Although most cinemas by now had disbanded their orchestras in favour of mighty Wurlitzers, the electronic organs whose keyboards rose from the old orchestra pits under a galaxy of coloured lights, the theatres still had live musicians for their overture and interval music. Leslie Bridgewater, operating from the Haymarket, arranged or composed all such music and engaged the necessary musicians for any

theatre that was housing a Tennent production. Binkie described Leslie's music as 'plinkety-plonk', and in the office he was privately known as Leslie Ditchwater, but the quality of his musicians was always high, as the finest artists didn't mind accepting this somewhat lowly work since it was well paid, not too onerous and, as the orchestra pits were usually covered over, could be undertaken anonymously, out of sight of the audience. In fact, during the war, when recording sessions and BBC work were at their lowest ebb, the Haymarket boasted a trio composed of Alfredo Campoli, Anthony Pini and Leslie himself, a group who would normally be commanding the highest fees as soloists or leaders of their own particular sections.

Each production had its own company manager, and a stage director, who was responsible not only for the technical details of the show but who also carried a brief to see that the actors did not deviate from the production as created by the director, or as he was then called, the producer. The stage director took understudy rehearsals and usually stood in for one or two of the senior roles himself, if he didn't actually walk on as a butler or chauffeur with a couple of lines at most to speak. Each production had its wardrobe mistress, master carpenter, property master and electrician, though these might be attached to the individual London house and were in reality paid by the bricks and mortar management. Of course, if a play went on tour 'prior to London', a duplicate team would be recruited, and as there were always tours going out before or after the London run, the staff was moved around like pieces in a Rubik cube in an endeavour to keep them in continuous employment. Much the same was true of the actors, to such an extent that one youth asking for advice as to how to break into the 'magic circle' was told, "You don't get a job with H. M. Tennent, you inherit it," a gibe that held more than a grain of truth.

All wardrobe requirements were under the direction of Lily Taylor, a diminutive figure who had worked on the famous Oliver Messel production of *Helen* which C. B. Cochran had produced at the Adelphi Theatre – the first achievement of that remarkable young man. Lily told me that before the opening they had had a week of dress rehearsals during which none of

the wardrobe staff had left the theatre, merely dropping off to sleep in odd corners when they couldn't keep their eyes open for a moment longer. She taught me the phrase, "You reach the limit of human endurance and then you start the dress rehearsal . . ." and through the years I've seen this paradox proved over and over again.

The job of negotiating salaries was divided between Binkie and Elsie – the star's percentage was pretty standard, and never higher than 10 per cent of the gross, the only delicate negotiations being over the question of billing. Each feature player's salary was negotiable, based on what he or she had received during their last engagement, but for the lesser players the expression would be "and the money is . . ." with no question of argument. Elsie was responsible for engaging the stage management staff, fixing the company managers, wardrobe mistresses and technicians. It was here that she earned her reputation for hard bargaining, not giving away a penny more than was absolutely necessary and checking every last petty cash statement or weekly expense account to make sure nobody was getting away with any hanky-panky.

While Harry concentrated on the bricks and mortar managements, Binkie used his charm and incredible energy on the stars, male and female, who guaranteed the success of the productions, wooed authors, directors and agents who provided the raw materials, and his diary was crammed with lunch dates and supper engagements. The Ivy and Scott's were favourite venues (Scott's in its original position in Coventry Street), while the Grill Room at the Savoy was much patronised for after-theatre suppers. Performances began at 8.30 or 8.45, and the supper parties would continue until two o'clock or later as a matter of course. Where Binkie found the energy to carry on all his nocturnal activities as well as his daytime labours was a secret he kept to himself, and I have also heard that he was a dedicated poker player, keeping it up sometimes all through the night. I could well imagine those blue eyes giving nothing away while he treated the card game much as he did the wheeling and dealing he was carrying on in the cut-throat business of the theatre world.

Elsie would be occupied with some of the lesser feature players and a list of special friends, including Murray Mac-

donald, the producer, who kept a small stable of 'oldies' whom he escorted to their or his dying day. Our bank manager arrived in the office every morning from the Midland in Leicester Square to take Elsie out for coffee (his daughter had briefly held my job but had failed to measure up to the required standard), leaving me free to concentrate on the younger players. So began a series of friendships with the rising generation, among them very specially Muriel Pavlow and Dulcie Gray, and it was through them that I really began to feel part of the magic world that existed behind the footlights and the painted scenery.

Although nothing compared to the activities of later years, even in 1937 the office seemed never to have a dull moment. Elsie Beyer opened the post and distributed it between her own, Binkie's and Harry Tennent's desks, while Banks the office boy emptied filing baskets and sorted out the papers. On Monday mornings I entered the figures of each production's receipts in a big loose-leafed folder ('the returns book') which thus recorded the fortunes and vicissitudes of every play, whether in London or on tour. Unfortunately these invaluable records have disappeared, otherwise they would have provided historians with the handiest possible terms of reference.

Every morning George, the linkman – a lovely eighteenth-century name for the uniformed commissionaire who stood outside the theatre as the audience arrived, taking his name from the boys who held the flaring torches (links) lighting the rich in their sedan chairs – made the journey to the bank with the previous night's takings from the Globe, and twice a week he went on to the accountants, Gillespie Brothers in Chandos Street, to collect the cheque books. I'd never seen 'personalised' cheque books before and thought they looked incredibly smart with the firm's name printed across the blue pages – three cheques to a page, already signed by Willie Gillespie or Bill Newton, the Company Secretary – and Harry or Binkie would add the second signature while Elsie stood beside them with a sheet of blotting paper to press over the wet ink. The Friday cheques would be distributed to the various company managers, George would go down to the bank again to cash the office wages cheque, and Elsie would sit behind her desk with our national insurance books in front of her,

sticking on the stamps and counting out the wages for the office staff and permanent members of the Tennent organisation. I hugely resented the weekly deductions – after all, I had private money and certainly never saw myself as drawing unemployment benefit – but the law said that you had to pay the contributions unless you were earning more than £8 a week. The day did finally come when Elsie handed me my cards with a note saying she hoped I would never have to use them again and congratulating me on having raised my salary to the level of this princely figure, but that was a very long time in the future.

There was a constant stream of visitors throughout the day, stars, directors, designers, agents concerned with the current show, young actors looking for work and coming out of the lift half fainting with shock from claustrophobia and utter nervousness. I very quickly took over the job of interviewing the actors, as the office boy couldn't really be expected to cope, and found it absolutely fascinating to meet the aspiring talent and discuss their training, experience and characteristics. In those days there was no official casting director, so if I liked anyone particularly I could pass their name and address or agent's name on to Elsie or Binkie, a job which soon became one of my favourite occupations. Later, when the war had taken the cream of our young men and we were left with the physically handicapped or medically discharged, the situation was practically reversed and it was we who did the wooing while the young men condescended to accept the jobs offered or turned them down with lofty disdain.

Once a young actor arrived to enquire if we were casting and I told him "We're doing *The Druid's Rest* and *A Month in the Country.*" "Oh, but I won't go on tour," was his reply and he stalked out of the office before I could clear up the misunderstanding.

Scripts were a jealously guarded commodity once a production was under way. Agents would ring up and ask to see a copy, but we never let any out for mass suggestions, though of course once a star had been contracted and given the play his agent could ring up and offer his other clients for consideration. This monopolistic attitude must have been pretty galling to the agents generally, except for a favoured few who owed

their privileged position to the stars they represented and so would get an advance peek at the casting problems. But we always felt we could cast a play ourselves better than any agent, and this accounted for the recurring names on the posters as the actors rose from juvenile to supporting player and eventually star.

Three plays were in preparation when I arrived at the Globe, but, though one of them was by Dodie Smith, *Bonnet over the Windmill* starring James Mason, they were all comparative failures and I didn't feel particularly involved with any of them – I had missed the excitement of their arrival and the subsequent decisions to produce them, and in any event the first couple of months were bewildering enough without trying to get involved with the upper echelons of the company's policy. But it was not long before a new script arrived – a virgin offering which made its impact on everyone immediately, and as Damon Runyon would put it, the backers were prepared to bet plenty of six to four that it was going to be a humdinger and a surefire 18-carat success. This was an untitled play by St. John Ervine, an established playwright and theatre critic, written for his friends Owen Nares and Edith Evans. Owen, had been a basic pillar of the Firm for years – going right back to *Call It A Day* – but Edith had never worked for them before. The play was the author's gift to those two great stars, and as he wanted the title to reflect their equal importance, it eventually came to be called *Robert's Wife*.

Like cutting the pages of a French novel, the thrill of reading a new play for the first time is a unique experience – you don't yet know what faces the actors will give the characters, or how the director will shape the scenes. If the author has done his job properly, the characters move and speak with their own voices, and the play grabs your attention from first to last. As nobody ever reads at acting speed, a normal script will not take more than thirty to forty minutes to read, after which a totally new pleasure begins, trying to imagine the right actors in the parts and visualising sets and costumes. If the play is less than perfect you embark on a new mental exercise – trying to trace where the development goes wrong, imagining how certain elements could be strengthened and training an instinct that can be developed over many years and productions. I don't

know how far Binkie influenced his authors – once a cast and director had been engaged, he would attend the first reading and then never interfere until the first run-through, when he would always put a finger unerringly on whatever might be in need of fixing. His taste was considered impeccable, but in my opinion he learned it originally from Harry Tennent, with his university and intellectual background.

Robert's Wife went on tour before coming to the Globe, and Binkie came back from Scotland with news of the play's triumph and a story about Edith Evans on the first night. Apparently during rehearsal she had always stuck on a particular line and at that first performance he could feel her tightening with apprehension in anticipation of the dreaded moment. When it came, she dried stone dead. Quite unable to pick up the prompt, she had risen from her chair, walked across the stage, picked up the script and looked at the line. Returning to her place, she spoke the line perfectly and nobody in the audience had noticed anything unusual.

How I loved that play! There is a 'spy hole' cut in the wall of the outer office, which was made originally so that Marie Löhr could look down on the stage when she first leased the theatre. By 1937 this had been partly blocked by filing cabinets, and you had to stand on a chair before you could open it. This made you very conspicuous, so I would sneak out to the back of the Upper Circle, pretending I wanted to use the lavatory, and watch the superb cast: Margaret Scudamore (Michael Redgrave's mother), Edith Sharpe, playing the devoted spinster parish worker (she continued to appear until she was seven months pregnant and nobody ever noticed anything unusual), David Markham as the pacifist son and David Horne pontificating as the most benevolent of bishops.

It was an immensely topical play, with the wife advocating birth control and the son preaching against war, while all the time Hitler was ranting at the German Nazi rallies and the final march into Czechoslovakia came right in the middle of the run. It was much easier to retreat into the security of the theatre than face the possibility of war, for by this time it was 1938 and we really shouldn't have been quite so surprised when the crisis came.

Not that we hadn't seen the signs. Mother and I had gone to

Vienna just after the *Anschluss* in 1935 and seen the blinds still drawn down over the Chancellery window behind which little Chancellor Dollfuss had been left to bleed to death; while a Hungarian family we met who made the most exquisite lingerie and *petit point* bags later called on us in London before emigrating to the Argentine. But, with four brothers likely to be called up in the event of war, I flatly refused to think anything so dreadful might happen, and in common with the White Queen felt that if I didn't believe something was possible then it just wouldn't be allowed to happen. Even so, everyone was talking of war, trenches were being dug in Hyde Park and the young men were wondering how they could get into the Forces if the worst really came to the worst. George Devine complained that he would never be able to join up:

"I'm short-sighted, I've got flat feet, and I'm much too fat," he complained.

"They should employ you to light London," quipped J. B. Priestley, "and then nobody could see it . . ."

So the summer of 1938 became an anxious period of watching the box office receipts fluctuating in relation to the news, while Mr Chamberlain clutched his umbrella and the French laid barbed wire coils along the Atlantic beaches in the fond hope that this would prove an insurmountable obstacle to a seaborne German invasion.

Then, during a matinée performance, Owen Nares stepped forward in the interval to announce that Mr Chamberlain was going once more to Munich, and the audience cheered so loudly that I had to rush out to the back of the Upper Circle to join in. I almost sobbed with relief when the Prime Minister came home, waving that ridiculous piece of paper, declaring that out of this nettle danger he had plucked this flower safety. I know Shakespeare has a word for almost everything, but I do think politicians should be clever enough to coin their own in moments of stress. Anyway, with the crisis temporarily over, the theatres settled down again to capacity business, and we were safe for another twelve months of blissful unawareness.

Chapter IV

While *Robert's Wife* was filling the Globe, John Gielgud opened his legendary season of four plays at the Queen's next door. I had seen John first at the Old Vic in *Richard II* when he was twenty-five, and our class was 'doing' the play for School Certificate. At first sight I had hated the pale effeminate boy he appeared to be, but by the end of the second scene I had fallen in love with the magical voice and as the play ended I was sobbing uncontrollably. Merely by describing his performance throughout the exam I sailed through with an A+ and now here he was, playing nightly on the other side of the walls of a theatre where I could come and go as I pleased.

Of the four productions the magic of *Three Sisters*, with the impeccable cast led by John, Gwen Ffrangçon-Davies, Peggy Ashcroft and Carol Goodner, remains for anyone who saw it as the supreme example of Chekovian interpretation. I didn't care much for the Tyrone Guthrie *School for Scandal*, which was suppposed to show the itch beneath the powder, but agreed with the critics who called John's Joseph Surface the highlight of acting in our time.

Before the end of the season I had got to know Genevieve (Gene) Jessel, the young actress who understudied Peggy Ashcroft and played Jessica in *The Merchant of Venice*. We would sit in Lyons Corner House in Coventry Street for hours after the evening performances, discussing John's magic and the emotional impact of playing a scene with him. Which explains why when one day a tall, elegant young man whom none of us knew appeared in the office enquiring for Mr Beaumont, the sight of his companion made us gasp. John Gielgud had arrived with John Perry to say he would like to direct a play his friend had written with the Irish novelist, M. J. Farrell, dealing with the affairs of an impoverished Irish family, called *Spring Meeting*.

"A sprat to catch a mackerel", murmured Morrie, but it

was more like a whale that had been landed, for that was the beginning of the association that was to make the three young men in question the most powerful triumvirate on the London scene.

Of course Binkie had worked with John Gielgud before, at the Little Theatre in Barnes, and even possessed a signed front of house picture mounted in one of the elegant leather bound albums which he continued to add to for the rest of his life, but this was the first time John had approached Tennent's to act for him in a managerial capacity. The play was accepted at once and went into rehearsal almost immediately.

Starring Zena Dare, with various former members of the Dublin Abbey Players, the cast included Margaret Rutherford as Auntie Bijou, the funniest creation that even she had ever produced. Clutching her hot-water bottle to counteract her 'little pain', Margaret romped into stardom and the hearts of the British public.

The next thing we knew was that Dodie Smith was bustling in and out of the office again with Alick Beesley, later to be her husband, and the news that John Gielgud was joining Marie Tempest in Dodie's newest play, *Dear Octopus*, a family saga dealing with the celebrations of a golden wedding and glorifying the unifying effects of Christmas. Every member of the cast was a star, Angela Baddeley, Valerie Taylor, Kate Cutler among them, and even a very young John Justin. He had heard that Dodie was looking for a juvenile among the aspirants in the audition tent, one of the features of the annual Theatrical Garden Party in Regents Park, held to raise funds for the Actors' Orphanage. He duly paid his five shillings and performed in the tent. Of course he got the part, but his stunning good looks would have made him stand out in the teeth of any ordinary opposition without having to resort to such tricks.

Dear Octopus opened in Brighton to a week of sold out houses and then moved into the Queen's with every prospect of repeating the success John had had with his classical season. In those days it was a polite fiction that authors would be tremendously surprised when called for by the public (they must all have sat up for nights thinking up memorable phrases) but on this occasion there was a different *ordre du jour*. 'Call sheets', telling the cast what to do, are posted on the

notice board at the stage door, and once the first-night calls have been sorted out by the director and carefully rehearsed, the list goes up so that everyone knows where to stand, who will take joint or solo calls, and then 'all on' until the applause dies down. To the amazement, not to say shocked surprise of the company, the call sheet announced that after the return to the second 'all on', Miss Dodie Smith would make her entrance from the upstage door of the dining-room set and take her place between Dame Marie Tempest and Mr Gielgud. She even had a new dress made for her by Motley for the occasion.

The curtain fell, the audience clapped their hands sore and while some of them may have been shouting for the author it was the brilliant cast supplemented by the three children, headed by Muriel Pavlow, who were being saluted. Nevertheless, the author duly made her way to her appointed place and reached out a hand to take Dame Marie's, but that lady was equal to the occasion. With the utmost delicacy and the clearest of intentions she lifted the folds of her leaf-brown chiffon dress and swept them aside, leaving the author in no doubt as to the depths of her temerity.

Dame Marie belonged to that breed of *monstres sacrés* that the theatre no longer seems to create. Tiny and autocratic, she ruled any company in which she appeared with a rod of iron. Chairs had to have boards placed beneath cushions so that skirts would not be creased and muslin wraps were made for every female artist who had to wear them from their dressing-rooms to the side of the stage where they would be removed by the wardrobe mistress or a dresser, and donned again for the journey back to the dressing-room. Legend has it that once when using the tiny Globe lift she shared it with a young actor who, quite unable to turn his back on her, faced her nervously, fumbling for the gates before letting her out.

"After that experience, young man," she said, "there's nothing for us but marriage."

Awed though the profession might have been by her personality, the response to the gala matinée arranged to mark her fiftieth year on the stage at Drury Lane on 28 May 1935 raised enough money to name a ward for her in St. George's Hospital, and when she died, the memorial service at St.

Martin's-in-the-Fields was graced by the entire theatrical galaxy. The service was organised by the firm in conjunction with the *Daily Telegraph* and on that occasion George Bishop, the critic, then the paper's gossip columnist, voiced an unexpected compliment:

"Tennent's" he said, "are renowned for the excellence of their casting, but they have never done a better job than on the personnel of their own office."

When *Dear Octopus* opened, Muriel Pavlow looked about eleven years old, but in reality was an experienced trouper of seventeen. Her fragility and delicate beauty ensured that she remained employed by the firm for the next dozen years and she and I became firm friends and frequent companions during the early days of the war, even sharing a bed in one set of grotty digs when she was on tour with a new play. On one occasion, with tears streaming down our cheeks, we found ourselves part of a cinema audience of about half a dozen, defying Hitler's bombs at a matinée of *Dumbo* and far more affected by the animated drawings than any frightfulness the Führer and his minions were hurling at us. Muriel was being wooed by Patrick Gibbs, later the film critic of the *Daily Telegraph* and when she was busy at the theatre he took me out a couple of times instead. As he was in Coastal Command and had been involved in the attack on the German cruisers Scharnhorst and Gneisenauer, he had collected a couple of gongs and it was very amusing to go to restaurants patronised by the swaggering stars of Fighter Command and see their surprised glances at the neatly fastened top button of Patrick's tunic.

But Patrick wasn't Muriel's only beau, and it was fun to play gooseberry and watch the enamoured swains fainting in rows as the result of her all-conquering attractions. When she was appearing as Bianca in a production of *The Taming of the Shrew* with Laurence Harvey at Stratford some years later, my American companion remarked, "There's only one thing to do with that girl – pour cream on her and *eat her*." But Muriel remained serenely heartwhole through all the adulation and dutifully went home every night to her parents in Rickmansworth until we were all gladdened to hear that she had finally succumbed and was going to be married to the perfect choice,

Derek Farr, a marriage that has already lasted over several decades.

It was during the run of *Dear Octopus* that John Gielgud asked if I would help him with his first book of memoirs, *Early Stages*. This had originally appeared as a series of articles in a women's magazine and needed expanding. He had heard of my shorthand speed and thought it would be much easier if he dictated the additions which I could then type out. Arrangements were made for the spare room in the office to be made available, and we had a couple of sessions, but whether he found improvisation unexpectedly difficult or was put off by my efforts to conceal the doglike devotion of a lifetime, the dictation came to an end and he wrote out the additions in long-hand, giving me the resulting mosaics to type.

Binkie on the other hand, never hesitated when he was dictating and could rattle off his correspondence at a steady 200 words a minute, which meant we could get through an amazing amount of letters with a minimum waste of time. He had a trick of writing memos on the backs of cigarette packets – he always smoked Du Maurier – and would arrive in the morning or after lunch with half-a-dozen notes that he would pass on to me. Having gone through the list he would exclaim "That's done," and toss the orange packet into the wastepaper basket. *I* might have been saddled with several hours' work, but as far as *he* was concerned, the job was done. He never wasted time reading a letter through before signing it, usually carrying on a telephone conversation at the same time, and certainly acted on Harry Tennent's advice not to keep a dog and bark yourself. His was the quickest brain I have ever met, and working later with a man who needed to think between every phrase drove me absolutely frantic. Binkie was never afraid of delegating jobs to others, so that the day to day running of the office was carried out by Elsie and the rest of the team, leaving Binkie free to concentrate on the creative side.

Once an author or star had come under his spell and experienced the care and meticulous attention to detail which was the hallmark of all Tennent productions, they didn't want to venture into other circles and were content to be cosseted and cared for, knowing he would never let them down.

Peter Saunders, in his book *The Mousetrap Man*, describes

how after the war he approached one famous actress – Margaret Rutherford, perhaps? – to offer her a part but she replied "No, thank you. Binkie looks after me". Athene Seyler told me how she once went to the office to discuss the part in a new play she had been offered. The conversation turned to money (Athene never used an agent), and Binkie asked what salary she had in mind. "Oh, I don't know," she answered. "The same as I had before, I suppose." Binkie was so charmed that he immediately gave her a £10 rise. No wonder they all adored him.

With *Early Stages* complete and only seven entrances in *Dear Octopus* to keep him busy, early in 1939 John arranged a series of charity matinées of *The Importance of Being Earnest* at the Globe Theatre. From the back of the Upper Circle I watched the incomparable production take shape – Edith Evans' Wagnerian Lady Bracknell, formidable even in rehearsal, and John's solemn and irresistibly funny Ernest. Capacity houses were assured so when the next two plays at the Globe, *We at the Crossroads* ("My dear, you can't do a play called *Wee at the Crossroads*") and a Welsh offering called *Rhondda Roundabout* both failed, it was only natural that *The Importance* should be used as a stop-gap for a limited season when John came back from Denmark.

The British Council had set up a summer tradition of taking English companies to Elsinore to play *Hamlet*, and as the plans to demolish the Lyceum Theatre were already announced, it seemed the ideal moment for John to leave the cast of *Dear Octopus* and mount a production of *Hamlet* at Irving's historic theatre which would go on to Denmark afterwards.

A marvellous cast was assembled, many of them from the 1935 company that had appeared at the New, but, Frank Vosper, the wonderful 'bloat King', having disappeared overboard during an Atlantic crossing, Jack Hawkins played the Ghost and Claudius as a stunning double, and Glen Byam Shaw and Fay Compton (as Ophelia, not Gertrude) together with Andrew Cruickshank completed a dazzling nap hand. In place of the unruly hairstyle of the previous version, John chose a bobbed wig and a high white collar which I thought made him look like a lady cellist but the performance swept away all such carping considerations. Guégué had told me that

when she was a girl Sarah Bernhardt had played *L'Aiglon* for a three-week season at her home town, Calais, and she had determined to see every performance. She went twenty three times on the trot and cried at exactly the same place every night and twice on matinée days. Determined to undergo the same experience, I booked to see every performance of *Hamlet* and found myself in floods of tears at exactly the same moment in the play – though it was "Now cracks a noble heart" from Glen that set me off – the emotion of watching John being far too intense to allow tears while Hamlet was still alive.

On the last night I changed from my best Paris evening frock into shirt and slacks and sat on the stage with my typewriter. Using specially thin sheets of paper and carbons I made twelve copies of the contents of every box and crate for the Customs, finishing the job in the small hours before going out to have breakfast at the Corner House in the Strand.

The weather was vile as it had been the previous year when Laurence Olivier and Vivien Leigh had performed with the Old Vic Company. After the outdoor performances had been rained off they had retired to the great hall and an improvised stage, but in John's case they struggled on in the courtyard and only cancelled one of the scheduled performances. The whole company felt as if some kind of era was drawing to a close and indulged in all kinds of horseplay and schoolboy extravagances, finally throwing everyone, including John, into the sea after the last performance. His postcard to me described the visit as "extracts from the Lyceum production with wind and rain accompaniments". It was to be many years before the British Council exercise could be repeated.

The Importance opened at the Globe on 14 August to rave reviews and capacity houses. I played the piano backstage for Algy (Jack Hawkins) as the stage music began before curtain-up and the pit musicians had no time to get up into the wings. (I played 'Autumn' by Chaminade and a snatch of the Mendelssohn Wedding March. Occasionally word would come round from Leslie Bridgewater or John Gielgud that I wasn't playing enough wrong notes.) In between these musical offerings seven times a week, I could stand in the wings and watch the first act (on the Wednesday matinée I had to nip back to the office). I was paid half-a-crown a performance which I

thought was pretty generous as it amounted to one-third of my basic salary. This was my first experience of actually taking part in a show and appreciating how performances could vary, depending on the mood of the audience or on what the actors themselves were feeling. Once John dried in the middle of his handbag scene with Edith Evans, excusing himself later with "I'm so sorry, Edith dear, but I was lost in admiration of your performance."

Once she dried while he was counting on his fingers the number of bedrooms in his country house and he was really desperate before she picked up the prompt. In the corridor outside their dressing-rooms, it was her turn to explain: "I'm so sorry, John dear, but I suddenly thought how funny it would be to play Lady Bracknell with protruding teeth."

She demonstrated. Gwen chimed in. "Yes, and Gwendolen's teeth would have to protrude slightly too," and everyone collapsed.

Imagination or fact? The laughter from the audiences during the first full week at the Globe when there was never an empty seat seems in retrospect to have been happier and more carefree than any laughter I have ever heard since. Did the laughter of the audiences in July 1914 have a special quality too that has since been lost or has the gift of total enjoyment gone from a world which has experienced Auschwitz and Hiroshima and can never wholly be happy again?

The next week beginning 28 August brought ever-increasing war fears – children were being evacuated to the country and trenches dug again in Hyde Park. Audiences began to fall away and on Thursday evening there was only a handful of people in the house. Drury Lane, where *The Dancing Years* had been playing to capacity business, taking £750 a performance, dropped to a mere £35. On Friday morning, when Hitler invaded Poland, all the Tennent stars came up to the office to discuss what should be done, among them Diana Wynyard, Rex Harrison and Anton Wallbrook. Anton was in tears – the first time I had ever seen a man weep in public – and it was decided to cancel the Saturday evening performances.

It felt odd to be going home as soon as the matinée ended, but it was just as well for on the doorstep I met my brother Brian, in uniform, on his way to report for duty at Hendon

airfield. For the past year he had been flying with 601 City of London Squadron, the long-haired week-end boys of the Auxiliary Air Force, commanded by Max Aitken. By the end of the war there would only be three survivors of the original team, including Max himself, and 'Mouse' Fielden, who later commanded the Queen's Flight. The blinding shock of saying good-bye had to be countered with a fierce conviction that the whole thing would somehow be called off again, and I kept repeating "It can't happen, it can't", like a Coué charm.

The next twenty-four hours we spent glued to the radio, trying to imagine a war that would reduce the world to a mixture of Passchendaele and Guernica – and wondering what had happened to all the optimism of umbrellas over Munich and "peace in our time".

On Sunday morning, Mother decided not to switch on the radio until the one o'clock news, believing there would be no further developments overnight, so I was washing my smalls when I heard a frantic call. She had sneaked down to the radio and switching on, had found herself in the midst of Mr Chamberlain's eleven o'clock speech: " . . . and consequently this country is at war with Germany."

This was followed by a list of official announcements, among the first an order closing all theatres and cinemas. I stood there stunned. A world at war might just be conceivable, but life without the theatre was unimaginable.

Suddenly the sirens wailed in alarm and the barrage balloons slowly floated up into the sky above Kensington Gardens. From our balcony we could see buses stopping and their passengers racing for the shelters that had been dug in Hyde Park. By this time the BBC had reverted to its normal programme and a light orchestra was playing something called *Woodland Pictures*. "It can't be a raid," I kept repeating. "It can't. If it were, the BBC wouldn't be playing this idiotic music."

As it turned out I was right, and it was only a false alarm (nobody seemed to have worked out how long it would have taken for a real bombing mission to cross the North Sea), and after a few moments the all clear was sounded; I took a snap of the barrage balloons floating over the Albert Memorial before they all sank back to earth like overweight homing pigeons.

This proved to be quite a historic document as it shows the cross at the top of the memorial in its original position facing north/south. Later it was knocked off by an anti-aircraft shell, and when it was eventually replaced after the war it was realigned to face east/west. The group showing Mother India was also damaged in the same raid and the lady lost her left breast. She continued to hold her veil proudly aloft to proclaim her mutilation until the same restorers who replaced the cross gave her a neat plastic job so that you'd never know to look at her now that anything of the kind had ever happened.

Next morning, going to the office as usual, though this time with my gas mask slung over my shoulder, everthing seemed extraordinarily quiet and it was uncanny to arrive at the Globe and find the big main doors still shut. I made my way to the office via the stage door and was met with the announcement that Mr Tennent intended to keep everyone on the pay-roll for a month while the situation was assessed.

One by one the various company managers arrived at the office, as well as some of the stars from the productions in rehearsal. There were routine matters to attend to, filing, entering the weekly returns, etc., and as the theatre was dark and there were no cleaners, Elsie Beyer issued the female staff with white cotton gloves as worn by stage hands when moving light-coloured scenery. We emptied ashtrays, dusted the office and swept the carpets in an endeavour to keep busy. We made blackout curtains and stuck strips of gummed brown paper criss-cross over the windows. The Theatre Managers Association (TMA) arranged for a deputation to visit the Ministry of Labour to find out how long the order would be kept in force, and ENSA, the organisation that would provide entertainment for the forces was hastily formed with Leslie Henson and various stars announcing that they could assemble a series of concert parties to entertain the troops at a moment's notice. It was all very British, stiff-upper-lip, and totally unreal.

On Thursday night I heard on the nine o'clock news that theatres and cinemas in "safe" areas were to be allowed to reopen. I arrived at the office next morning wild with excitement. Oddly enough, nobody else seemed to have heard the announcement – it wasn't to become official until the follow-

ing Sunday – but Binkie telephoned the Home Office and discovered that this was indeed the situation. Local authorities would decide whether to allow the openings or not – some cinema owners going so far as to say that cinemas would be safer than theatres as only alternate rows of seats would be used.

In a moment the whole office was transformed. Everyone sprang to the telephone as dates were booked, company managers contacted and agents advised that their clients would be working again. We spent all Saturday in the office and I felt as though I had been given a reprieve from a death sentence – the theatre was alive again.

The Importance was the first away, on 14 September, opening at a matinée at Golders Green, considered 'safe' in spite of its nearness to Hendon airfield, but with the gallery closed as a precaution, while Marie Tempest departed for Blackpool with *Dear Octopus*. The provinces were certainly in for a theatrical treat, and the railways were starting on the booming business that was to keep them packed to bursting point for the rest of the war.

Chapter V

After a quiet summer, the Tennent autumn programme for 1939 had been the most ambitious the firm had ever lined up. Noël Coward was to appear with Leonora Corbett in two new plays of his own, *Sweet Sorrow* (later retitled *Present Laughter*) and *This Happy Breed*; Binkie had persuaded Daphne du Maurier to dramatise her novel *Rebecca* herself – after all, he argued, her famous actor father Gerald must have taught her *something* about the theatre – which John Gielgud was to do with Jill Furse, the exquisite young actress who was being hailed as the new Meggie Albanesi; Edith Evans, Gwen Ffrangçon-Davies and Peggy Ashcroft, together with Ralph Richardson, were to star in a production of *The Cherry Orchard* directed by Michel St. Denis, with Cyril Cusack as Firs, and three understudies from the Old Vic Studio, James Cairncross, James Donald and Peter Ustinov. All these productions had been in rehearsal and were abandoned with the closing of the theatres. Of *The Cherry Orchard* cast, James Cairncross was the only one on a two weeks' notice clause, and so got paid the princely sum of £6. Nobody else got anything.

Remembering the enthusiasm for light entertainment – *A Little Bit of Fluff*, *The Bing Boys*, *Chu Chin Chow* – which had filled the London theatres during the First World War, it was decided that this was what would be wanted in the present climate. Black-outs, hooded headlights, barely visible traffic signals, all added up to a clear indication that once inside the theatre the public would want bright lights, pretty girls and plenty of laughter. The first new production, therefore, was to be an intimate revue directed by Harold French, and starring Beatrice Lillie, entitled *All Clear* – a nice bracing phrase which would reassure any nervous theatregoers and entice them into the safety of the theatre. Bea was to be joined by Fred Emney, Bobby Howes and a small cast of supporting performers, together with four dancers who would also take part in the

sketches. Harold had been the highly successful director of *French Without Tears* among other smash hits and was under contract to the firm – the only instance of this kind of engagement.

But putting on a revue is a very different matter from the technique required for a straight play and the firm had no expertise in the new field, in spite of the talents of the various contributors and the magnitude of the stars making up the company. Fred Emney, a heavy not to say over-weight comedian insisted on contributing his own personal *pièce de résistance* which he had performed successfully for years at the piano in cabaret. Entitled '*Mothballs*', it had never been written down, so he came up to the office and dictated it to me for submission to the Lord Chamberlain. What may have corpsed a night-club audience already high on champagne fell as flat as that same champagne the morning after when dictated in cold blood in the clinical atmosphere of the office. I never cracked a smile throughout the exercise. It didn't seem to work very much better in the theatre either. Nobody is infallible, as I discovered later when I read the letter from Harry Tennent rejecting a ballad entitled '*A Nightingale Sang In Berkeley Square*', and even the top numbers that were used didn't seem to make much impact. Bobby Howes sang '*Have You Met Miss Jones?*' but didn't turn it into a popular number. In spite of getting rave personal reviews Beatrice Lillie couldn't create a smash hit single-handed. Although the formula of the intimate revue was eventually proved to be exactly what the public wanted, Binkie admitted ruefully that this was something entirely outside his experience; the firm never touched the medium again until after the war when Laurier Lister showed them how to do it at the Lyric, Hammersmith. However things did look up a little when *The Importance* came back to London and resumed its interrupted run at the Globe.

This was the period of the phoney war when everyone was trying heroically to get into uniform and volunteer for the non-existent front. The French had something called the Maginot Line (known jeeringly and all too prophetically as 'le ligne imaginaire') which was supposed to protect us all, and the Air Force was limited to dropping leaflets over Germany, though if an empty beer bottle was added to the consignment

the pilots said it whistled exactly like a bomb. Nobody wanted any extra men. Brother Brian was furiously relegated to a training squadron as being too old at 33 for fighter pilot duties, and I attended fire drills and first-aid sessions as I was over the age to be compulsorily called up and would be exempt from service anyway on the grounds of belonging to a reserved occupation.

Fire drills were pretty hysterical inventions. The main weapon was a stirrup pump which operated out of a bucket filled with water. Manned by a three-person team, the first operator filled the bucket and controlled the tap from which the water came, the second stood with a foot thrust into a 'stirrup', which balanced the contraption, and pumped vigorously, while the third lay prone and directed the thin stream of liquid in whatever direction the conflagration was supposed to be raging. Sheridan peeing on the burning Drury Lane Theatre probably created an equally effective flow, but, sublimely ignorant of what was going to hit us, we obediently called 'water on' and 'water off' as required by regulations. I never operated a stirrup pump in anger, but the technique did come in handy after the war when we rented a villa in the South of France and the only way to flush the loo was to fill the cistern with the hose from the garden tap. 'Water on' and 'water off' worked beautifully.

Surprising figures showed up in uniform. Murray Macdonald who had directed *Robert's Wife*, was among the first, appearing as a major decorated with the MC, incredibly won in France in 1918 when he had been seventeen (or so he said). Rival impresarios, Henry Sherek and Stephen Mitchell, were on the reserve and so were called up immediately, their absence considerably strengthening the expanding Tennent empire. They both had valuable authors in their stables, while Henry also had an American connection through Gilbert Miller. Stephen Mitchell had produced Emlyn Williams' play *The Corn Is Green* when the firm turned it down. According to Emlyn, Binkie felt people didn't want plays about education, but conceded that if Emlyn would appear in it himself with Sybil Thorndike, the star names would ensure success. Initially Emlyn had refused, thinking he was too old, but Stephen had talked him round and created a world famous

modern classic. It was then agreed that Tennent's would present Emlyn's next play, *The Light of Heart*, "by arrangement with Stephen Mitchell", who was also allowed to put up fifty per cent of the capital. After the war, when Stephen came back into management, Emlyn stayed with Tennent's, though the balance was somewhat redressed when Stephen produced Rattigan's double-bill, *The Browning Version* and *Harlequinade*, when Binkie (and John Gielgud) had turned them down.

Another important connection was an American, John C. Wilson, Noël Coward's personal manager and an associate of the Theatre Guild, the important producing company in New York. The first time Jack Wilson arrived in the Globe offices after I had joined the firm was to co-produce *Amphitryon 38*, starring the legendary Lunts, Alfred and his English-born wife, Lynn Fontanne. "Our Miss Gibbs" informed me loftily that she always looked after Mr Wilson when he was in London so I could do Mr Beaumont's work for the duration of the American's stay. Jack was cast in the same mould as Binkie and Terence Rattigan – immaculately turned out, handsome, charming and bursting with transatlantic courtesy in his dealings with stars and secretaries. His relationship with Noël Coward is fully charted in the Master's *Diaries*, but of course, all we saw at this time was the highly successful business façade with no hint of the tragedy to come. When he returned to New York, Linda Gibbs equally loftily informed me that she would now resume her duties as Mr Beaumont's secretary, whereupon to my own surprise I threw a temperament. My complaints brought about the desired results and I was confirmed in my acting capacity as Binkie's secretary. Linda Gibbs was put in charge of theatre contracts and repertory bookings, while Elsie Beyer was appointed General Manager: great excitement, as this was the first time a woman had been given such an important job.

On Jack Wilson's second visit, to co-produce Noël Coward's fairly unsuccessful *Operette*, Miss Gibbs' nose had been very much put out of joint since he was accompanied by his exquisitely beautiful new wife, the former Princess Natasha Paley. But the third venture, *Design For Living*, which opened at the Haymarket, hit the jackpot and proved the truth of the old adage.

One of the most beautiful theatres in London, the Haymarket had belonged to an enlightened manager, Frederick Harrison, who on his death created a trust, leaving the building to the employees who had worked so faithfully to serve it, including the box office manager and the stage director. The ghost of Mr Buckstone, a previous manager, is said to appear at regular intervals, benevolently overseeing the fortunes of his beloved theatre, and occasionally a shadowy figure is glimpsed by the more psychic members of the company. The Haymarket provided the ideal setting for the Tennent type of presentation, and, although there was never any written agreement, if Tennent's only had two productions running in London, with one at the Globe, the other would almost certainly be at the Haymarket. The only disadvantage was that as the theatre always housed a smash-hit, with a long line forming continually at the single-windowed box office, it was virtually impossible to get the staff to answer the telephone . . .

Design had been produced originally on Broadway with the Lunts and Noël Coward in the lead, but in London it starred Rex Harrison and Diana Wynyard, joined by the newest Continental heart-throb, Anton Walbrook, who had startled London originally in a German film with Paula Wesseley, *Masquerade*, in which he appeared as an unscrupulous artist, specialising in "naughty" pictures. He had then been cast as the Prince Consort in *Victoria Regina*, the Housman chronicle about George V's grandmother – the first play about royalty to be licensed by the Lord Chamberlain while such close descendants were still living. Anton had quickly established himself as a matinée idol, a position consolidated by his appearance in various other films, the most famous perhaps being *Dangerous Moonlight* when he played Richard Addinsell's 'Warsaw Concerto', which became the top of the wartime pops. All his subsequent stage performances were given for the firm, and in *Design for Living* his continental charm provided the perfect foil for Rex's English understatement. I didn't like Diana's Gilda, thinking her too cold for the part created by Lynn Fontanne, and when she sank on the sofa with Anton at the end of Act II, I was horrified to see her cross her legs . . . but perhaps this was a sop to the censorship of the

period.

At the end of the run of *The Importance*, Edith Evans agreed to appear in a play by Clemence Dane called *Cousin Muriel* in the spring of 1940. She was supposed to play the piano in this and declared that she was going to look as though she were really playing – none of that sitting facing the audience. The plot called for her to lift one hand from the keys and take a bag held out by a maid while still playing with the other, and Richard Addinsell picked out the opening of a Bach suite as fitting this particular manoeuvre. Edith had a dumb piano carried to her flat in Albany and practised under the guidance of my music teacher, Miss Louie Heath. I was to play the real music in the usual back stage position. On the first night Miss Heath brought her friend, the president of the Society of Women Musicians, without telling her anything of our trickery. At the end of the first act the friend exclaimed, "I had no idea Edith Evans was such a fine musician!" One up to Edith, Miss Heath, and perhaps even a little to me.

Casting for *Cousin Muriel* required finding a juvenile to play opposite Peggy Ashcroft. One of my "civilian" girl friends had lodged for some time in the boarding house run by John Clements' mother in Vicarage Gate, and we had all gone out to Palmers Green to see her son's *Hamlet* – a remarkable exercise considering the stage appeared to be slightly smaller than his mother's kitchen. He had had to play most of the time sitting in an armchair to make room for the other actors, but even so his talent was remarkable. I suggested him therefore as a likely candidate and he had duly presented himself at the Globe. After his interview I enquired about his chances. Binkie replied that he was too odd-looking and they were going to give the part to Alec Guinness. I was outraged. John certainly didn't possess your ordinary juvenile features but Alec's long chin and jutting out ears didn't make him into a chocolate box heart-throb either. It was two years before John Clements came to work for the firm, this time as a star, and oddly enough, once more at the Globe.

Edith had been mainly attracted to the part in *Cousin Muriel* because she was supposed to be a glamorous creature, able to twist her middle-aged cousin round her little finger. She wore exquisite clothes, an attractive hair style, and in one scene

appeared in a white organdie creation in which she said she wanted to achieve a fire-in-ice effect. Although Edith had been greatly praised for her playing of grotesques such as *The Witch of Edmonton* and the fierce gypsy woman in *The Old Ladies*, Binkie had the wit to see that she secretly saw herself as Gertrude Lawrence, and gave her every opportunity to indulge her desires. I never ceased to be amazed by her ability to transform her asymmetrical features into an effect of total beauty. One eye was set at least half an inch lower than the other, and, with thick ankles and flat feet, she moved awkwardly and gave no impression of feminine charm until she was on the stage. Then the result was as devastating as the effect produced by international beauties such as Vivien Leigh or Lynn Fontanne. Her faithful dresser, Katie Elliot, said that Edith would stand in front of a mirror looking at herself and repeating "Edith Evans, you're a beautiful woman", and the transformation would begin to glow from inside. (Of course she was a Christian Scientist, which perhaps helped.)

Tennent's organised a big Red Cross matinée at the Palace Theatre in the early part of 1940, the King and Queen's last public appearance in a theatre during the war, with all the stars of stage and screen contributing. Edith performed the Millamant-Mirabel scene from *The Way of the World* with John Gielgud, wearing the costumes Oliver Messel had made for the Tyrone Guthrie production of *The Country Wife* at the Old Vic, and I saw Edith's transformation at close quarters. I persuaded John to let me 'hold the book' and prompted those two luminaries for the first and last time in my life. Edith sent Katie scurrying all over London for white face powder – she wanted a sugared almond complexion – and the resulting beauty made me regret more than ever that I had been too young to see her play the full performance at the Lyric, Hammersmith.

As the phoney war showed no signs of hotting up, early in November the British Council approached John with the idea of going abroad for them with a repertory of two or three plays. All kinds of possibilities were discussed – *Hamlet*, using the Lyceum production was an obvious starter, and after that

The Importance, with Sybil Thorndike substituting for Edith Evans. They even talked of going to South Africa, but the time involved ruled this out from the beginning. The plan finally boiled down to five weeks in Italy, one week in Paris, one in Belgium and Holland, with two weeks in Scandinavia. Wild with excitement and dying to play my wrong notes in all those exotic places, I persuaded Binkie that I could be released from the office and allowed to go out as company manager. "Of course you'll have to walk on as a lady-in-waiting in *Hamlet*," warned Binkie, but with Gene Jessel to back me I was utterly confident of my ability to do this convincingly, and bought a stout pair of shoes in the next Rayne's sale to see me over the Italian marble floors and the French *pavé*.

The correspondence grew ever more animated, costs were calculated down to the final farthing and then in January the whole thing collapsed – just as well, as otherwise we reckoned we'd have found ourselves playing in Paris at the exact time of the fall of France. The Sadler's Wells (now the Royal) Ballet were not so lucky. They were caught in Holland by the main German advance and got out on the last boat, leaving all their scenery and costumes behind, which meant they couldn't present several of their main attractions until after the war.

With the foreign tour cancelled, John went out with Bea Lillie to entertain the troops for ENSA, appearing in Coward's *Fumed Oak* and an adaptation he made himself of Chekov's *Swan Song*, a one act play about an aged actor. He dictated the text to me in the office and I was only sorry I never got round to seeing it on the stage. After the forces performances they played some commercial dates. By this time John wanted to add *The Dark Lady of the Sonnets* to the programme so I was duly instructed to write to Bernard Shaw for permission. He sent the letter back annotated in his meticulous writing: "Where is this lunacy to take place?" I rang his secretary to explain and was almost struck speechless when he answered the phone himself in a wonderful Irish lilt. As it was addressed to me I had planned to keep the letter with the Bernard Shaw postscript for my collection, but Binkie collared it as he did everything that came into the office in Shaw's handwriting. I never managed to acquire a single postcard. Suddenly one morning there was a tremendous flurry in the

office. John Gielgud had been passed A1 at his medical examination and his call-up papers had come through. The idea of losing England's leading actor was absolutely unthinkable, quite apart from the fact that he would probably prove useless at anything practical in the military line. Binkie had always assured him he would never have to get into uniform and now sprang into action. He discovered the right office to approach and scuttled off to Hobart House in Grosvenor Gardens, emerging triumphantly with an order granting John exemption for the duration (I can never drive that way to Victoria without a *frisson* as I remember that narrow squeak), and as a result John declared that he would only appear in the classics for the rest of the war. He joined the Old Vic Company and appeared in the Granville Barker inspired production of *King Lear* and the Oliver Messel designed version of *The Tempest*. James Agate was very rude about this, saying that in the first scene John looked like the Albert Memorial on top of the Albert Hall, but I loved the costume Oliver had made with his own hands for Ariel, stuck all over with pipe cleaners, and the lumpy fishy Caliban of Jack Hawkins. He was married to Jessica Tandy at the time, an exquisite Miranda, and it seemed terribly bad luck when she went off to America with their child when he was called up and fell in love with somebody else.

With John's declaration of dedication to the classics, there was now no question of his appearing in *Rebecca* and plans for the production were revised with Celia Johnson playing Mrs de Winter and Owen Nares substituting as Maxim. Ronnie Ward played the part Jack Hawkins should have created. Italia Conti had recommended a young actor to play Robert the footman, saying he had more talent than Jack Hawkins had shown at his age, and this was how Jack Watling came into the Tennent stable. Margaret Rutherford discarded Auntie Bijou's cosy dottiness for a spine-chilling performance as Mrs Danvers, and Isolde Denham, married to Peter Ustinov, understudied Mrs de Winter and took over the part when Celia left the cast.

Once more I was playing the piano backstage. Owen Nares suffered from the same pronunciation problems as Churchill, so one of my cues came out as 'I don't scheem to have scheen

you sinch thish morning'. I even made a fleeting appearance, supposedly one of the musicians packing up at the end of the ball scene, and stood in the hall with Barney Gordon and Cecil Clarke, the stage management team, while the upstage double doors opened and closed again after a split second. By sprinting madly to the Piccadilly underground and running all the way to the pit entrance of the Old Vic I could arrive just in time to hear John's rendering of the cloud capped towers – a schizophrenic existence which was extremely satisfactory. The summer evenings lengthened, the blackout became a forgotten inconvenience and then, without warning, Hitler embarked on his *blitzkrieg* and advancing across Europe overran country after country.

Mother had learned High Dutch (as opposed to Afrikaans) at school and once more we sat glued to the radio, listening to the sounds of war as Holland was devastated. The Germans were using the air to issue misleading instructions to the civilian population and the counter was for the local announcers to impress their voices on their listeners.

"This is Dirk, or Hendrik, or Andreas", they would insist, "listen to my voice. Don't follow any instructions unless you hear them from me or one of my colleagues . . ."

Then there would be an audible crump, and sometimes voices calling that parachutists could be seen – five, ten, fifteen, dropping at a time. We had been in Holland just before the war and seen the lines of cars arriving from Nazi Germany filled to bursting with Jewish refugees – the men in tight-lipped resignation and the women with diamond bracelets stretching from wrist to elbow – the only way they could bring any of their money out of the country. I wondered how many of them were still in Amsterdam.

"Don't worry," we had been told when the war began, "the Maginot Line will check the German advance. They'll never get past it to the Channel ports."

Now we discovered that the Line stopped at the Belgian frontier and that the Belgian king had decided to surrender to Hitler. The way to Calais and Dunkirk was open. After the miraculous evacuation we learned that there had been quite a fair proportion of theatricals among the prisoners who would spend the war behind barbed wire and exercise their talents in

the prison theatres. I once asked Hilary St. George Saunders, the historian and official chronicler of the RAF who would find anonymous fame as author of the Battle of Britain pamphlet, to write the story of the actors' war and he promised to do so if I would collect the necessary information. I'm always sorry that we never got round to it – it would have made a glorious tale.

Chapter **VI**

Mr Churchill's historic phrases were rolling out of the radio and making headlines in the papers – Spitfires and Hurricanes took to the skies, and through a cloudless August and September we watched the Battle of Britain drawing closer and closer to London. One lunchtime I was among the excited crowds in Trafalgar Square watching the vapour trails high overhead coming towards us in a straight line – a moment later, tiny pinpoints in the sunlight showed the approach of the fighters and the crowd cheered as the line of bombers executed a smart U-turn and turned tail for France and safety. On the morning of the famous Sunday, 15 September, I was once more washing my smalls when I heard the chatter of machine-guns and looking out of the window saw a plane disintegrate and a parachute begin to drift slowly downwards. Fortunately I couldn't see which markings were on which plane. The first Canadian airmen arrived in London without my youngest brother, who had been turned down on account of his eyesight, and without the eldest, who was too old for active service. We celebrated by opening a bottle of Napoleon brandy my mother had bought at an auction before the war, but even this couldn't console the boys for the fact that they had been stationed at a place called Middle Wallop. "Our wives will never believe us," they said disgustedly. And then the Blitz on London began.

The first few attacks were merely samples of what we would experience throughout the winter – the air raid warnings would sound well after dark but contrary to the original statements that performances would be stopped immediately, everyone took it as a matter of pride to carry on as though nothing untoward was happening. By this time *Thunder Rock* by Robert Ardrey, a very moving mystery a little on the lines of *Outward Bound*, had transferred to the Globe from the Neighbourhood Theatre, a small private venture in South

Kensington, directed by Herbert Marshall (the professor of Russian, not the Hollywood actor), starring Michael Redgrave. The pattern was soon established that if a warning was given and the all clear had not sounded before the end of the play, the audience would be invited to stay in the theatre and an impromptu entertainment would be mounted by the cast and any visitors who happened to be around. Michael invited me to come in from the Queen's next door and play his accompaniments while he sang popular songs and ballads. Once Peter Ustinov was persuaded to come and join us. He was in uniform but seemed extraordinarily shy and at a loss as to what to do. Eventually he hid underneath a table and made all the noises that would come out of a radio if you twisted the dial across the wave-lengths – static, German, French, and incomprehensible babbles. He had us all in fits of laughter for as long as he could be persuaded to carry on.

My brothers were very insistent that my mother should go to the country away from the air raids, or at least move into a modern concrete block, so to oblige them we visited a few in Abbey Road and elsewhere but finally came to the conclusion that Albert Hall Mansions with its system of open wells might prove more resistant to blast and decided to stay put. Binkie on the other hand was in a very vulnerable position in a basement at 142 Piccadilly. His dining-table was under a huge skylight which Sibyl Colefax had disguised with inch-thick carved oak fretwork which didn't offer the slightest form of protection. John Gielgud and John Perry had moved in with Binkie when their flat in St. John's Wood was requisitioned for Gibraltarian refugees. They were all preparing dinner in the kitchen when a bomb fell on 145, skylight and fretwork came crashing down and huge splinters of glass embedded themselves in the table. A lucky escape. A day or two later, I helped Binkie pack his belongings and was amused to find he had dozens of carved wooden animals to float in his bath – a pride of Aloysiuses, as Evelyn Waugh might have described them.

The list of theatres damaged was surprisingly small considering the way they are packed together and the numbers of bombs that actually fell on London. The Queen's was an early casualty. A small bomb fell in the churchyard of St. Anne's, Soho, opposite the theatre, bursting open the scene-dock

doors and shearing one leg off the dummy piano of the *Rebecca* set. But this was nothing compared to the damage caused by an anti-aircraft shell that exploded in the foyer, cutting through the cantilever to the main stairs and putting the building out of action for the remainder of the war. A fire bomb destroyed the Shaftesbury, then on the site of what is now the fire station opposite the Palace on the eponymous avenue. On 15 October Drury Lane itself was hit by an oil bomb, which set fire to and ruined the auditorium, though it didn't interfere with the ENSA activities. A land-mine – a horrid invention that floated down on its own parachute to maximise the effect of the explosion – fell through the roof of the Palladium but fortunately the parachute became entangled in the theatre grid and the bomb disposal lads were able to remove it safely. The Piccadilly had a narrow escape when another land-mine exploded in Denman Street, our own casualties being Peggy Ashcroft who sustained a cut leg while she was having her hair done, and Binkie's mother, Mrs Schwerzee, who was living at the Regent Palace Hotel – she had incautiously looked out of her window and got a bad gash on her head. *A Month in the Country* was rehearsing at the Lyric at the time and the cast's disgust was inordinate when, covered in dust and grime, they saw Binkie arrive among them, full of concern for their well-being but without a hair out of place or a speck of dust on his immaculate suit. The Little Theatre in John Adam Street was wiped out, and the Old Vic sustained a direct hit, but that was the sum total of the theatre damage in London.

One by one the shows closed, leaving only the Windmill to carry on with its nude presentations to the waiting queues of servicemen and for the rest of the autumn and winter once more all the productions went on tour, performances beginning at all kinds of outlandish hours to beat the bombers. Pantomimes started at ten-thirty in the mornings, but start they did: nothing was going to defeat the spirit of the British people.

With nothing to do in the evenings I went in search of other employment and ended waiting at table in a private canteen in Hertford Street, run by a Mrs Stewart-Richardson, a Greek lady whose cousin, Miki Iveria, had been Yvonne Arnaud's

regular understudy and played an important part in Peter Ustinov's first play, *The House of Regrets* at the Arts Theatre Club. Here we served any members of the forces who happened to call, notably Michael MacOwan's company of actors in uniform, who were stationed nearby; and a good many policemen and air raid wardens would drop in for a hasty cup of coffee or a lightning meal. Dorothy Paget's butler came in occasionally to help wash up – no detergents in those days and pure soda can be death to your hands and nails, so his cooperation was much appreciated. We had a narrow escape one evening when a bomb fell in Queen Street. We all heard the whistle, and resulting "crump", and when the noise died away the canteen presented a curious sight. All the customers had quite rightly disappeared under the tables while the waitresses remained standing wondering what on earth had happened. Sadly one of our regulars was buried under the house that was hit, but although he was dug out the traumatic effect turned him into a diabetic. Not all casualties are measured in terms of amputations and physical damage.

A small 50 lb. bomb exploded in a tree just outside the Albert Hall and blew out all our plate glass windows on the fifth floor, in spite of the criss-crossed brown paper stuck over them. Our heavy velvet curtains protected the rooms from the flying splinters and débris, so apart from the resulting mess no serious damage was inflicted, the broken panes were quickly replaced and we continued to occupy the flat on the grounds that lightning would be unlikely to strike twice. Little did we know . . .

One night during an air raid after the theatre Gene and I waited in Lyons Corner House in Leicester Square until the all-clear sounded and then came out to find the sky red from horizon to horizon. The docks were burning. When I got home, I took a newspaper out on to the balcony and was able to read the print from the glare of the fires eight miles away – I thought of Pepys' diary and his "horrid red conflagration" but even he would have been shocked by the effects of that night's devastation. It was odd to wake up in the morning after a "blitz" and go to work as if nothing had happened, remarking only on the amount of broken glass littering the streets, already being swept up by the shop owners, busy putting out

"business as usual" signs where the damage had left the place wide open. Once I saw a Westminster dust-cart in Piccadilly with a huge steel girder sticking out of the back – the dustmen had scooped it up as a matter of course, and all bomb damage seemed to be cleared away almost within twenty-four hours – damaged buildings were boarded up and everyone attempted to carry on as normally as possible. But nothing could disguise the horrible smell of a blitzed site – the combined effect of cordite, burned wood and decaying vegetation that created a sinister atmosphere of death and corruption.

A strange reaction to the blitz was that, if one went into the country to get a good night's rest, it seemed almost impossible to make contact with the locals who hadn't had the same experiences. When we heard the sound of aircraft engines we learnt to say "theirs" and "ours" with complete conviction, though experts told us there was no way of distinguishing between an English and a German bomber, and it was months before our own force was strong enough to make retaliatory raids across the channel. Rumour had it that Churchill was so determined to keep up public morale that when no anti-aircraft guns were available, he ordered the naval guns from Greenwich and Deptford to be mounted on lorries and driven round the London streets, firing at intervals. There was nothing they could hit, but the sound of the gunfire was so reassuring that we all believed it was a splendid form of counter-attack and cheered every time the bangs sent dust spinning down from the picture rail or rattled the flimsy glass that had replaced our original panes.

But by Christmas the worst of the blitz was over and the London theatres were quick to reopen, though initially playing for matinées only. Touring had always carried on in the Provinces, with business fluctuating wildly if a town was unexpectedly subjected to an aerial attack, so Binkie invented a marvellous form of insurance. Everyone was paid a basic £10. a week salary with a 'points' system that gave them a share of the box office receipts, rather than a straight percentage. Expenses were calculated minutely, the management's obligations including staff salaries, advertising and a ratio of the production cost, and after that it was possible to work out what each share would be worth at any level of box

53

office receipts. The system was only abandoned when Binkie found that actors were getting more than they would have been paid on the usual flat salary basis, but it was an extremely fair system when it was important to keep theatres open, actors in work, and not to place too much of the risk on the shoulders of the backers.

One of the new ventures was a memorable production of *The Devil's Disciple*, mounted with Robert Donat and originally a dashing 'James Stewart' as his opposite number, but when it moved into the Piccadilly, he was replaced by Roger Livesey of the ginger hair and gravelly voice. When we all started playing golf again after the war, Roger demonstrated both his incredible slice and his pithy language. Swish would go the club, followed by a ricochet as the ball departed in the wrong direction and 'bugger' would be sounded in a rich bass-baritone. 'James Stewart' changed his name to Stewart Granger and proceeded to chalk up fresh records in the annals of film making.

John Gielgud's regular secretary, who worked in the box office at the Queen's, had retired to the country to look after an aged mother, and Binkie asked if I would like to become John's secretary in addition to my job of looking after him, with the result that I took over the duties of answering fan mail, sending out signed photographs and paying John's salary in to the bank every week. I was horrified to discover he had no savings account and determining that he would never feature in a bankruptcy proceeding, made him open a deposit account from which he would have funds to pay his income tax. For the first time I discovered how volatile he could be and how changeable his ideas as to what he wanted to do next. Finally, when he had vacillated a dozen times, Binkie pinned him down to doing a revival of *Dear Brutus* which I had adored when I was a schoolgirl but found disgustingly sentimental in the light of the current international crisis. However, a marvellous cast was assembled with Muriel Pavlow playing the dream child, Nora Swinburne, Ursula Jeans, George Howe and other stalwarts to back him up and he was wonderfully raffish as the painter in the second cast and beautifully waspish with Margaret Rawlings in the first. After the play opened I met his father on the No. 9 bus which he and I often

shared on our way to work (he would walk one stop to join me outside the Albert Hall as this meant he saved a penny on his bus fare to the City).

"Well, did you enjoy the play?" he enquired and I answered, "I think it's only to be enjoyed by someone who is eight or eighty."

"Well, I'm eighty," he said. "And I didn't enjoy it."

"But I did admire the acting," I acknowledged, and he agreed that the cast at least had been impeccable.

Later John took the production on tour for ENSA, and arrived at the Canadians' camp at Borden. When the "dream child" sequence began there was a loud scraping of boots and half the audience left the Garrison Theatre.

"Jesus Christ, they're crackers," one backwoodsman was heard to mutter, and I doubt if they ever repeated that theatrical experience again.

Being a devotee of radio drama I had been charmed by the adaptations of the *Just So Stories* which Cecil Trouncer had been reading for the BBC, and using something of the same technique I made a radio adaptation of *The Suicide Club*, which I showed to John without really wanting anything other than his opinion of what I had figured out. One afternoon he greeted me with the news that his brother Val, then head of drama for the BBC, had asked him to do two radio plays. "I'll do yours," he said, as casually as if he was announcing he would put on his hat before going out. "Get Val on the phone."

We rang the BBC and I was still floating on Cloud Nine when I heard the project being clinched. John made the broadcast with the usual stellar cast – Cecil Trouncer included – and my mother's colleagues at South Africa House joined together to give me a gold charm in the shape of a tiny ladder "because I had got my foot on the bottom rung." My mother provided the bracelet, and I added a charm ever after to represent every translation or adaptation of mine that was produced, until the numbers became too unwieldy and the price of gold charms put them out of my range as a trinket collector.

The other script John chose was *The Great Ship*, a verse drama by Louis MacNeice, likening England to a great galleon

that would sail bravely through every storm, and I was delighted to find myself in such distinguished company.

In addition to his theatrical activities, John was much in demand for concerts and fund-raising activities, and I would hear him run through his lines for such epics as *Morning Heroes* or *Cyrano de Bergerac*. The former reduced me to such paroxysms of emotion that by the time he finished and enquired if he had got it right I had to confess that I hadn't been able to follow the text through my tears.

Noël Coward had abandoned his double bill when the war broke out and subsequently seemed to disappear into a limbo of unexplained official activity which everyone believed was connected with the Secret Service. During the phoney war he was constantly popping over to Paris or somewhere equally glamorous and then would burst into the office unannounced, bounding with energy, unfailingly courteous and charming. Through his French connections he acquired a copy of the 1940 Paris smash-hit, *Histoire de rire* by Armand Salacrou and as I had always translated any correspondence that arrived from France, in much the same manner as he might hand over another letter, Binkie gave me the Salacrou script and asked me to make an English version.

In those days it was the custom for French plays to be heavily adapted for the English scene, the idea being that the two temperaments and senses of humour were so different that if a play was set in, say, Paris or Bordeaux, you promptly transferred the whole thing to Dublin or Scunthorpe, on the grounds that it would make it more accessible to an English audience. A literal translation merely enabled the adaptor to demonstrate his culinary skill and cook the resulting mess into something that might become an English success but was usually unrecognisable as a foreign importation. All I did, therefore, was to produce a faithful rendering of the French original for future fiddling and was immensely cheered when Noël took the trouble to seek me out and declare it the best translation he had ever read. Sadly the fall of France put paid to any further negotiations and the play was presented after the war by a different management in a different translation, but this treatment of a lowly secretary was symptomatic of the

Master's kindness and understanding. I have always been grateful to him for giving me the courage to cultivate what was to become an important aspect of my own career. After a two year silence great therefore was the excitement when he announced that he was about to produce a new play with a part for Margaret Rutherford and that he was off to Portmeirion in North Wales to put it on paper. He was as good as his word and a week later he was back, beaming, with the script – *Blithe Spirit* – and Margaret was delighted with her part.

Records say that the play opened on 2.7.41 and ran for 1997 performances, but that was only the start of its career and it must run *Private Lives* very close as the author's most popular play. The original cast – Cecil Parker, Kay Hammond, Fay Compton and Margaret Rutherford produced a display of ensemble playing that could only be compared to the integration of the Amadeus Quartet or the Beaux Arts Trio – in Cecil's hands Charles Condomine didn't seem at all dull and he held his own against his matrimonial partners with consummate ease. The greeny-grey make-up created for Elvira and Ruth was made up by the gallon, and the chiffon dresses the girls wore had to be renewed so often during the run that the dozens of half-worn ones hanging in the wardrobe (to be made available for repertory productions later) looked like so many ghosts of Bluebeard's wives. Not wanting to use any time-worn stage trickery to cover the entrances and exits of the spirits, Noël called in Jasper Maskelyne, then the representative of the famous partnership of Maskelyne and Devant who used to run a permanent theatre of illusion next door to the former site of the Queen's Hall. "Do you want them to disappear *completely*?" asked the magician, but after going into the complications of the mechanism required, the final solution was an orthodox black-out.

When the play went to America, Jacqueline Clarke, who had created the part of the little maid who causes all the trouble, went with it and eventually left the cast to return to England. By this time America too was in the war, Jackie's ship was torpedoed and the passengers were rescued and taken back to New York. Jackie made her way to the theatre, arriving just before the end of the last act when the off-stage voice is heard singing 'Always', the little song that heralds her

final entrance. Jackie sang for the girl who had taken over from her and transfixed the entire cast who thought some kind of ghostly manifestation really had taken place.

After playing to capacity at the Piccadilly, the play moved to the Duchess where it continued to play to full houses, proving Binkie's theory that the percentage of seats sold will be the same no matter the size of the theatre – if you think a 50 per cent capacity house in a large theatre would have filled a smaller one, you're quite wrong. You would still have a 50 per cent capacity audience.

Disaster struck us from an entirely unexpected quarter. At midday on to 10 June 1941, Harry Tennent collapsed on the steps of the United Universities Club where he went to lunch every day and was rushed off to hospital. Elsie Beyer gave us the news that he had had an aneurism (I didn't even know what that was, let alone how to spell it) and by eight that evening he was dead. Over the past year we had noticed him slowing up considerably, and Binkie was taking over more and more of the day to day activities, but nothing had prepared us for the shock of losing our Managing Director. The soul of courtesy, kindness personified – it was his relationship with his staff that coloured the entire firm's operations. He trusted everyone, relied on their good sense and cooperation – and his loss was shattering. What would become of the firm? When details of his estate were published, everyone was shocked to learn that Harry only had £8 in his bank account, but although royalties from his songs are still bringing in substantial amounts, to all intents and purposes he died a poor man.

The Board were of the opinion that Binkie was too much of a playboy to take over the firm and wanted Willie Gillespie, head of Gillespie Bros., the firm's accountants, to become managing director, but we in the office knew that Binkie had proved himself more than capable of running the show. We all wrote letters of resignation which he took to the board meeting that was to decide the matter. If the vote went against him, he would produce our letters as his ace in the hole, but when he came back to the office he was wearing a broad grin. Ceremoniously he produced the unopened letters, tore them across and dropped them in the wastepaper basket. We offered congratulations, but he declared he would only be able to

make a success of the job if we all rallied round and helped him – although we were all perfectly aware of the technique, when he chose to use his charm on us we were just as susceptible as everyone else.

So here I was, secretary to the Managing Director, and the next thing was Willie Gillespie interviewing everyone in the office to discuss salaries. The first year of the war, Harry had decreed that no increases should be paid, but we would all be given a bonus if business was good, and in due course everyone received the equivalent of a 25 per cent rise. When at the end of the second year, in April 1941, business was booming and there had been no drastic fluctuations owing to air raids, we all maintained that the previous year's bonus should be taken as our basic salaries, an argument that was accepted, so that by now I was getting £5 a week. I considered that on top of this I should get an additional ten shillings, appropriate to my new position, and said so. Willie demurred and suggested five shillings. Then suddenly my name seemed to ring some bell and he asked if I was any relation to Brian Black the famous rugger international and place kick?

"Yes," I replied. "His sister."

"Where is he now?" asked Willie, much interested.

"He was killed last year in a flying accident", was the reply.

"In that case," said Willie, "you'd better have the ten shillings."

Somehow the firm had a knack of making a favour sound like an insult, and it was to happen again in different circumstances before I came to the end of my time with them.

Chapter VII

Like Prince Hal, overnight Binkie changed his attitude – no one could say his nature – and firmly assumed the seat of power which he was to occupy without a break for the next three decades. With the advent of the new wave of dramatists in the sixties, perhaps his control of the London theatre became less all-powerful – he wasn't interested in kitchen sink drama anyway – but commercial television gave him the alternative outlet he needed and by switching to the new medium he made a fortune for himself and the company he worked for. He told me, after several years of successful productions, that he had never commissioned a script that hadn't been produced – a record which very few television drama departments could match. But this is to anticipate, and in the summer of 1941 nobody could have foreseen the immediate future, let alone the events of a quarter of a century away.

As already explained, Emlyn Williams' play, *The Light of Heart*, had been produced in association with Stephen Mitchell – this was the one about the aging actor, ruined by drink, who is being nursed back to stardom in a production of *King Lear* by his devoted daughter. Godfrey Tearle gave a magnificent performance with Angela Baddeley extremely moving as the daughter, but when Godfrey gave in his notice (I think it was because he wanted to go fishing) and no similar star was available, Emlyn rewrote the part for himself, changing generations, and making the alcoholic into the girl's brother. Not quite so convincing perhaps, but it worked after a fashion and in those wartime days we were used to make do and mend.

So now the first new play produced with Binkie at the helm was Emlyn's latest, *The Morning Star*, once more with Angela, this time playing a "clippie", the new name for female bus conductors who were making their first appearance on

London Transport.

A week later Edith Evans opened in another glamorous role in *Old Acquaintance,* John van Druten's play about two women writers, later brought to the screen with Bette Davis and Miriam Hopkins. Muriel Pavlow had her first grown-up role in this, emerging as a radiant teenager (with a love affair to boot), and Mother lent the firm her grey squirrel fur rug to drape over Edith's apparently naked body at the opening curtain when such an article was unobtainable elsewhere. War-time restrictions were beginning to make themselves felt in the theatre and all materials were now rationed, some things becoming almost impossible to obtain. One of the stage managers proved to have a rare talent for painting utility china to look like priceless porcelain, and silk stockings had to be darned and darned again. I returned to my schoolgirl crochet hook and mended ladders invisibly for myself and any deserving friends. In summer we painted our legs with stocking-coloured preparations and drew seams up the back with eyebrow pencils – it was not yet fashionable to appear in bare feet and sandals and everyone still wore hats and gloves on every outing and occasion as a matter of course.

But the brightest star Binkie added to the Tennent stable was undoubtedly Vivien Leigh. She made her first appearance for the firm in a lavish production of *The Doctor's Dilemma* with décor by Cecil Beaton, directed by Irene Hentschel, who had always been successful with women's plays. Vivien created a vision of loveliness, surrounded by superlative actors, including Cyril Cusack as the irresponsible and irrepressible Dubedat. His Irish charm and outstanding talent seemed to promise a happy association with the firm and he would probably have joined the long line of regular leading men if he hadn't come a bad cropper on St. Patrick's Day when the play had only been running a few weeks. Unfortunately he celebrated his national saint's day with such enthusiasm that he was utterly incapable of appearing at the evening performance. Equally reprehensibly, his understudy, who was playing a small part in the last act, had omitted to learn the part and had to go on with the book, a heinous offence which led to the most almighty row I ever remember happening in the office. Cusack was promptly sacked and retired to Ireland, where he

fathered a clutch of beautiful Irish actresses who eventually made their mark on the London stage, but his own career suffered a setback which took him several decades to overcome.

Why do actors drink? It's a boring fact of the profession that so many of the best seem to find it necessary for bravado, necessity, or through a flawed character, to pour the stuff down in incredible quantities, and remembering the historical precedent of Edmund Kean, get blind drunk every night and ruin their health, figures, marriages and careers. Philip Stainton, a wonderful "heavy" who gave an unforgettable performance of Sorin in *The Seagull* with Paul Scofield and Mai Zetterling, boasted that he drank eighteen pints of beer a day. He died before he was sixty five. Stage hands develop "beer guts", and proudly display the effects of spending a large percentage of their enormous salaries on alcohol during the evening while they wait for the end of the performance with nothing to do except drink or play cards. Tragically, it is supposed to be funny to get drunk, and the real hell-raisers such as Erroll Flynn, Robert Newton and Wilfrid Lawson have become legends of the drinking league. They all died young and showed nothing of the personal discipline that has kept the major stars of our time, Gielgud, Olivier and Richardson, spry and well, enabling them to work on into their seventies and eighties. Perhaps the medical profession will find a way of countering this terrible addiction so that by swallowing some magic pill or injecting some powerful specific the alcohol may be neutralised and the patient develop an aversion to the horrible stuff, but the Demon Drink seems to have a powerful fascination which very few actors can resist. At all events it proved the downfall of Cyril Cusack – his place was taken by Peter Glenville, who was fortunately available.

The son of Dorothy Ward and Shaun Glenville who had established a famous partnership in pantomime as Principal Boy and Dame, Peter had been given exemption from military service on medical grounds and had a brilliant career as a leading juvenile, with all his mother's flamboyance and his father's talent. His considerable technique came in handy one afternoon when an air raid warning sounded during a matinée

and from far away the sound of the guns firing could be heard coming nearer and nearer as the invaders flew up the river. Stoically unmoved the audience never flinched until Dubedat's line, "my ears hear things that other people's ears can't," when a ripple of amusement released the tension that was sweeping through the house.

Vivien's beauty had burst on an astonished London when Sidney Carroll, then chiefly known for his work at the Open Air Theatre, Regent's Park, had discovered her and taken her to lunch at the Ivy, the theatrical restaurant where all the tables were allocated strictly in order of precedence. Ivor Novello and Noël Coward automatically rated the tables nearest the entrance, and less important luminaries were graded down the room until the nonentities and minor managements ended up beside the swinging service doors. Carroll and his young protégée had to traverse the length of the room before they reached their table, leaving dead silence behind them as each chattering group was struck dumb, not only by the fabulous being who was being paraded for their inspection but also because nobody had the faintest notion who she was. *Gone with the Wind* and various other films soon saw that she rated the star table herself and by 1942 she was acknowledged as one of the world's most beautiful women.

After the successful London season Vivien took the play on tour and gladdened the hearts of her fans in the blacked-out cities of England. At that time she wasn't plagued by the ill-health that darkened her later years, but even so, she succumbed occasionally to the usual winter chills and her understudy had to go on for her a couple of times, turning in a very creditable performance. She was really the stage-manager and it was typical of the Tennent economy that even with a star of Vivien's importance it wasn't considered necessary to have a special stand-by. There isn't even a maid's part in the play to justify the employment of an additional actress, and Binkie never believed in paying somebody for sitting around all evening doing nothing.

During the tour Vivien had to register for national service though, like myself, she was automatically exempt from call-up as a member of a reserved profession. The play was in Blackpool at the time and Vivien made a mistake in the date,

but the girls at the Labour Exchange were so excited at finding her in their midst that they took her name anyway and saved her the trouble of coming back on the proper occasion.

My own registration was a hurried affair which involved dashing out of the office, streaking (the word had a different meaning then) to an address in Oxford Street, and then giving my particulars to a breathless lady who apologised for keeping me waiting, even for five minutes. Once the official business was over, and she had confirmed that I certainly wouldn't be called up, she burst out with the question she had all along been dying to ask.

"Tell me, how old is Patricia Burke?" Unfortunately I hadn't the faintest idea and left her to check her facts with the Information Desk of the *Daily Telegraph*.

Laurence Olivier by this time was serving in the Fleet Air Arm but as he was stationed "somewhere in the south of England", he managed to get leave most week-ends and visit Vivien. He and Ralph Richardson had joined up together, but I don't think either of them got as far as operational flying. Richardson scored a nap hand on one memorable occasion when he forgot to check the hydraulic fluid in his brakes before taking off and landed safely only to find he couldn't stop and the machine went on to plough slowly through the ranks of the aircraft parked around the tarmac. Onlookers said the slow motion destruction was an incredibly funny sight but quite understandably their lordships at the Admiralty were not amused. There was probably an audible sigh of official relief when the two friends were returned to civilian life and the entertainment industry.

The highlight of 1942 for everyone, however, was the incomparable production of *Watch on the Rhine*. This Lillian Hellman play had been highly successful on Broadway where it had been presented by Herman Shumlin, starring Lucille Watson and Paul Lukas. It was exactly the type of play that fitted best into the Tennent tradition and Emlyn Williams was asked to direct it – his first assignment on a play written by someone other than himself. Like everyone else, he fell in love with the script and apart from making a few minor alterations to enable the English audiences to follow the Americanisms (this was some thirty years before *Dallas*, and theatre

audiences were not expected to be familiar with the transatlantic idiom), he left the text alone. He set to work with a fabulous cast including Athene Seyler and renewing the association between Diana Wynyard and Anton Walbrook. There are three children in the play, two supposedly very attractive, and one, the youngest, an oddity who describes himself as "not beautiful". The pretty ones were easy to cast – Brian Nielsen and Irmgard Spoliansky, both fair-haired, blue-eyed Ayran types – but the other child presented a grave problem. So many of the stage children had been evacuated to safe areas outside London that the usual choice was no longer available. Suddenly one morning I had a phone call from a Dutch actress, Betsy Kiek, to say she had just seen a Belgian child called Yvan Deley in an amateur production who seemed the ideal answer and sure enough, he turned up and was immediately engaged. The trouble was that like so many Belgians he had a hearty appetite and grew alarmingly, so as the play ran for well over a year, he eventually had to be replaced as his size made him no longer credible.

The smoothness of the production and its instant success gave no hint of the backstage drama that apparently had been building up during rehearsal. Not being experienced with other people's plays, Emlyn had a feeling during the first week that some members of the cast didn't like him and were virtually ignoring all his suggestions and directions. He took his misgivings to Binkie, who reassured him.

"I haven't heard a word from anyone," he said. "If they really are unhappy they'll soon tell me", and Emlyn went back to rehearsals with a quiet mind.

Once again I was playing the piano for an off-stage solo from Anton, and attended the final rehearsals in consequence. The closing scene was so unbearably poignant that the stage managers maintained nobody had ever actually *seen* the printed page. Anton was in floods of tears himself and little Spoliansky became agitated.

"Tell me, Mr Walbrook," she asked. "Are you going to cry like this every night?"

"Certainly not," snapped Anton. "In rehearsal *I* cry, in performance it is the bastards in front who cry."

And cry they did. One afternoon John Gielgud came to the

matinée and glancing at him through the curtain peephole Diana commented "John is awash". I looked myself a moment later and found that he had clapped his handkerchief to his face and was holding it there, gazing at the stage with the tears rolling into the now sodden linen. Of course he is well-known for his capacity to cry at the drop of any hat, and during one book recording not only reduced everyone in the studio to tears but was in floods himself. Taxed with this afterwards he said, "Oh yes, I cry very easily. I cry for trumpets, I cry for Queens . . . Oh dear, I suppose I shouldn't say that . . ."

Charles Goldner, as the villain, ran a sweepstake on the box office figures every night – most of the cast, being stars, were on a percentage and entitled to be given the figure. He always won for he made his first entrance from the french windows centre stage, came down to kiss Athene's hand and then straightened up, his bulging eyes sweeping the house from stalls to gallery, and counting any empty seats that might be visible in inconspicuous corners.

The only other time I saw that trick performed was during a production of *Two Gentlemen of Verona* when the dog that Michael Aldridge had bought from the Dogs' Home in Bristol, and who had behaved perfectly during rehearsals, was so startled at seeing the auditorium full of people on his first entrance that he walked down to the footlights, stared straight out in front, surveyed the theatre from floor to ceiling as if counting the house and got the biggest round of the evening.

Another new star was added to the Tennent firmament when by arrangement with Stephen Mitchell, the firm presented Terence Rattigan's *Flare Path*. Written as a result of Terry's experiences in the RAF as a rear-gunner, it was the first of the wartime plays to dramatize Air Force conditions in the theatre and portray the emotional strain the young pilots endured, not in the violent single combat of the Battle of Britain days, but the much harder conditions of the bombing raids when the crews were airborne for anything up to sixteen hours and under constant pressure from take off to landing.

In common with everyone else we in the office were besotted with the Air Force and its heroes and I even ran an

office "Spitfire" fund to which everyone in the firm's employ contributed one penny in the pound of their weekly salary on a purely voluntary basis. The money collected went towards the purchase of one of those fabulous fighters. A script I read about this time summed up the situation perfectly in one memorable line.

Two girls share a flat and the phone rings.

"If that's for me," says one girl, "say yes to the army, yes, thank you to the navy, and yes, please, to the Air Force."

So Terry's play had an adoring fan club in the office even before it faced the public.

Like Binkie, Terry was the personification of charm. Always immaculate, he wielded a long cigarette holder in the Coward manner, and used a gold Fabergé cigarette case with careless ease. (Later Binkie was to acquire one of these as the obligatory status symbol.) The final run-through of the play before it went on tour was attended by half the office staff, and nothing on earth would have kept me out of the theatre. Noël Coward was among the spectators and when the rehearsal was over, attacked Terry violently, saying he had sentimentalised the play by allowing the missing Polish airman to return from the dead to provide a happy ending. Terry, very upset, and yet prepared to do the right thing if it would improve the play, went round asking everyone present if they agreed. Even my opinion was solicited, and I hope I gave the right answer.

"You've written a comedy," I said. "Haven't you?"

"Of course."

"Then you can't possibly kill off a leading character and turn it into a tragedy."

I had learnt my theatre technique in the classic French tradition. This decrees that you must state your theme within the first few lines so the audience gets the message and then you mustn't upset them with unpleasant surprises. I think I was about fourteen when I realised that the Porter in *Macbeth* has to pretend he guards the gates of hell because Macbeth and his lady are damned . . . Terry left the play alone and it ran for over 670 performances.

As a playwright Terry was the god of my idolatry and his technique and construction always seemed impeccable. He told me about his experience with his first smash-hit, *French*

Without Tears, which had been sold to Bronson Albery, then a producing management as well as the owner of the three theatres of the family group, the New (now the Albery), Wyndham's and the Criterion. Casting difficulties had held back the production for nearly two years until a play at the Criterion failed and Albery had nothing else to put in quickly. He had reluctantly agreed to all Terry's suggestions and the play was due to open after only two weeks' preparation. For the record, the cast was headed by Rex Harrison and Kay Hammond, with Roland Culver, Guy Middleton, Robert Flemyng and Trevor Howard among the supporting players.

As they were opening 'cold', i.e. with no provincial try-out, they had invited an audience for the final dress rehearsal made up of the employees of the firms associated with the construction of the scenery, costumes, lighting, etc. The entire play had gone without a single laugh and at the post-mortem afterwards everyone declared that it was hopeless and the script must be rewritten. Although agreeing, Terry flatly refused to rewrite the play overnight and substitute the new text with only one day's rehearsal. He would only do this if the opening could be postponed for a fortnight, a condition Albery was not prepared to meet. The net result was a change in the last line. Diana Lake, the part played by Kay Hammond, has been playing fast and loose with all the young men in the cast, and having been firmly rejected by all of them, prepares to meet the newest student arrival. A young actor, George Astley, had been engaged to cross the stage, followed by an enormous dog. In obviously "gay" accents, he was to say, "Come along, Alcibiades," and the audience was expected to roar with laughter at Diana's discomfiture. At the dress rehearsal there hadn't been a titter. So the dog was dismissed, the line eliminated and George was replaced by a very small boy who walked across the stage in silence. On the first night that moment provided the final roar that set the seal on a triumphant production.

The year closed with Robert Sherwood's *The Petrified Forest* starring Constance Cummings, Owen Nares and a newcomer, Robert Beatty, in a stunning production by Murray Macdonald. We had all seen the film that brought international stardom to Humphrey Bogart, but the play was so compelling

that it disproved the theory that once a film had been shown there would be no audience for the same material in the theatre. Oddly enough, *Forest* seemed to be dogged by as many disasters and deaths as the ill-fated Shakespearean tragedy whose very name is bad luck to mention in the theatre. Not only did several members of the cast die during the run, but one of the black actors knifed his wife, and as if by remote control disaster struck even Leslie Howard, who had played the lead in the film, when the plane in which he was travelling was shot down over Spain. Apparently there were so many people seeing him off at Madrid airport that the German spies there thought the VIP was Churchill.

Raymond Mander and Joe Mitchenson, the theatrical historians, were both playing small parts in the Sherwood play and one day, after another disaster, the stage manager called Ray over. Lifting up the stage cloth he pointed to the fatal words 'Macbeth, Act II', printed underneath. No further explanation was necessary.

Chapter VIII

The *Macbeth* stage cloth had come from the first presentation of a new venture which was perhaps the most famous of Binkie's creations – the non-profit-making side of the business known originally as Tennent Plays Ltd, called into existence to take advantage of the non-payment of entertainment tax. Tax exemption had been legalised as long ago as 1934, the first to benefit being the Old Vic, but while it was expected that many other companies would follow the pattern set in the Waterloo Road, very few had done so. This was perhaps because the aims of the organisation had to be educational (later changed to 'partly educational') but also because of a clause which laid down that in the event of a surplus being made and the company wishing to cease trading, such surplus was to be handed over to a similarly orientated body. This was one reason why Sir Barry Jackson at Birmingham refused to apply, and it is interesting to note that Glyndebourne didn't bother to go through the motions either, since it was entirely financed at that time by its founder, John Christie. Another exception was the Shakespeare Theatre at Stratford-upon-Avon as it was considered that they were so successful it was not necessary to give them any such moral support.

By 1942 Entertainment Tax was being charged at 33.3 per cent of the box office receipts (compared to the modern 15 per cent VAT, which is bad enough) and it seemed absurd that the principle that allowed tax exemption to Shakespeare when performed in the Waterloo Road by John Gielgud should not be valid when that same star appeared in a Shakespeare play at a West End theatre.

There was a further consideration that affected Binkie's reasoning. This was the Finance (No. 2) Act of 1939, which was designed to limit the profits made by firms operating under wartime conditions and prevent them making the huge fortunes that had been amassed during the First World War.

By its terms, companies were limited to profits based on their previous year's trading and any excess (EPT) was to be charged at 100 per cent. For any financial genius interested in the subject, the Finance Act of 1946 brought in a variation by stating that from 1.4.39 to 31.3.40 and from 1.1.46 to 31.12.46 the tax figure would be reduced to 60 per cent and during the period when the full amount was charged, 20 per cent would be credited for post-war repayment, but all such refunds had to be ploughed back into the business. This punitive tax was abolished by another act in 1953.

As the year in question – 1938 – had been a slack one for the firm, its EPT figure was something like £1,000 and any profits in excess of this attracted 100 per cent taxation, so Binkie cast around for means to preserve the capital being generated by the firm's expanding business, to say nothing of minimising the risks of mounting elaborate productions with large casts. The answer obviously was to form a non-profit-distributing company. Acting on advice from Bronson Albery, then a governor of the Old Vic, Binkie submitted a proposal to CEMA (Council for the Encouragement of Music and the Arts), the predecessors of the Arts Council, then under the chairmanship of Lord Keynes, and it was agreed that they would sponsor the new venture, allowing it to announce that it was "in association with CEMA".

The organisation would operate from the Globe Theatre offices, using all the existing staff and managerial facilities, though none of us would be paid anything extra for doing the extra work. The firm would be allowed to charge a management fee (then £25 per week) per production, which would be free of tax. The new company was incorporated on 6 July 1942 with Lord Keynes as chairman, and a structure drawn up by F. A. S. Gwatkin of McKenna and Co, the firm's legal advisers. In its original stages the company was financed by a loan from the firm, a loan which was subsequently repaid without interest or profit. Not a penny of subsidy was given to the non-profit-distributing company either by CEMA or any other governmental body, and in the light of the present enormous sums handed out to theatres, orchestras and opera houses by the Arts Council, it is difficult to understand just why there should have been such an outcry and such endless

accusations that Binkie was profiteering and using government money for personal gains.

In his book *The Mousetrap Man*, Peter Saunders has given an account of the efforts made after the war to curb the Tennent empire by ending the activities of Tennent Productions Ltd, as by then it had become, while Charles Landstone, in his book *On Stage*, describing the workings of CEMA in wartime, paints a highly jaundiced picture of the way the association with Tennent Plays operated. Charles, who declared that he wouldn't demean himself by referring to Mr Beaumont as Binkie, seemed to have a total fixation where the workings of the tax free company were in question. The profits (or rather, surplus) accumulated seemed to him immoral and misapplied, in that his own ambitions lay in the provinces where he felt the repertory system represented the best and finest training ground for young actors arriving from the various drama schools, who were able to learn their professional business in the culture-starved backwoods of wildest Wales or darkest Cumberland. During the war the efforts made by CEMA to bring culture and relaxation to such far-flung outposts deserved the highest praise, and artists of the calibre of Sybil Thorndike and Lewis Casson toured mining villages and endured horrors of discomfort and improvisation worthy of the pioneering days of the barnstormers in the Far West of America.

Charles was somewhat mollified by the gift of a much-needed van to replace CEMA's broken-down vehicle and further cheered when Binkie seemed to endorse the CEMA policy by setting up two repertory companies, one in Brighton and one in Glasgow, where a host of promising youngsters backed by experienced artists provided useful training for future stars. None the less, the whole tone of Landstone's book reveals his total disapproval of the profit motive and the general implication is that if any theatrical enterprise makes money there is something tainted about the resulting lucre. He was obviously insanely jealous of Binkie and this could probably have been explained by the fact that Binkie had emerged triumphantly from whatever may have been his humble beginnings, while Charles remained distinctly second-class. Although much beloved, he never

attained the dizzy heights of the man he so haughtily condemned.

In any event the new company met with no opposition during the first year of trading and the initial storm blew up from a quite unexpected quarter a year later over another Gielgud production, *Love for Love*, at the Phoenix Theatre. The first complaint raised concerned the payment of salaries. On the assumption that if no tax was payable, then authors and stars would be paid their percentages on the gross box office takings, these amounts were calculated and paid out in good faith until the financial officers of CEMA became aware of this horrifying generosity. At the time Binkie was in North Africa with his second concert party, entertaining the troops, and the wrath of Civil Service bureaucracy fell on the capable shoulders of Elsie Beyer. Stalling the irate authorities until the boss's return, Elsie pointed out that a contract was a contract and she had no authority to alter the terms of an artist's engagement.

A further complaint was that *Love for Love* was "bawdy" and therefore by no stretch of the imagination could be described as educational, though one young South African sailor I sent to see it as his first experience in the theatre was so carried away by its impact that he walked the streets for the rest of the night, swearing that he had never actually come down to earth. Questions were asked in the House, reminiscent of earlier complaints regarding another Restoration play, *The Country Wife*, at the Old Vic (for which Oliver Messel had designed the exquisite scenery and costumes). As both plays predated the setting up of the Lord Chamberlain's office, they were not subject to censorship.

Eventually Binkie returned and appeared before a Select Committee of the House of Commons and it was then agreed that in future percentages should be paid on the net receipts "after the deduction of tax or tax equivalent" and honour was satisfied. At one stage it had even been suggested that the association with CEMA should be ended – no hint of commercialism being allowed to contaminate the cultural image – but once the situation had been amended the status quo was allowed to stand.

None of this of course was anticipated when John originally

planned his production of *Macbeth*. True to his war-time classical dedication he wanted to appear in a Shakespeare play and as the Old Vic Theatre had been put out of action, Binkie agreed to back the undertaking, initially for a long provincial tour. But when conditions made it possible to bring it into London, he had cast round for means to minimise the risks of a disaster and had found the solution in the creation of Tennent Plays Ltd. Throughout the run of *Dear Brutus* John was planning the production, giving me copious notes to type, and eventually choosing two talented newcomers, Michael Ayrton and John Minton, to design scenery and costumes. Carrying out their designs presented a formidable challenge to Lily Taylor and the Tennent wardrobe staff, as the boys had had no previous theatrical experience and had created a series of stunning pictures that didn't necessarily relate to the human form or the cutting of any known fold or fastening. They had envisaged massive figures clothed in voluminous costumes with bulging calves and rippling biceps. What we had instead were weedy sub-standard Category C actors draped in limp painted canvas (the only material available in bulk from which to clothe the cast), although the colours were exciting and the general conception perfectly in tune with the play.

For a long time John couldn't make up his mind about the Lady, and finally announced that he would hold auditions in order to find a suitable new star. Among the letters was one application for the part of "Lady McBeth" enclosing a photograph with the pathetic p.s. "I do take my glasses off often." Eventually he settled for Gwen Ffrangçon-Davies who had been his exquisite partner in the romantic smash-hit, *Richard of Bordeaux* as well as in *Three Sisters* and *The Importance of being Earnest*.

From the first the disasters that seem to dog the Scottish play began to accumulate. First, William Walton disappeared. His agent had no idea where he was and as the music he had been commissioned to write had been conceived as an accompaniment to all the witches' scenes, which were to be spoken rhythmically against a recorded score, nobody could rehearse anything final until the composer had set down what had been agreed with the director. One day the office boy came into my room saying: "There's a bloke outside who says he's supposed

to be composing the music for *Macbeth*."

"Mr Walton, Mr Walton," I cried, hurrying out to meet him, "where have you been? Where is the music?"

"I haven't written it yet," he replied.

"Not written it!" I gasped. "But we need it right away."

"It won't take long," he replied and proceeded to explain that composing the twenty-odd minutes of music required would barely take him a week, and he was as good as his word. He attended only one run-through of the play, made careful notes and when the score was delivered, every fanfare and musical bridge was correctly timed to the very last second. A piano version was made to enable the witches to rehearse their "Double double" bits and eventually the whole thing was recorded by HMV on acetate one-sided 78s with thirty members of the LPO conducted by Ernest Irving. They over-ran the recording session by an incredible amount of overtime and poor John had to produce a personal cheque as nobody would leave the studio until every last penny had been paid. Came the day when there was a run-through of the play with the music, and in the empty theatre I felt like Ludwig of Bavaria listening to the final versions of *Tannhäuser* or *Lohengrin*.

John had put together a tremendously complicated effects score with wind howling at all the climaxes, bells ringing, doors being hammered on, etc. and the only way all this could be coordinated was for two operators – Mary and Viola – to manipulate the panatropes – gramophones with pick-up arms that could be spotted on to any given groove of the 78s – with the effects records on one machine and the Walton music on the other. John kept changing his mind and adding or sub-tracting effects with the result that finally there were one hundred and forty separate cues for effects, while the music was fed in to complement or underline the action. After the final matinée, John came to Viola and asked her to add another wind cue to the plot.

"But Mr Gielgud, there's only one more performance," wailed the harassed stage manager.

"Yes, I know, but I *would* like to hear it just once," said John, and who could resist him?

As I have said, there was the usual accumulation of disasters,

but in this particular production it included an incredible number of deaths. One of the witches, Beatrix Fielden-Kaye, died in her bed at the Midland Hotel, Manchester, after the final dress rehearsal, and there were to be four more before the production closed. But in spite of all the difficulties there were some tremendous excitements. Because of the scarcity of good young actors, John had combined all the messengers into one part, played by Alan Badel, then barely twenty and already giving the clearest indication of possessing star quality. He also played the part of Seton, Macbeth's body servant, so that it was possible to establish a relationship which was repeated later in their unforgettable performances as Lear and the Fool.

"I had to be good," said John, "with Alan's beady little eyes boring into me," and he was full of admiration for his young protégé.

The play opened in Manchester and as the first night would be on Friday and Charles La Trobe, the Stage Director/ Company Manager, would be far too busy to cope with financial matters, Elsie Beyer allowed me to travel to Manchester to act as his assistant, and pay 'treasury', the collective word for salaries and petty cash. This meant I could see the two final dress rehearsals and the first night. Rationing by this time was in full force. You got something like tenpence-worth of meat a week, plus one egg, and in addition you were allocated a number of "points" per month to spend on tinned goods. Because Elsie was on fire watch at the Globe she was very friendly with the manager of Hammett's, the grocery store opposite (no fire bombs for *his* roof) and he was extremely generous in the matter of tinned goods and extra rations. He would always allow her extra amounts of Spam, the disgusting version of luncheon meat which we were allowed at that time, together with the odd precious tin of sardines and other goodies. I travelled to Manchester with a suitcase crammed with Hammett's illegal offerings and during the two all-night sessions, cut sandwiches and made endless pots of tea and coffee for the benefit of the cast and theatre staff. At one stage of the second rehearsal, Binkie and I were cutting yet more sandwiches in the Pit bar, behind two sets of double doors, covered in two sets of so-called sound-proof

curtains. Through all this the Gielgud tones were suddenly audible. "Listen to John saving his voice," said Binkie, and we both burst out laughing.

John gave an opening night performance completely on nerves – he had been so busy with the production (to say nothing of having to rehearse a new Witch), that he had had no time to give much thought to his own performance, and the result was electrifying. But the Saturday matinée found him so tired he hardly knew what he was saying and in the final battle scene he dropped Alan Badel over the edge of a rostrum, instead of flinging him firmly aside. Alan, being Alan, fell as he would have done if he had really been dead and hung upside down on the rostrum to the end of the play, without moving a muscle. Willie Walton and I were watching horrified from the back of the dress circle and by the time the curtain fell I was waiting in the wings with a glass of water and an aspirin. Alan swallowed both but said he felt none the worse for his experience – no wonder that within a matter of weeks he was serving in the Airborne Division and was one of the six sergeants who survived the ill-fated drop on Arnhem.

On the Sunday morning when I reported to John's hotel room to deal with his letters and telegrams, my knock was answered by an almost inaudible "Come in". My alarm must have been written on my face for as I entered John reassured me. "It's always like this after *Hamlet* too," he croaked, and then proceeded to dictate a long letter to John Perry. By the end of our session the familiar tones were slowly coming back, but it was just as well he was able to rest for the next twenty four hours.

After a twenty one week tour, and the formation of Tennent Plays Ltd the play moved into the Piccadilly Theatre where it got mixed notices – most of the critics decrying Gwen's Lady Macbeth, and commenting on her lack of stature in the part. The exception was James Agate who came out strongly in favour of her temperamental rendering, declaring that she was a Pict, and so had every right to appear without Mrs Siddons' commanding inches. Always very short-sighted, Gwen had an accident during the run when on her way home through the black-out she bumped her nose on the iron railings outside Albany where she was using Edith Evans' flat. She clapped her

hands to her face and when she opened the door and turned on the light, found herself covered in blood. "That stuff that Ted [the property master] makes up at the theatre is pretty good," she thought. "It looks exactly like this."

Alan Badel was called up just as I met a young actor called David Peel who presented himself at the office saying he had been discharged on medical grounds from the Royal Welsh Fusiliers. A few nights later I heard him reading some poetry on the air quite beautifully, so when Alan left I suggested David for the part and he was immediately engaged. He only had a few hours to rehearse and was terrified he would be unable to learn the lines in time. To reassure him I typed out all he had to say on a couple of sheets of paper but unfortunately I missed out one line with the result that he had the greatest difficulty in remembering it. Charles La Trobe, the unflappable majestic stage director who was taking the rehearsals wasn't in the least put out. "Don't worry, my boy," he said. "If you don't say it, somebody else will . . ." In the event, of course, David was word perfect and through this happy introduction we became inseparable.

Possessed of an incredibly beautiful head, with an attractive and flexible voice to match, David might have become a matinée idol but for one thing; he suffered from duck's disease, having disproportionately short legs under a very long body. I think his father had Egyptian origins – David got his dazzling good looks from his mother – and he spoke French fluently with an absolutely perfect accent. When he walked me home after a performance we would declaim long passages from Racine or Molière, or swap favourite poetry, capping each other's lines as we reeled off Victorian favourites like 'The Slave's Dream' or 'Curfew Shall Not Ring Tonight'.

He had an inexhaustible fund of theatrical anecdotes, one of my favourites being the one about the old actor and the prostitute shivering beside a street vendor's brazier on a winter night.

"Here we find ourselves, my dear, members of the two oldest professions in the world, ruined by bloody amateurs." Another favourite was the one about the old actor, very much come down in the world, engaged to understudy and greeted by an excited callboy as he reported at the stage door.

"Mr Jones, Mr Jones, you're on . . .", and then making his way to his dressing-room, calmly making up and then sending for the stage manager.

"Now, my boy. Where is the stage and what is the play?"

Then there was the old chestnut about the actor who has been engaged to rehearse for two weeks on approval (which meant that at any time during the first fortnight he could be fired), getting a telegram on the 13th day, convinced that this was the dreaded cut-off, opening the envelope and then exclaiming in total relief, "Thank God, my mother's dead."

David had also worked for Robert Atkins, the legendary actor-manager who staged Shakespeare in the Open Air Theatre in Regent's Park and took over the direction of the Memorial Theatre in Stratford-upon-Avon. He could imitate Robert's distinctive tones better than anyone, though it must be confessed it was an easy voice to reproduce. Everyone who has ever worked for Atkins has endless stories of his remarks, my own favourite being one of Michael Bentine's, dating from the time when that genius was a struggling juvenile and cast as Demetrius opposite the statuesque Helen Cherry. "Put in some lifts, my boy" advised Robert, and Michael experienced his first uncomfortably high heels. Tottering uncertainly on to the stage he was greeted by a roar from the auditorium. "You're supposed to come from Verona, my boy. Not bloody Pisa."

It was David who introduced me to a French play called *Altitude 3200* and suggested we should translate it. The piece had been filmed before the war with Jean-Louis Barrault as the juvenile lead and David had liked it enough to get a copy of the original French text. Now we approached Eric Glass, then the representative of the French Société des Auteurs and found we could get the rights through someone called the Custodian of Enemy Property who administered foreign copyrights, the French being temporarily under foreign rule and unable to look after such things themselves.

Enthusiastically we made a version eventually called *Landslide*, cutting the original thirteen characters down to nine and planning the parts for all our friends – Dulcie Gray and Michael Denison, Hugh Burden, Richard Attenborough and Sheila Sim. In the event both Michael and Dickie were called

up before we went into rehearsal, but Dulcie and Sheila both appeared, with Peter Hammond playing the part originally intended for Dickie.

Norman Higgins of the Arts Theatre, Cambridge, agreed to let us put on the play but was months in making up his mind and giving a firm date, so in reply to one of David's despairing letters as to when we were going to start I burst into verse:

> When Norman names the happy day
> I'll send you warning right away
> But till that moment brings release
> You must possess your soul in peace.

Eventually the "happy day" came round and we were to open on 19 July – another coincidence in the line of fortunate dates. John had agreed to direct the play "for free" and Rolf Gérard, who eventually became the resident designer at the Metropolitan Opera House in New York said he would create the set in return for the majestic fee of £25. John, who by this time was appearing in *Love for Love*, left all the casting to us and we collected a bunch of bright young friends who reported for rehearsal, quaking with nerves, on the stage of the Phoenix, kindly lent for the occasion. Rehearsals were nerve-racking for the "authors" as well. At the very first read-through, John interrupted the opening lines with an impatient, "No, no, that won't do at all," and I had to break in.

"They're only calling to each other off-stage," I explained, "It doesn't really matter what they say," and he allowed them to continue.

But we rewrote the text for him so often that the stage manager got hopelessly lost and quite unable to follow what was happening. "Some of this is different," she wailed when once more a scene had been completely turned round, and the expression became a favourite catchword.

Once John told Julian Dallas (who changed his name to Scott Forbes when he went to America) that he should be more *farouche*.

"What does that mean?" asked the luckless Julian.

"I haven't the faintest idea," was the answer, and there the matter rested.

80

In due course we travelled to Cambridge, and got through all the usual agonies of the dress rehearsal, but John couldn't be present on the first night. We had arranged that I would ring him at the theatre after our own performance to give him an account of the reception, and I was all steamed up to tell him that the audience had loved it, but by the time I got through I was crying so much I could hardly speak. As I was holding the telephone I had heard one playgoer say to another, "There, that's what I call a play," and it had completely finished me off.

Business for the whole week was excellent and it was easy for John to persuade Binkie to present the play for a run in the West End. Unfortunately the only theatre available proved to be the Westminster and then only after an interval of several weeks. The cast loyally were prepared to wait, except for Julian who was offered a part in a play called *The Fur Coat* opposite Jeanne de Casalis, and his departure seemed to alter the whole balance of the play. Even so, the notices were encouraging and we might have had an honourable run but for the sudden renewal of night bombing in January – known as "the little blitz" which, combined with a particularly foggy spell put paid to the business.

We lost our windows at Albert Hall Mansions once again on the night the spire of St Mary Abbot's church in Kensington caught fire, and a stick of bombs fell across our building, one exploding in a tree on the edge of Kensington Gardens, and another digging a deep hole just near the statue of Energy west of the Serpentine. We had been waiting for the All-Clear in a small room in the middle of the building, a long way away from the outside windows and after an appreciable period of quiet, Mother and I cautiously made our way to the drawing-room windows overlooking the park to see if there were any fires. I was in time to see the bomb explode and thought "just like the gun flashes in *For Whom the Bell Tolls*" before falling flat on the floor. Apart from a few superficial cuts and bruises we were both unharmed but the blast had wreaked havoc in the flat. The heavy eight-foot mahogany doors had been blown off their hinges, the lead lights in the main hall were hanging in festoons, the black-out curtains had disappeared and there was dust and powdered glass everywhere. Mother groped her way to the larder, found a bottle of gin and poured

us each a tumblerful. It's the only time in my life I have drunk gin "like water", but it was immensely warming.

After checking up on the rest of our flat-mates and reporting our own safety to the wardens, we decided nothing much could be done until daylight, and settled down in the same little room, fully dressed, to get some rest. Suddenly there was a lot of shouting – "Everybody out!" – the porters had found a time-bomb in the central block.

With only minutes to choose from among your possessions, what do you salvage? Fortunately we each had a packed suitcase with emergency overnight supplies, but what else should I take? Eventually I picked up my diamond earrings and my only pair of nylons. After spending the night in the Royal School of Mines, I contacted Dulcie Gray in the early hours and she put her flat in Dolphin Square at our disposal. When I rang Elsie Beyer to tell her of our experience her only comment was "Get your mother settled and then come on to the office."

The time-bomb was duly removed and after a couple of weeks we were able to go home, but it was impossible to heat the flat properly afterwards and every winter for the rest of the war we shivered in the howling draughts that roared through the damaged window frames, but at least that was the last of our bombs.

Chapter IX

In common with everyone else, we were tremendously snooty about the quality of the shows produced by ENSA, the official body centred on Drury Lane and directed by Basil Dean, one of the best hated people in the business. His sadistic treatment of actors was legendary and nobody could understand why he had been given the job of supervising the wartime entertainment for the troops which would seem to require a more philanthropic approach. He was married to Victoria Hopper, the girl who had made an enormous success in *The Constant Nymph* and rumour had it that she had travelled all through the Middle East on a forces tour with her trunks marked V.D., but this may have been a libellous invention.

My only encounter with Dean on a personal basis came many years later when I was invited by J. B. Priestley to convalesce after an operation at his lovely home in the Isle of Wight. Dean had been thoughtfully provided as my escort and chauffeur and he couldn't have been more charming. I asked Jack about his own experiences of the famous sadism and the answer was that Basil had never tried it out on *him*. I could imagine the two geniuses eyeing each other balefully during rehearsals like two enormous tom cats, each daring the other to make the first move, but respecting each other too much to risk an out and out encounter.

As the war moved away from London and we all settled down to an air-raid-free existence, the men serving at home were definitely wanting something better than the concert parties provided by ENSA. The standards guyed in the television series *It Ain't 'Arf 'Ot Mum* weren't so very much of an exaggeration – top performers like Gracie Fields and colleagues couldn't possibly visit every site and camp, and oddly enough it was the straight plays that the troops seemed to enjoy most. All through the war we used to send com-

plimentary tickets for the current shows to all the units stationed in and around London, with the result that the serving men acquired a taste for drama and on the mountain and Mahomet principle, the Tennent Sunday shows were born. Financed by Tennent Plays Ltd, nearly seventy individual performances were given between January 1943 and May 1945.

John Clements was first in the field early in 1943 with a specially mounted production of *Private Lives*, in which he starred with Kay Hammond. Elsie Beyer became the organising officer of the operation. She persuaded Brunskill & Loveday to build and paint eight-foot sets that could be easily packed in a small truck and sent ahead for assembly on the Saturday. Cast and wardrobe would be picked up from the stage door of the Globe on the Sunday morning, travelling in a crew bus to the air force stations within a radius of ninety miles of London, the maximum range the company could travel before and after the show, though occasionally we did have an overnight stop, returning to London in time for the office opening at ten o'clock.

John Clements also had a concert party, recruited on an *ad hoc* basis, performing revue sketches and black-out gags, the body of the company consisting of himself, Michael Shepley, Brenda Bruce, Avice Landone and anyone who was available to appear as a guest star. Rehearsal time in London being very limited, John had an expression "it'll be all right on the bus" which just about summed up the situation, for the running order would be finally settled during the journey and new-comers given an extra word rehearsal, but the performances looked as though they had been prepared for months and were as slick and professional as if they had come straight from the West End.

After *Private Lives, Flare Path* joined the list of attractions, the cast playing in town during the week and then giving their services for the Sunday shows with the utmost goodwill. Following these successes, Elsie thought it would be a good idea to put on a special production of *George and Margaret* and I joined the team as wardrobe mistress and property master. Michael Shepley directed and we had a duplicate cast with Muriel Pavlow or Brenda Bruce playing the juvenile lead, and

84

Emrys Jones, John Blatchley and Isabel Dean among the regulars.

On arrival at the station – Manston, Northolt, Bradwell Bay, North Weald and a whole list of others – the stage management would unpack and put up the set, do the lighting and lay out the props (*George and Margaret* includes after-dinner coffee, drinks and a full breakfast – washing up done in cold water, ugh!), while the actors went to tea in the mess and chatted up the Entertainments Officer and anyone available. There would then be a quick technical run through in the set – usually to find stage exits and dressing-rooms – and then an early evening performance. This would be followed by a huge party in the mess, sometimes with dancing, and in the days of wartime restrictions our eyes would bulge out of our heads at the spreads provided. It was a highly emotional experience on another level, for although the Battle of Britain tensions were over, casualties were still high and faces would be missing between one visit and the next.

In due course, *While the Sun Shines* joined the attractions and because Brenda Bruce was engaged to Roy Rich at the time, she arranged for us to go to Tuddenham, a satellite station of Mildenhall in Norfolk, where Roy was in charge of FIDO, the box of flaming jets that could clear fog from the runways for returning planes but which the pilots found almost more frightening than the actual bombing raids.

In view of the distance from London, we were to spend the night on the station, the men bedded down in the officers' quarters, and we girls boarded out among the WAAF. During the performance we heard the sound of engines and the audience that had been laughing delightedly at the play suddenly 'left' the theatre. All their attention was directed to the runways, and we heard first one and then another plane roar off into the night until eight in all had taken off, after which the audience reaction returned to normal. Nobody mentioned the raid during the party after the show, but next morning at breakfast everyone was smiling – we had brought them luck – all the planes had returned safely to base.

Because it was conveniently near to London and had a huge theatre, we took all the shows to Tangmere – I went along for the ride even if the play wasn't *George and Margaret* and did my

social stuff in the mess before and after the performance. In those days we girls were extremely proud of our Jacqmar scarves which had various designs on them relating to the three services or other patriotic emblems. They were a sort of yardstick and if you didn't have at least one, you couldn't be riding very high in the popularity stakes. The pilots adored these scarves and would beg them, together with any spare silk stockings, to keep them warm in the air – in the days of modern aircraft with air conditioning and pressurisation it is almost impossible to remember that the entire war in the air was fought in freezing conditions with ears popping at unexpected altitudes and black-outs during power dives. Cold was one of the worst hazards the crews had to face and all kinds of unorthodox additions to the standard flying suits would be pressed into service.

I fell very heavily for one of the pilots at Tangmere and he always singled me out as soon as I arrived with a show and we would giggle and dance together and generally have a wonderful time. Although everyone was always very excited on these visits, sometimes one or other of the pilots would seem to be even more worked up than usual (sad that it is no longer possible to say "gayer") and later we would hear that he had gone missing on the following sortie. On one visit to Tangmere I found "my" pilot in this higher-than-a-kite mood and even more affectionate than usual. When I boarded the bus, my Jacqmar scarf had changed hands, and a few days later, we heard that he too had "bought it" on a routine patrol. I never asked, but I do hope he was wearing my scarf.

When the war was over, the RAF gave Elsie Beyer a gold bracelet made of links surmounted by RAF wings and arranged for her to be nominated for an MBE which she duly received. It was nice that all her efforts should have received official recognition but I think we all felt it had been a privilege to take part in the shows and if anyone was to be given a medal it was each and every member of our audiences no matter what function he or she had carried out during the war.

Binkie's war service took a totally different direction. As a member of a reserved occupation there was no way in which he would be called up and as soon as the air raids began he joined up as an ARP warden. On his first patrol he had been

ticked off for smoking in the street – "They can see a match at 10,000 feet" – (something I have never bothered to check), but on his second duty night he was set to man the telephone at the local headquarters. A very long message came through about special anti-gas arrangements for babies in perambulators, and with his immensely slow and laborious handwriting it took him forty minutes to record. This message had to be passed on to about twenty-odd posts, and doing some rapid calculations, Binkie reckoned this would take a minimum of sixteen telephone hours.

"Give me a typewriter and a team of Boy Scouts," he said to his commanding officer (a First World War Colonel), "I'll make sixteen copies and you can dispatch them in the time it would take to do it all on the phone to one post."

Next morning he received a polite note from the Home Office to say his services would no longer be required, and that was the end of his Home Front active service. However, later he was able to contribute personally in a completely different way. By 1943 Anthony Quayle had been appointed ADC to General Mason-Macfarlane, Governor of Gibraltar and Tony sent Binkie a message to say there would be a warm welcome for a concert party on the Rock for which transport could be arranged. Binkie recruited a team including John Gielgud, Edith Evans, Elisabeth Welch, Kay Young, Leslie Henson and Norman Hackforth, and the group spent ten days on the Rock at Christmas and had an enormous success. Binkie brought a basket of fruit home which he distributed round the office, and my share was a banana, so the following Sunday I gave a tea party at the flat to half a dozen friends, including Hugh Burden and Muriel Pavlow, and we solemnly divided the banana into equal shares and had a nostalgic taste of the fruit we hadn't even seen for over three years.

Just before they were due to take off, Binkie suddenly had a nervous seizure – supposing there was colour prejudice on the Rock and Liz Welch were to find herself barred from the same hotel as the rest of the team? He sent a discreetly worded cable to Tony Quayle, and almost simultaneously was asked to send another for Zena Dare, as her son had been reported missing and she was in agony to try and find out more details. Two days later a cable arrived: "Regret no hope for the person you

mention . . ."

"Oh, God," cried Binkie, with no thought for anything but his tour, "what are we going to do about Liz Welch?"

"But Mr Beaumont," I said. "Doesn't this refer to Zena Dare's son?" Sadly I was right, and Liz encountered no racist prejudices during their stay in Gibraltar.

Another result of the Rock visit was that Tony Quayle persuaded Mason Macfarlane to use his influence to get John Perry posted as his personal ADC, so the following year every string was once again being pulled to arrange a return visit. This time it was to stretch to three months, as the group would visit the various centres in North Africa where the Allied Forces had set up their combined headquarters prior to the invasion of Italy. The team included Vivien Leigh, who recited "You are old, Father William," in a modern crinoline dress reminiscent of Scarlett O'Hara, and Dorothy Dickson, shortly to become Tony Quayle's mother-in-law. All the arrangements had been made and everything was set for the off when two days before they were due to leave, a message came from the Air Ministry to say that the special plane required to take the group to Gib. would not be available – obviously the invasion plans were hotting up, though no official reason was given for the cancellation.

Leander's efforts to swim the Hellespont to meet up with Hero were puny compared to the energies Binkie now devoted to sweeping aside all denials and forcing the Air Ministry to honour the promises made to Mason Mac. Finally, at five-thirty in the afternoon Binkie came back to the office after yet another session to say that the only hope would be for complete copies of all the correspondence relating to the visit to be on the desk in front of the members of the council who arranged air transport before nine o'clock next morning. There were about a dozen letters, some running to two pages, and about eighteen members of the council, so as there was no question of using carbons, each letter had to be typed out eighteen times. The three of us – Elsie, Binkie and I – looked at each other. We decided Binkie should type the short letters, Elsie would take the medium-length ones and I would embark on the two-pagers when Linda Gibbs, preparing to go home, discovered the assignment and declared her willingness to

help. Somewhat reluctantly we agreed, the jobs were re-divided and we all set to work, preparing to collate the letters in date order as each typist finished. Linda Gibbs came downstairs with her hat on, carrying a bunch of copies. As she turned to go, Elsie Beyer reacted. Linda had typed her two-page letters on the back of the first sheet – an unacceptable presentation – they would all have to be done again. "Don't let's tell her," I whispered. And we typed away without her all through the night.

The evidence was carried to High Wycombe, the Council agreed that the plan had gone too far to be cancelled, and the group duly assembled at Paddington to catch their train to an unknown destination where their plane would be waiting. (Subsequently we discovered this was Blackbushe.) Up until the final whistle, there was no sign of Dorothy Dickson. She is notoriously vague, but this was going a little too far even for her – if she missed the plane there was no hope of her joining them later. I stood at the station entrance (fortunately the train was on platform 1) and as the guard blew his whistle I saw Dorothy stepping out of a taxi. I flung a pound to the driver (about three times his fare), grabbed Dotty by the hand and literally pulled her across to the guard's van. She scrambled in as the train began to move off and I ran triumphantly down the platform, waving the good news that she was on board.

After ten days on the Rock, the group proceeded down the coast through Morocco and Tripoli as far as Suez, where the night before the fleet sailed, they played to the invasion forces. Unfortunately, nobody seems to have kept a record of the actual places visited and as it must all have been very hush-hush, there is no way now of reconstructing their route from Gib. (rum, bum and 'The Warsaw Concerto') to Cairo (wine, women and song) but among the hosts who entertained them was General Eisenhower, just appointed El Supremo of the Allied Forces and in residence in Tripoli. He had refused an invitation to attend the show on the grounds that he had had to make it a rule not to accept private entertainment – if he accepted one he would have to accept so many others that he would have no time to attend to his duties, but he invited the company to supper at his villa after the show. After a little initial shyness, everyone relaxed and ended up round the piano

giving him a potted version of the entertainment. At the end of the evening he thanked them, and then said he could neither sing nor recite, but he did have a party trick, and proceeded to fall flat on his face. Not every concert party can have been similarly honoured by a future President of the United States of America.

Chapter **X**

If Pearl Harbour brought America into the war, one side effect of that ill wind the Japanese couldn't have anticipated was the decision the Lunts made to bring their current offering, *There Shall Be No Night* to London. This legendary pair, a husband and wife team, were the acknowledged king and queen of Broadway. I had seen them in New York before the war in another Sherwood play, *Idiot's Delight* (filmed with Barbara Stanwyck and Clark Gable) and John C. Wilson had presented them in *Amphitryon 38* in June, 1938, in association with the Tennent office – the occasion when Linda Gibbs had transferred her allegiance to him in preference to Binkie. Although Alfred Lunt was American with Danish ancestry and Lynn was British born, their complete integration as a team resulted in performances of the highest artistry and perfection of timing. Occasionally a young British couple would attempt to follow their example and appear in the same play. Immediately they would be jeered at for aiming to emulate "the Lunts", and somehow none of these matrimonial partnerships achieved the same impact and emotion.

Although *Amphitryon*, adapted by S. N. Behrman (the 38 didn't refer to the year, since it was produced originally in New York in 1937, but to the adaptor's calculation that this was the thirty-eighth version of the original story), had a dazzling set by America's leading designer, Lee Simonson, with a prologue showing Jupiter and Mercury reclining on a plaster of Paris cloud, and providing Lynn with an opportunity to show her femininity to the utmost, it failed to please the London audiences, and put Binkie off doing plays with Greek themes for years to come. There was a legend that Greek classical mythology was incomprehensible to the English public, but perhaps modern travel to the Aegean may have changed all that and somebody will some day revive what I always thought was an enchanting production. However, for

their war-time presentation, the Lunts came back with another Sherwood play, dealing with the Russian invasion of Finland.

With London full of American troops, the Lunts allocated four tickets at every performance to be given free to their uniformed compatriots, and apart from that, the theatre was sold out every single night. In the famous "returns book" which I typed up every Monday, the pattern was astonishing. Capacity at the Aldwych was £415, and the box office return each night was exactly that figure. The only variant was the final total, after deducting library commission which depended on the numbers of tickets the agencies had sold for each performance. I never saw this pattern repeated anywhere else, though there were many other smash hits that ostensibly played to capacity just as consistently.

The Lunts too came on the Sunday circuit and appeared at Warboys, then an American Air Force base. The theatre wasn't as well equipped as those on our usual ports of call and the only way to the stage was through the auditorium. Toilet facilities were in the mess proper, so the artists had to climb in and out of the windows to reach them. When I explained this to Lynn, hesitatingly, she merely smiled. "Just give me a bucket, honey," she said, and that beautiful lady continued to make up with the aid of my tiny handbag mirror.

After the war, Lynn and Alfred continued to divide their time between London and New York – Coward and Rattigan both wrote plays for them, and Peter Brook directed them in an adaptation of the Dürrenmatt play, *The Visit* which opened the rebuilt Royalty Theatre in Kingsway. They made a special trip to London to attend Binkie's memorial service and can truly be said to have remained his faithful friends for the rest of his life.

In addition to the commercial activities, the non-profit-making company, following on the success of *Macbeth*, was embarking on an ambitious programme. A trio of plays was chosen, "to represent English classic comedy, Russian masterpieces and the new voice of our own country." I can't imagine who dreamed up that resounding phrase – it probably marked the end of one press agent's career prior to the engagement of the next. By the end of the war, "Popie" had

been replaced by Richard Clowes, a firm friend of both the Johns, Gielgud and Perry, a brilliant journalist and wit, joined in 1942 by Vivienne Byerley, his secretary and soon my close friend. The plays were to be *Love for Love, A Month in the Country*, adapted by Emlyn Williams, and *They Came to a City* by J. B. Priestley, who was sharing with Churchill the honour of expressing English doggedness through his radio talks. The undertaking was to be sponsored by the Co-op movement, probably the first instance of commercial backing for the theatre, and as far as that organisation was concerned, the last time they cooperated in a managerial venture. The play had visionary Utopian overtones, and because of the CEMA association, the script was duly sent to their drama panel. To quote Charles Landstone again, he felt the title might more properly be *I Have Read This Before*, an allusion to one of Priestley's earlier "time" plays which had been so successful. However, there were compensations. John Clements appeared as the ardent visionary, with a radiant young Googie Withers at his side, and a veteran of the music hall, Ada Reeve, provided many of the comic interludes.

Emlyn's adaptation of the Turgenev was to have been played by Peggy Ashcroft, squired by Michael Redgrave and my new friend David Peel, but when she was hurt in the bomb explosion in Denman Street and was replaced by Valerie Taylor, David was considered too young and the part was given to Tom Gill. David departed to Stratford-upon-Avon and enjoyed himself playing Romeo and Orsino and never worked for the firm again. It was the third production, *Love for Love* that really hit the jackpot.

As a juvenile at Oxford, John had played Valentine and now he staged the play with settings by Rex Whistler. Rex by now was in uniform, and as his time was limited, he was only able to do the sets. Over dinner with John, he sketched out his ideas on the back of a sheet of John's own notepaper, and the result was so successful that he completed the drawing next day in the office, putting in the final details with a mapping pen and a bottle of Indian ink, so the historic document was finally completed under my very eyes.

Ruth Keating, who had designed the sets for *Dear Brutus*, suggested a colleague, Jeannetta Cochrane, to do the cos-

tumes, and she produced an authentic collection that, made up by B. J. Simmons, lasted for the two year run of the play and many other subsequent productions of Restoration plays. *Love for Love* opened in Manchester and John wrote: "I've just realised that I could have doubled Valentine and Ben . . ." but perhaps it was just as well he didn't try. One young understudy, newly discharged from the forces, was Peter Bridge, who later became a successful West End impresario, and the leading juvenile was Rosalie Crutchley, whom I had seen at the Oxford Playhouse dazzling everyone with her incredible dark beauty. Seeing her in Jeannetta's creations Russell Flint was equally overcome and wanted to paint her in his studio – great kerfuffle resulting since no costume or prop is normally allowed to leave a theatre during a production – and special permission had to be given. It was while preparing *Love for Love* that John came into the office one day and finding Binkie's door shut enquired who was in conference.

"Robert Donat and his agent are discussing *Heartbreak House*," explained Elsie.

"That's a part I've always wanted to play," remarked John. Then after a pause he added, "Oh, but Ralph Richardson would be so much better than I should."

For his make-up as Shotover, GBS wanted Donat to look like the old sea captain in Millais' *Northwest Passage* and I was instructed to find a reproduction. Fortunately I knew the picture belonged to the Tate Gallery and somehow the museum managed to find a photograph, although so much of their material was stored "somewhere in the country" in safety. Years later I discovered that the model for the picture had been Trelawny, the flamboyant swashbuckler who had been the friend of Lord Byron and the Shelleys. It was he who supervised the cremation of Shelley's body and rescued his heart which he then carried home to Mary.

Whether John was being over-modest or not, I don't think anyone could have bettered Donat in the part. His spiritual quality, his exquisite voice, and the tenderness he showed towards Deborah Kerr as Ellie Dunn, added up to an unforgettable performance. Edith Evans and Isabel Jeans played the captain's daughters and it is only fair to say that when Tennent's set their mind to being glossy, there was no

management able to match, let alone exceed, the constellations of stars they always managed to present. The standards set by those revivals can only be compared to what is now being done at the National or Royal Shakespeare theatres, where almost unlimited public money is poured out in order to finance similar revivals. The Tennent "empire" was a focus of envy and criticism at the time, in exactly the same way as the "commercial" managements nowadays complain that all the stars are tied up with the subsidised companies . . . *Plus ça change* . . .

To set the crown on an entirely successful year, December saw the production of Terence Rattigan's *While The Sun Shines*, and once again the Tennent talent for casting seemed to find a new peak of perfection. Sadly so many of the cast seem to have died young that a modern audience would know nothing of the skill that assembled Michael Wilding as the Englishman, Hugh McDermott as the American, Eugene Deckers as the Frenchman and Ronald Squire as the Duke. Jane Baxter, the perfect English ingenue, who had created the part of Frankie in *George and Margaret*, was flanked by Brenda Bruce in her first important West End part, and the success of the play was so immediate that the production costs were paid off during the four weeks pre-London tour.

But however effortless and joyous the whole undertaking may have seemed, it had the usual background of sheer hard work and technical brilliance that marked all Terry's writing. Having completed the first draft, he told me that he had read the play through, decided it didn't work, torn it in half, dropped it in the wastepaper basket and started again. The laughter of the audiences seeing uniformed characters they could immediately recognise disporting themselves in Terry's witty situations, delivering Terry's inimitable lines, sent me out to the back of the Upper Circle on every Wednesday matinée as often as I could pretend I urgently required to visit the loo . . . and with 1154 performances to its credit the Globe didn't require another production until December of 1946.

Looking through the list, oddly enough 1944 seems to have been a less than successful year, though with the carry-over of the previous season's smash-hits, nobody could say the office was idle. The first new venture, though we didn't know it at

the time, was to provide a landmark in the firm's fortunes and bring about a very big change in my own situation.

Emlyn Williams' new piece, *The Druid's Rest*, called for two young Welsh boys of the same type that Emlyn himself had played so brilliantly in his early plays, and at his suggestion, Daphne Rye was dispatched to Wales to hold auditions and seek out any likely talent. Advertisements were placed in the local papers and Daphne interviewed dozens of potential Proteans with the requisite qualifications. She came back triumphantly with her discoveries, Stanley Baker and Richard Burton. They were both engaged at once and went on to fame and fortune as film stars, though at that time it looked as though Richard at least would eventually head the list of theatrical knights and take over the mantle worn so bravely by the Gielguds and Oliviers who had preceded him. Photographs show his incredible beauty, which came mainly from those mad pale blue eyes burning against his dark colouring, and the voice even when he was a teenager had a musicality which no subsequent vicissitudes have been able to mar.

Immediately after the end of the run, Emlyn engaged him to appear with Edith Evans in a film he was making, *The Last Days of Dolwen*, and then Richard returned to the firm to appear in a new play. Meeting Emlyn after he had discussed his contract with Binkie, Burton proudly announced that he was now to be paid £12.10s a week.

"That's ridiculous," cried Emlyn. "You're a film actor now. Go back and tell Binkie you must have £15."

Burton duly put in his request and the Boss remarked, "I see you've been talking to the Welsh pit pony again." But Burton got his £15.

As a result of her talent spotting achievements, Daphne was made casting director for the firm, and half my job and much of the fun disappeared. I certainly didn't wish to be a shorthand typist again and the fact that nothing was said openly, but that Daphne merely became an established figure in the office didn't help. She continued with the firm until she fell in love with and married Sam Ainley, son of Henry Ainley, an incredibly handsome actor with a superb voice. Marriage didn't find favour in the Boss's eyes, and eventually Daphne

departed to the Costa del Sol where she opened a series of highly successful restaurants. At the time she went the waspish Dick Clowes was heard to remark that it was the first occasion on which a sinking ship had abandoned rats.

Two less than successful high-brow entertainments followed. The first was a revival of *The Cradle Song* directed by John Gielgud with Wendy Hillier giving an exquisite performance, flanked by groves of budding *jeunes filles* as nuns and novices, headed by Yvonne Mitchell. It provided employment for the chronically idle sex, the male appeal being provided by Julian Dallas of *Landslide* fame.

The second play was by Eric Linklater, *Crisis in Heaven*, an extraordinary mish-mash in which the inhabitants of Olympus become concerned about the future of Earth with its warring factions. They decide that only the offspring of the keenest brain, represented by Voltaire, coupled with the fairest of women, Helen of Troy, can solve the problem. Adèle Dixon embodied the redoubtable Amazon produced by this unlikely union and appeared as a policewoman trying to establish what the post-war BBC announcers invariably described as Lauren Orda. At the end of the play she prayed for courage, and in burst the blind actor, Esmond Knight, to provide the answer. Stripping off her navy blues, Adèle then appeared in a becoming off-the-shoulder white tunic and the nuptials of the young couple brought the proceedings to a triumphant conclusion. The run of the play was less triumphant and it came off after a mere thirty eight performances in spite of the all-star cast, led by Dorothy Dickson and Ernest Thesiger. As he was sadly contemplating the evidence of the box office figures I tried to console Binkie by saying, "Surely you're glad you produced *Crisis* and *Cradle Song* rather than *Arsenic and Old Lace* or *The Man Who Came To Dinner*," naming two highly successful comedies that both enjoyed long runs under the aegis of a rival impresario, Firth Shephard.

"I'd much rather have produced them as well," was his reply, which I suppose summed up his philosophy, but somehow neither of them would have been right for the Tennent image.

Yet another play to join the list of flops was *An English*

Summer, called originally *Fighters Calling*, an RAF story set mainly in the operations room of a Fighter Station. The popularity of films such as *The Sound Barrier* and *Reach For The Stars*, as well as the documentary *F For Freddie*, had proved the public's passionate interest in everything to do with the flying service. It therefore seemed like a good idea to have a play dealing with the same subject, but in spite of a most realistic set, with what had previously been the secret lay-out of the ops. room shown on stage for the first time, it didn't catch on, though later we gave it another chance at the Lyric, Hammersmith, with the story rewritten and the characters strengthened.

Raids on London were by now a thing of the past, but we had two more trials before everything was over – the horrors of the doodlebugs and the V2s which I found much more upsetting because they gave no warning of their arrival. Fortunately for me, I had been having dinner with some friends on the top floor of a house in Lyall Street that faced east the first time we heard the odd sound of the V1 engine. Rushing to the window, we were in time to see the tiny aeroplane chugging its way towards us and then the engine cut, the thing tilted downwards and a few seconds later there was a loud bang. Thanks to this experience I could judge how near or far the danger was when I heard the sound again and before long everyone knew that it was possible to count ten between the time the engine cut and the ultimate bang. Apparently there was some defect in the petrol system which caused the ignition to cut when the nose was tilted downwards and if the engine had continued to run until the final explosion, the destruction would have been even greater. The RAF found they could shoot down the V1s reasonably easily and there was a story of a pilot flying alongside one and using the wing of his own plane to flip it over and send it crashing to the ground. The V2s on the other hand gave no warning at all and it was really horrid to hear the sudden bangs, though always accompanied by the guilty feeling of relief that it had missed you again.

And then suddenly it was 6 June – D-Day, and the whole atmosphere of the country changed. Invasion pictures filled

the press and fresh anxieties were born as the battle swung slowly from the Normandy beaches towards the Ardennes and ultimate victory.

Chapter **XI**

The first success after D-Day was *Uncle Harry*, one of the rare plays which Binkie returned to after an initial disaster. It had originally been tried out with Eric Portman, but nobody was satisfied with the production and it had closed before opening in town. Now it was restaged with Michael Redgrave, newly returned from his stint in the navy (I remember him coming into the office in his immaculate sailor suit, carrying his gas mask over his arm to avoid creasing his collar) and it was an instant success, achieving a respectable number of perform-ances at the Garrick. This was the first time one of the firm's productions had visited that theatre notorious for an architec-tural oversight – the whole structure had been virtually complete before the discovery that the designs had omitted to provide for dressing-rooms. A second block had to be hastily pressed into service, which explains the passage-way between the stage door and the main building.

However, it was left to the non-profit-making side of the firm to crown the achievements of the year with the second Gielgud season at the Haymarket. John decided to revive *Hamlet* with Peggy Ashcroft as Ophelia followed by *A Mid-summer Night's Dream* and *The Duchess of Malfi* in order to provide her with two more starring parts. The plays were to be directed by outside luminaries: *Hamlet* by George Rylands from Cambridge, the don known to all his pupils and friends as Dadie, and *The Dream* by Neville Coghill from Oxford. Both would provide the scholarly approach and emphasis on the verse-speaking which were always the hallmarks of John's productions, leaving him free to concentrate on his own performances.

The idea of having a permanent company employed for several plays brought ecstatic support from the Arts Council, as CEMA had now been renamed. In the person of Charles Landstone they rejoiced at seeing a commercial management

adopting the principles the Drama Department had been preaching for so long, but a glance down the cast lists of the various Gielgud productions shows that in fact he had virtually set up his own company of actors from the beginning – his own style of acting being admirably set off by such stalwarts as George Howe, Max Adrian and of course Peggy and Gwen.

The *Hamlet* was given Jacobean costumes with a very heavy permanent set that never seemed ideal for any of the interiors and was a positive hindrance for anything smacking of the outdoors, though perhaps the academic approach would maintain that this gave it greater historical authenticity.

I took advantage of a week's holiday to travel to Manchester to see the play during the try-out. John Byron was performing the same play at Stratford-upon-Avon and David Markham was also doing it at the Oxford Playhouse, so I decided to fit in all three performances in the same week – starting with the best, like a wine tasting in reverse, though the other interpretations helped to highlight all the elements in the Gielgud version which nobody in our time has so far been able to surpass.

After attending John's first night I arranged to call in at the Midland next morning and collect all the telegrams of good wishes, which I would then answer and send back for signature and despatch. I had been staying at The Bells of Peover, a beautiful black and white inn just outside Manchester and nearly missed my train when the hotel staff omitted to call me. However, there was quite a wait at the station before the Birmingham train left Manchester and I was able to retire to the local "ladies" in the interim. To my horror I found wartime shortages had extended to the absence of toilet paper, but wasn't it lucky I had the telegrams? Wild horses could never drag from me the names of the senders of the ones I used.

The day of the last two performances at the Haymarket eventually arrived and having watched bits of it so often I decided I would wait until the evening and then see the whole thing through, especially as John had said he would save himself during the matinée. I arrived half-way through the afternoon to find the entire theatre backstage shimmering with excitement. John's idea of saving himself had resulted in a

performance of such intensity that everyone had crowded into the wings to watch throughout. The saying goes that no actor can entirely fail as Hamlet, but for my money John is the only actor of our time to fulfil every possible requirement for the part. The critic Alan Dent coined the expression "exquisite Gielgudry" and exquisite is the perfect word to describe the polish and gleam of his performances as Hamlet and Richard II. He was always so undeniably *royal*, whereas actors of the Burton and O'Toole generation are always so distressingly plebeian, the modern fashion being to aspire to *primus inter pares*. John was quite simply *primus*, and everybody else knew and respected his position.

The fan letters poured in during the run and provided one or two amusing incidents. One schoolboy wanted an explanation of a very obscure line and asked for a gloss.

"I've absolutely no idea," said John. "It's one of Polonius's. Better ask George Howe."

George was no more helpful.

"I haven't a clue," he said. "But I always say it with immense conviction."

The Dream suffered to my mind by comparison with the Oliver Messel pre-war creation with Vivien Leigh, Robert Helpmann and Ralph Richardson at the Old Vic, and the exquisite speaking of the verse by John and Peggy wasn't really enough to make it a milestone. John was unhappy about his make-up and costume and shed a most elaborate perspex helmet decorated by Hugh Skillen in favour of a flaming red wig which may or may not have been an improvement. But some moments were unforgettable.

We had a real little Indian boy in the production – something I hadn't seen before – and Peggy's description of his mother's death was the most beautifully spoken line I have ever heard. Somehow she managed to put regret, wonder and incomprehension into the one word "die" – she, being immortal, didn't understand what had happened – and I remember it to this day, in the same way as anyone who saw Burton's Henry V remembers the way he read the casualty list after Agincourt and the way he coloured the name "Davy Gam, Esquire." Like Proust's madeleine those two readings can conjure up an entire production and like entries in a commonplace book

they can be taken out and savoured over and over again with no loss of thrill or pleasure.

John chose *The Duchess of Malfi* (he still wouldn't do *Venice Preserv'd*) as the next vehicle for Peggy, but he looked uncomfortable as the wicked Duke while Leon Quartermaine, the most saintly of men, who had been a vision of integrity as Banquo, paraded magnificently as the Cardinal, but didn't look capable of hurting a fly, let alone of contributing to the horrible deaths that overtake so many of the leading characters. Cecil Trouncer gave probably the best performance as the enigmatic Bosola, but the play suffered from the middle-aged cast.

It was not until John decided to produce *The Circle* that the triumph of *Love for Love* was repeated, though perhaps *The Importance* would be a better comparison. Yvonne Arnaud, the Belgian actress with the squeaky voice and inimitable comedy technique was an adorable Lady Kitty and the other parts suited the rest of the cast to perfection. Yvonne was a somewhat buxom figure and was immensely proud of the fact that she had the same measurements as Queen Elizabeth, now the Queen Mother. On another occasion, for a new play *Jane*, one Hartnell coat had to be changed as she had chosen pillar-box red and the tent-like cut of the garment provided an all-too-apt comparison. I bought the coat from the wardrobe for a nominal sum and found some inches had to be removed from the hem at the back where the material had had to be sculpted to fit the actress' curves. My five foot eight filled the rest of the draping very satisfactorily.

The legendary seasons at the New Theatre presented by the Old Vic led by Laurence Olivier and Ralph Richardson remain as highlights of 1944 and 1945 theatre-going for anyone lucky enough to have seen them. *Peer Gynt* with Richardson as the perfect Peer, galloping over the hills with his dying mother, played by Sybil Thorndike, and Olivier's marvellous appearance as the Button Moulder, were matched by the latter's *Richard III* (subsequently filmed) and the double bill when he began the evening as the stricken Oedipus, uttering one of his famous howls on his blinded entrance, and afterwards flitting all over the stage as Mr Puff in Sheridan's *The Critic*. It comes as a shock to read that play and find how little was provided for

Tilburina and her attendant to say, for Margaret Leighton and Joyce Redman made the scene as hilariously funny as anything in the play sparked by Sheridan's dialogue. Of course I saw everything the company presented – interestingly enough Bronson Albery for whom the theatre was eventually named, had voiced his doubts about English actors being able to appear in a repertory of plays as the French did, thinking their memory training wouldn't prove adequate to the strain. However, when it came to the crunch the English actors didn't seem to experience any difficulty.

And then suddenly the war was over. D-day, the invasion, the months of waiting for news of casualties and fears for the safety of friends, all culminated in a huge explosion of relief and cheering, with crowds dancing in the streets and outside Buckingham Palace. Somehow I couldn't join in the general rejoicing. The end of the war seemed to make the deaths so final – as though subconsciously it had still seemed possible that when the fighting was over the dead would be restored to life. I went into St Martin's-in-the-Fields to give thanks, but found myself weeping uncontrollably for the losses which became even more poignant in the context of the cheering crowds outside – Gene Jessel drowned when her ship was torpedoed on the way to South Africa, brother Brian sleeping in the Air Force cemetery at Upavon, Geoffrey Nares lying somewhere in North Africa, new friends like Bobby de la Tour disappearing in the Normandy landings, and the major losses for the theatre like Rex Whistler and Stephen Haggard. Of course the war in Japan was still to be won and my sailor brother was very much in the thick of things, so VE Day marked only the first half of the final victory. There were to be another three months of anxiety before the mushroom cloud burst over the horizon heralding peace.

Black-outs were torn down, shop windows could light up again, and the illuminated signs outside the theatres could once more display the names of the stars and the plays in which they were appearing – I don't remember being thrilled by any of it – we were far more concerned with the terrible stories coming out of Germany as the concentration camps were liberated and the horrifying pictures of the skeletal figures in their obscene prison garb and clogs were shown on the cinema

screens. A delegation of MPs went on a tour of the camps to testify to the authenticity of the pictures and one gesture in the sequence struck home as almost nothing else could – the way one woman MP had to hold a handkerchief over her face – the stench must have been almost the worst part of the entire experience.

But like the lifting of the barriers between England and France with the defeat of Napoleon, the floodgates opened between the cultural lives of London and Paris and the names of Jean Anouilh, Jean-Paul Sartre, André Roussin and Louis Ducreux brought a whole new lease of exciting plays to the London stage. In celebration of victory in Europe, the British Council arranged that the Old Vic would do an exchange with the Comédie Française – the first time in the history of the Maison de Molière that a foreign company would appear in their august hall – and I was asked if I would like to go to Paris during my summer holiday in June to act as technical adviser and interpreter for the French end of the negotiations. I took off for Paris with huge excitement and a suitcase full of goodies such as tea and tinned sardines that I managed to scrounge for I knew my French friends had been suffering even greater hardships in the food line than we had.

Crossing the channel was an experience in itself – we had to wear life-jackets throughout in case the ship hit a mine, and the train journey to Paris was like travelling through a nightmare – everywhere piles of fallen masonry, débris of houses half-filling the roadway – long lines of carriages and goods waggons rusting in sidings with the tracks overgrown with grass and weeds – you could have played hopscotch in the bomb craters most of the way, and it didn't look as though anyone had made the slightest attempt to tidy anything up. The contrast between this devastation and the incredible speed with which damaged houses and shops were patched and boarded up in London was poignant, and marked the difference between the brisk efficiency of the English attitude and the apathy of the French under the German occupation. I was travelling to Paris with John Burrell, one of the Old Vic directors, and as soon as we arrived we went straight to the offices of the British Council where to my immense surprise I discovered that the Paris representative was my cousin Ian, the

oldest male member of my generation whom oddly enough I had never met. Ian had always had theatrical interests and had been one of the original directors of Motley, the firm consisting of the Harris sisters and Elizabeth Montgomery who had scored an immediate success with the costumes and sets for John Gielgud's *Richard of Bordeaux* and had done so much work for him ever after. Ian had even been married to a young actress who appeared with John in *Noah*, but now he was living in Paris and married to a French wife with two stepsons. He had been a great friend of Michel St Denis, and together they had manned the Free French radio station in London which broadcast to both the Occupied and Unoccupied zones.

Ian led us off to the offices of the Comédie Française to meet the administrator, Pierre Dux, one of the handsome juveniles of my schoolgirl adoration, and for the first time I penetrated the holy of holies, the *bureaux de l'administration*. Everyone was politeness itself, help and cooperation were extended in every direction, and it was obvious no stone was going to be left unturned to ensure the success of both visits. John Burrell spoke no French and after many enquiries had been passed through either Ian or myself, asked how many dressing-rooms the theatre possessed. After all, he said, in addition to the leading men there were Dame Sybil, Miss Leighton, Miss Redman, etc. etc. There was a short pause. Pierre Dux held a rapid consultation with the Stage Director and I caught mutterings of "the little room at the end" – "If I clear out of my own office" – and finally the answer came. "Forty-two." As the cast in London were packed two and three to a room in the cramped backstage quarters of the New, there was an audible gasp of surprise from the English contingent.

Later we visited the stage to see the scene dock where the material for the London visit was being prepared. I had heard that owing to shortages of canvas and timber, most of the scenery at the time was being painted or photographed on to specially woven "canvas" made of paper, and the London fire authorities were adamant that in no circumstances could such material be allowed into a London theatre. The stage director assured me that they were remaking the scenery with fire-proofed pre-war canvas and timber and to prove his point struck a match and held it to the piece of scenery under

construction. So intent were we all on watching the effect that the stage hand didn't notice how far down the match had burnt and dropped it with an exclamation as it singed his fingers. At that moment a voice remarked, "In England even the stage hands have to be fire-proofed," and everyone laughed. It was my first meeting with Jean-Louis Barrault. He cordially invited me to come and see his production of *César et Cléopatre* the following night, regretting that neither this nor the more spectacular *Soulier de Satin* would be included in the London visit.

The stage director gave me three days' leave of absence to visit my "best friend" in the country and promised to have all the publicity material and technical requirements ready for me on my return. He was as good as his word, and on top of everything, had packed them in a satchel bound with red tape made of the paper canvas which had been the original cause of my concern, a historical piece of wartime economy which I still have.

I stayed at the Hotel du Louvre opposite the theatre and experienced some of the deprivations the French had had to undergo during the war. The first morning I asked for "thé complet" and was served with a pot of undrinkable greenish liquid with a small piece of French bread. Thinking the coffee might be better, the next morning I asked for the French national beverage – again it was disgusting, and I was told it was made from roasted acorns. If you were lucky you got roasted barley which was quite palatable, but they didn't have any, so after that I asked for "eau chaude complet" and stirred a spoonful of condensed milk into my jug of hot water. Fortunately we were allowed to eat at the American mess in the Hotel de Castiglione and the food there was on a pre-war level – it was too bad I couldn't take all my friends in as well for a surreptitious meal.

That winter in Paris was one of the coldest on record, and the girls of the Folies Bergères finally went to the manager and said they could no longer work in the nude unless he could provide them with some heating. The poor man had no way of complying with their very reasonable request, so said they could all wear fur tippets to stave off the worst of their suffering. The effect was so devastatingly erotic that the

American commanding officer commandeered a trainload of coal and had it delivered to the theatre in order for normal working conditions to be restored.

The Comédie Française season opened in London on 11 July with Jacques Dacqmine creating a sensation as Hippolyte in *Phèdre*. He wore stylised Louis XIV costume with bare feet and black anklets – the first time I remember this being done – and the seductive effect was immediately copied by all our handsome male – and female – stars. Angus McBean has recorded the event for posterity and the cultural exchange was a wonderful landmark in Franco-British relations.

In the sixties and seventies, Peter Daubeny's World Theatre Seasons brought the Comédie Française to London on many occasions and finally *Le Soulier de Satin* was shown to an admiring public with the divine Généviève Page in the leading role, but the scenery for the touring productions was always simplified to the point of tattiness so that they lost some of the impact the Paris productions possessed. I have always regretted that I didn't see the Claudel in its original incarnation.

I was always so pro-French and argued so hotly in favour of the country and people that when I finally established my reputation as a translator my wittier friends began to call me Noir, though I was never able to persuade them to add the feminine "e". They still won't.

Chapter XII

Of course over the years there had been changes in the set-up at the Globe. Office boys disappeared at the beginning of the war and instead a series of young girls were engaged to make the tea, do the filing and generally make themselves useful. As the pressure of work increased, the staff was occasionally augmented by Betty Woolfe, the wife of one of our company managers, who was an ardent actress but having worked for the Carl Rosa Opera Company in the manager's office was an excellent secretary and general factotum. The only way to keep her happy was to give her acting jobs every now and then, and she would pop off in the evening in time to report to her theatre. Nobody else ever left the office until the Boss departed – for just as Ivor Novello was always "The Guv" and Noël Coward "The Master", Binkie was known to everyone in the firm as "The Boss". When pressure of work was high, and the working day lengthened, sandwiches would be sent for, mostly from the Moulin D'Or, a favourite Soho restaurant much frequented by actors, and we would keep ourselves going with pots of tea until ten o'clock or later. It was taken for granted that this timetable was part of our engagement, together with any extra time needed on a Saturday or Sunday when there was too much to get through.

Nobody was ever paid overtime for this total devotion and we would probably have been horrified if anyone had suggested asking for more pay, let alone striking in order to get it. I remember once falling asleep in the train at eleven o'clock in the morning when we were going down to Ford to spend Easter with my sailor brother, and on summer holidays the first weeks was always spent entirely horizontal, so much were we exhausted by the strains and stresses of the daily routine.

However, with Betty Woolfe in the office we did have an invaluable extra body – she played Beer, the new maid, in our

Sunday production of *George and Margaret* and eventually appeared as Mrs Pearce in *My Fair Lady* at Drury Lane, never missing a performance and lasting throughout the entire five year run. She eventually achieved worldwide fame in her eighties when she became the poster grandmother for British Airways and adorned all kinds of advertising material both on the box and on hoardings – she had never had any children of her own so it was a wonderful compensation to become a surrogate mother and grandmother at her time of life and rake in vast sums of money in the process.

Now, with the war over, Binkie invited John Perry to join the firm, originally in some fairly unspecified capacity, but eventually he became a director and when Binkie died came out of retirement to run the business for the new management. This arrangement put Elsie Beyer's nose completely out of joint, just as my own position had been overturned by the appointment of Daphne Rye as casting director.

I had always enjoyed the fun of trying to introduce talent to the firm and using every known form of trickery to foster the chances of particular favourites. Remembering how Binkie had persuaded Betty Jardine, an actress in her thirties, to audition for Dodie Smith in a gym tunic for the young girl's part in *Bonnet Over the Windmill*, I tipped off Dulcie Gray when she was trying for the part of Alexandra in *The Little Foxes*. For her first interview she had appeared wearing a fur-trimmed winter suit on one of the hottest days of the summer as she considered it produced a "period" effect. Unfortunately the fur muff and veil gave her an extremely sophisticated appearance and Binkie dismissed her as too old.

"Please see her again," I begged. "She's absolutely right for the part," and when Binkie agreed, I rang up Dulcie.

"For God's sake remember the girl's fifteen," I urged, and she turned up next in a candy striped pink and white Horrockses number with pink bows in her hair.

"You have now gone too far," I said grimly and ushered her unsmilingly into the office. But she got the part.

It was during the run of *The Little Foxes* that Dulcie asked her fellow juvenile, Richard Attenborough, how long he had been on the stage. Dickie, the veteran already of numberless film and stage performances reflected a moment. "It must be

getting on for six months," he finally declared.

So much for Equity and the present rules for making entry into the profession as difficult as possible. They would never now countenance the Tennent scholarships – contracts running for twelve months, the first carrying a salary of £750 and the second £500, awarded by the non-profit-making company, to two graduates from the Royal Academy of Dramatic Art. These young people were used as understudies if there was no suitable part going, and had the immediate opportunity of working with top stars and directors, or later, joining us at Hammersmith when the Company of Four was formed. Many of these youngsters went on to become stars – Barbara Jefford, Brewster Mason, Paul Daneman among them – and in spite of the belief that Tennent's had all their stars under permanent contract, the RADA graduates were the only artists actually engaged in this manner by the firm. Eventually I considered the system should be extended and put in an impassioned plea that Paul Scofield should be given a similar deal. I knew he had two young children and it seemed ridiculous that he should not be given the same kind of security. A few days later, riding in a taxi with Binkie and John Perry, Binkie gave me the pussycat smile he reserved for moments when he had been particularly clever.

"You've got your way," he told me. "Your young man's just signed a contract," and Paul worked for the firm for the next dozen years.

After all the work I had done in the talent-spotting field it was all the more galling to find I was being excluded from the field I most enjoyed and relegated to a shorthand and typing situation. After a couple of sleepless nights I plucked up courage to tackle Binkie and ask if it wasn't perhaps time for me to think of changing my job.

"What do you want to do?" he asked.

"I think I'd like to be a casting director," I replied.

"You mean, like Weston Drury?" asked Binkie, naming the most important figure in the British cinema.

Being completely ignorant of the ways of film makers, and not at all sure where I would start looking for a casting job, I started to stammer something incoherent when Binkie cut me short.

"We've taken a lease on the Lyric Theatre, Hammersmith," he told me. "We're going to run it as a shop window for actors coming back from the forces. Murray Macdonald is going to be the administrator. How would you like to be his assistant?"

I nearly burst into tears. Although I only knew a little of what was being planned, that little was enough to give me a rough idea of the entire operation and I realised this was indeed the answer to my prayer.

"I can't think of anything I'd rather do," I said. And so it was agreed. I would become the Assistant Administrator of the Company of Four with a rise in salary and would be present at every step of the planning of the venture that would begin operations as soon as everything was organised.

The following Saturday morning Elsie Beyer announced that my desk would be wanted for Mr Beaumont's new secretary on the Monday morning and I had to carry eight years' accumulation of private belongings and papers down in the lift and up four flights of stairs to my new office in the Apollo Theatre. This time I was perched above the topmost gallery and the Upper Circle was a whole world and a different staircase away.

The Company of Four was the brainchild of Rudolf Bing, then the general manager of Glydebourne Opera, but more widely known as the first Administrator and inspiration of the Edinburgh Festival and later general manager of the Metropolitan Opera in New York. Following some pioneering work done with children's theatres in Sussex, he had persuaded John Christie that there was room for an experimental theatre of quality in London and found the ideal venue at the Lyric Theatre, Hammersmith. This lovely little Victorian jewel had had a chequered career, culminating in the achievements of Nigel Playfair's régime in the 1920s, among them the record-breaking production of *The Beggar's Opera* with sets and costumes by Lovat Fraser, the Zinkeisen version of *The Way of the World* in which Edith Evans created the definitive Millamant, and the intimate revues, *Riverside Nights*, which launched the Baddeley sisters on their respective careers. (When the newly built theatre reopened in 1979, one item missing from the historical exhibition was the Zinkeisen

poster and I feared it had been lost forever. To my great joy I subsequently discovered it in the bathroom of John Perry's house in the country.)

After the war the lease had been acquired by J. Baxter Somerville, the genial eccentric with sandy hair, an infectious giggle and a passion for bricks and mortar, which he seemed to acquire in all kinds of improbable places, ranging from the Theatre Royal, Brighton, to the repertory theatre at Llandrindod Wells, where he ran a series of summer seasons. He must have had more overdrafts than your average Soviet Olympic team has gold medals, but he was unfailingly cheerful and presumably left all the worrying to his bank manager. His other passion was trotting over the Sussex Downs on a Welsh cob, sufficiently stocky to support his over-large person, and in due course I knitted him a fine pair of golf stockings to wear during this exercise.

When he arrived to inspect the Lyric stage, J.B. (as everyone called him) told me, the first thing he saw was a dead cat, and although the place had been cleaned up somewhat before we arrived, it was still a very grotty number in terms of amenities. There was no hot water in the dressing-rooms, the footlights still worked on water dimmers as originally installed, and there was a permanent leak in the back wall of the stage caused by an overflow from the wet fish shop in the market which ran alongside the building. Our scenic designers learned to camouflage the contours of the leak by painting them to look like landscapes or architectural features, and the antiquated lighting system was gradually replaced by modern equipment, though by "modern" was really meant equipment that had been discarded from other theatres or touring items that were surplus to requirement. One story I heard was that the main power intake was operated by the engine of an Underground train that had been "won" by our multi-talented chief electrician, Bill Walton, a genial over-weight character who added methods learnt as a scrounger in the army to very real inventive genius and eventually ended up as the founder and director of his own company, Stagesound.

Being short on theatrical experience, Bing failed to get his project off the ground and realised he needed help. Starting at the top, he took the idea to Binkie, who immediately appreci-

ated the possibilities of the scheme. He suggested bringing in Norman Higgins, of the Arts Theatre, Cambridge, to provide another touring venue in addition to Brighton. Later two more were added, the Theatre Royal, Bristol and the New Theatre, Cardiff. The plan crystallised into a combination of fours: four weeks rehearsal, as opposed to the usual three which most artists declared inadequate, four weeks on tour, and a four weeks run at the Lyric, Hammersmith. Tyrone Guthrie, then Administrator of the Old Vic and consequently in charge of the theatre at Bristol was added to the managerial quartet and nobody could think of a better name than The Company of Four, inspired by the title of Gaston Baty's 'Compagnie des Quinze'. The English version sounded clumsy but seems to have proved memorable, and it has been copied by various groups of different numbers ever since.

Murray Macdonald, who had had a highly successful wartime job as the director of the Garrison Theatre, Salisbury, was engaged as Administrator and the offices at the top of the Apollo Theatre, where Walter Hackett's management had operated, were made available at a rental of £2 a week. The only furniture consisted of a couple of huge roll-top desks, which proved to be full of dusty relics of the former management – dress collars, handkerchiefs, old programmes – and two revolving chairs.

Here, in my new capacity as Assistant Administrator of the Company of Four, I took up residence in a room decorated in the Moorish style, lined with mirrors, exactly like the dining-room in my old school at St. Albans. There was a tiny alcove in one corner, which I comandeered originally for my own office, with a kettle for making tea, and a telephone with one outside line and a push-button communications system connected to the rest of the theatre. The radiators worked on the steam heat principle which meant that they hissed and crackled on Monday mornings when they came on again after the Sunday switch-off, and in summer the traffic roaring up Shaftesbury Avenue provided a choice between being deafened or stifling behind closed windows.

The policy was to be to produce new plays, with new directors and designers and to provide jobs for actors returning from the Forces. The West End was choked with long-

Christmas, 1939.

Top left: Dad.
Top right: Mother.
Above left: Me and my sister when young.
Above right: My father when young.
Right: Five down and one to go.

Edith Evans.
Above left: Cousin Muriel, with Frederick Leister.
Above right: The Importance of Being Earnest, with John Gielgud.

Below: Robert's Wife, with Margaret Scudamore.

Margaret Rutherford.
Above: Rebecca, with Celia Johnson.

Below: Blithe Spirit, with Cecil Parker, Jacqueline Clarke,
Fay Compton and Kay Hammond.

Design for *King Lear*, Roger Furse.

Vivien Leigh:
the picture that
helped her get
the part in
Gone With the Wind.

Opposite:
Vivien Leigh
in *The Doctor's Dilemma.*

Above: with Peter Glenville.

Below: With Geoffrey Edwardes,
John Turnbull, Frank Allenby,
Cyril Cusack, Morland Graham
and Austin Trevor.

John Gielgud. *Above left:* As himself. *Above right:* as Oberon.
Below left: In *The Circle* with Rosalie Crutchley.
Below right: *Hamlet* at Elsinore with Fay Compton.

Binkie pulls the strings
(Emlyn Williams and Angela Baddeley on stage).

Launching The Company of Four at the Savoy.

Above: Lady Playfair with Murray Macdonald and Tyrone Guthrie.

Below: Margaret Johnston, Hugh Beaumont, Marie Ney and KB.

Right: KB with Peter Brook at the first night of *Adventure Story* (Isabel Jeans has come between us).

Above left: Caste. Clement McCallin's ghost drives Brenda Bruce and Bill Owen under the table while Frith Banbury looks on.
Above right: The Brothers Karamazov. Elizabeth Sellars and Alec Guinness.

Below: The Holly and the Ivy. Daphne Arthur, Herbert Lomas, Cecil Ramage, Maureen Delaney, Jane Baxter, Bryan Forbes, Margaret Halstan.

The Seagull.
Above left:
Isabel Jeans and
Ian Hunter.
Above right:
Mai Zetterling
and Paul Scofield.

Right:
Tuppence Coloured:
Max Adrian, John
Heawood and the
Emett front cloth.

Above left:
The Reluctant
Debutante. Anna
Massey finds happiness
with Jack Merivale.

Above right: The Lunts.

Left:
Troilus and Cressida at
the Memorial Theatre,
Stratford-upon-Avon.
Laurence Harvey,
Anthony Quayle and
Muriel Pavlow.

Captain Brassbound's Conversion. Flora Robson, Malcolm Russell, with Michael Cacoyannis on the ground.

Heartbreak House. Robert Donat and Deborah Kerr in a modern 'North West Passage'.

The Eagle Has Two Heads. Eileen Herlie and James Donald.

Point of Departure.
Mai Zetterling and Dirk Bogarde.

Above: The Only Orpheus.
Dirk Bogarde and Hugh Griffith.

Right: Legend of Lovers.
Dorothy Maguire and Richard
Burton.

"Comedy Smash!"—Garland, Jrl.-Amer.
"Tip-Top."—Hawkins, World-Tel. & Sun
JUNE HAVOC in
AFFAIRS OF STATE
with REGINALD OWEN BARBARA O'NEIL and SHEPPERD STRUDWICK
MUSIC BOX Thea. 45 St. W. of B'way. Cir. 6-4636
Evgs. 8:30: $4.80, 4.20, 3.60, 3., 2.40, 1.80. Mats. Wed. & Sat. 2:30: $3.60, 3., 2.40, 1.80, 1.20 (Tax Incl.)
MAIL ORDERS PROMPTLY FILLED

GILBERT MILLER presents
VIVIEN LEIGH LAURENCE OLIVIER
ANTONY and CLEOPATRA
CAESAR and CLEOPATRA
ROBERT HELPMANN W. HYDE WHITE
HARRY ANDREWS NIALL MacGINNIS
Directed by MICHAEL BENTHALL
ZIEGFELD, 54th St. at 6th Ave. CI. 5-5200

2 SHOWS TODAY: 2:40 and 8:40
BAGELS AND YOX
A Musical Laff Riot!
HOLIDAY, Broadway & 47th St. CI. 5-4787
Eves. Incl. Sun. Matinees SAT. and SUN.
2 Shows New Year's Eve: 8:45 & 12 Midnite

Leland Hayward presents
ETHEL MERMAN in
CALL ME MADAM
with PAUL LUKAS
Music & Lyrics by IRVING BERLIN
Book-HOWARD LINDSAY & RUSSEL CROUSE
Directed by GEORGE ABBOTT
Dances by JEROME ROBBINS
IMPERIAL THEATRE, 245 West 45th Street
Evgs. Orch. $7.20; Mezz. $6; Balc. $4.80, 3.60, 3., 2.40
Wed. Mat. Orch. $4.20; Mezz. 3.60; Balc. $3., 2.40, 1.80
Sat. Mat. Orch. $4.80; Mezz. $3.60; Balc. $3., 2.40, 1.80

NOW THRU NEW YEAR'S EVE!
CHARLES BOYER CHARLES LAUGHTON
CEDRIC HARDWICKE AGNES MOOREHEAD
DON JUAN IN HELL
CENTURY, 7Av. & 59. Today 2:40. Tonite 8:40
MAIL ORDERS NOW
for Spring Season
4 Weeks Only—BEG. SUN. MAT. MAR. 30
Evgs. Tues. thru Sun.—Orch. $4.80; Balc. $4.20, 3.60, 3.00, 2.40, 1.80. Mats. Sat. & Sun.—Orch. $3.60; Balc. $3.00, 2.40, 1.80, 1.20. Tax Incl. Make checks payable to GREGORY ASSOCIATES.
Enclose self-addressed stamped envelope and mail to Gregory Associates, 152 West 42nd St., New York 19, N. Y.

Opens MON. Jan. 14 Mail Orders Promptly Filled
CHANDLER COWLES & BEN SEGAL present
FANCY MEETING YOU AGAIN
A New Comedy by
GEORGE KAUFMAN & LEUEEN MacGRATH
with Leueen MacGRATH Walter MATTHAU Margaret HAMILTON
Glenn LANGAN Ruth McDEVITT Reynolds EVANS
Staged by GEORGE S. KAUFMAN
Open'g Night: $7.20, 4.80, 3.60, 3.00, 2.40. Eves. Thereafter: $4.80, 3.60, 3.00, 2.40, 1.80. Mats. Wed. & Sat.: $3.60, 3.00, 2.40, 1.80, 1.20. Tax Incl.
ROYALE THEATRE, 45th Street West of B'way

"As engaging a comedy as we are likely to see for a long time." — GIBBS, New Yorker
AUDREY HEPBURN in
GIGI A comedy by Anita Loos from Colette's Novel
FULTON, 46th St. West of B'way. Cir. 6-6380
Evgs. at 8:40. Matinees WED. and SAT. at 2:40
Good Seats $1.20 and $1.80 All Performances

HILARIOUS COMEDY HIT!
" 'Glad Tidings' has an impudent sense of humor."—Atkinson, Times
"The first-nighters gave 'Glad Tidings' a rousing reception. They blistered their palms applauding."
—Coleman, Mirror
HAROLD BROMLEY presents
MELVYN DOUGLAS SIGNE HASSO
GLAD TIDINGS
Comedy by EDWARD MABLEY
with HAILA STODDARD
LYCEUM Thea., 45 St. E. of B'way. LU. 2-3807
MAIL ORDERS FILLED
Evgs. 8:40: $4.80, 4.20, 3.60, 3.00, 2.40, 1.80. Mats. Wed., Sat. & Jan. 1: $3.60, 3.00, 2.40, 1.80, 1.20.
NEW YEAR'S EVE PRICES: $6.00 TO $2.40

DRAMA CRITICS' PRIZE MUSICAL!
GUYS & DOLLS
A MUSICAL FABLE OF BROADWAY
starring
ROBERT ALDA VIVIAN BLAINE SAM LEVENE
46th ST. THEA. W. of B'way
Eves. 8:30. Ci. 6-4271
Evgs. $6.60, 4.80, 4.20, 3.60, 3., 2.40, 1.80. Mats. Wed. & Sat. $3.60, 3., 2.40, 1.80, 1.20
ISABEL BIGLEY

'A STUNNING PERFORMANCE"-Kerr, H. Trib.
I AM A CAMERA
A New Play by JOHN VAN DRUTEN
with Julie HARRIS William PRINCE
EMPIRE Theatre, B'way at 40th St. PE. 6-9540
Prices: Mon. thru Thurs. Eves.—$4.80, 4.20, 3.60, 3.00, 2.40, 1.80, 1.20; Fri. & Sat. Eves., also New Year's Eve—$6.00, 4.80, 4.20, 3.60, 3.00, 2.40, 1.80, 1.20
Mats. Wed. & Sat.—$3.60, 3.00, 2.40, 1.80, 1.20
Tax Incl. Evs. 8:40; Mats. 2:40. Mail Orders Filled
Special Holiday Mat. Tuesday, Jan. 1

Opens WED. Evg. at 8 Sharp
SEATS NOW ON SALE
MAIL ORDERS PROMPTLY FILLED
THE THEATRE GUILD presents
DOROTHY McGUIRE
RICHARD BURTON
In The London And Paris Success
LEGEND OF LOVERS
by JEAN ANOUILH
Adapted by Kitty Black
with HUGH GRIFFITH NOEL WILLMAN EDITH KING BRUCE GORDON
Directed by PETER ASHMORE
Scenery designed by Eldon Elder
Costumes by Mildred Trebor
Evs. (Exc. Op'g) Mon. thru Thurs. Orch. & Boxes $4.80 Balc. $3.60, 3., 2.40. Fri. & Sat. Evs. Orch. & Boxes $5.40. Balc. $4.20, 3.60, 3., 2.40. Mats. Thurs. & Sat. Orch. & Boxes $3.60. Balc. $3., 2.40, 1.80. Tax Incl.
NEW YEAR'S EVE: Best Seats $6.00 Incl. Tax
Enclose stamped, self-addressed envelope with check or money order. Specify 2 alternate dates
PLYMOUTH Theatre, 45th St. West of B'way

"EXTRAORDINARILY FUNNY LINES."
—Ward Morehouse, World-Tel. & Sun
THE THEATRE GUILD presents
LO AND BEHOLD Gay New Comedy
by JOHN PATRICK
with LEO. G. CARROLL LEE GRANT JEFFREY LYNN
Directed by BURGESS MEREDITH
Evgs. 8:40. Mon. thru Thurs. $4.80, 3.60, 3., 2.40. Fri. & Sat. $5.40, 4.20, 3.60, 3., 2.40. Mats. Thurs. & Sat. 2.40, $3.60, 3., 2.40 Tax Incl.
NEW YEAR'S EVE: Best Seats $6.00 Incl. Tax
Please enclose stamped, self-addressed envelope with mail orders. Kindly specify 2 alternate dates
BOOTH Theatre, 45th St. W. of B'way. Cir. 6-5969

GLORIA SWANSON DAVID NIVEN ALAN WEBB
NINA A GAY NEW COMEDY!
ROYALE, 45 St. W. of B'way. Cir. 5-5760
Evgs. Mon. thru Thurs. $4.80, 4.20, 3.60, 3., 2.40, 1.80
Fri. & Sat. Evgs. $6.00, 4.80, 4.20, 3.60, 3., 2.40
Mats. Wed. & Sat. $3.60, 3., 2.40, 1.80, 1.20 (Tax Incl.)

Seats Tom'w - Opens THUR. Jan. 3
PAL JOEY A MUSICAL PLAY
Music by Richard RODGERS Lyrics by Lorenz HART Book by John O'HARA
Starring
VIVIENNE SEGAL—HAROLD LANG
Entire Production Supervised by
Robert ALTON
Mail Orders Filled—Open'g Nite: $9.60, 6.00, 4.80, 3.60, 3.00. Other Evgs.: $6.60, 4.80, 3.60, 3.00, 2.40
Mats. Wed. & Sat.: $3.60, 3.00, 2.40, 1.80, 1.20
BROADHURST THEA., 44th St. West of B'way

"Packs atmosphere, romance, comedy, lusty singing, and fast-paced dancing into a most enjoyable show." — Coleman, Mirror
JAMES BARTON in
PAINT YOUR WAGON
with OLGA SAN JUAN TONY BAVAAR
SAM S. SHUBERT Thea. W. 44th St. Cir. 6-5990
Evgs. Orch. $7.20; Mezz. $6.00, 4.80, 3.60; 2nd Balc. 2.40. Mats. Wed. & Sat. Orch. $3.60; Mezz. $3.60, 3.; 2nd Balc. $2.40, 1.80. Tax Included.
MAIL ORDERS PROMPTLY FILLED

Leland Hayward presents
HENRY FONDA in
POINT OF NO RETURN
A New Play by Paul Osborn
Based on Novel by John P. Marquand
Mon. thru Thur. Eves.: $4.80, 4.20, 3.60, 3.00, 2.40, 1.80.
Fri. & Sat. Eves.: $6, 4.80, 4.20, 3.60, 3.00, 2.40. Mats. Wed. & Sat.: $4.20, 3.60, 3.00, 2.40, 1.80. Tax Inc.
ALVIN THEATRE, 52nd St. West of Broadway

"SEASONS FIRST BRIGHT EVENT." — Life
REMAINS TO BE SEEN
Comedy by Howard Lindsay & Russel Crouse
with JANIS PAIGE—JACKIE COOPER
Howard Lindsay—Warner Anderson
MOROSCO Thea. 45th St. W. of B'way. Cir. 6-6230
Evgs. 8:40. Mon. thru Thur. $4.80-1.80. Fri. & Sat. $6.00-2.40. Mats. Wed. & Sat. $3.60-1.80. Tax Incl.

"Inspired . . . makes the theatre something worth venerating again."—Atkinson, Times
THE THEATRE GUILD presents
UTA HAGEN in
MARGARET WEBSTER'S PRODUCTION of
BERNARD SHAW'S
SAINT JOAN
CORT THEATRE, 48th St. East of Broadway
Evgs. $4.80-1.80. Mats. Thur. & Sat. $3.60-1.20
Extra Mat. New Year's Day Jan. 1
Seats Now $1.20-$3.60 Proceeds Actors' Fund
MOVES TO Century Theatre 7 Av. & 59 St. Tues. Jan. 8

ROGER RICO
MARTHA WRIGHT
in The Pulitzer Prize Musical Play
SOUTH PACIFIC
MAIL ORDERS PROMPTLY FILLED
Eves. 8:30: $6.00, 4.80, 3.60, 3.00, 2.40, 1.80.
Wed. Mats. 2:30: $3.60, 3.00, 2.40, 1.80, 1.20.
Sat. Mats.: $4.20, 3.60, 3.00, 2.40, 1.80, 1.20. Tax Incl.
MAJESTIC Theatre, 44th St., W. of B'way

"HILARIOUS!"—Coleman, Mirror
STALAG 17 COMEDY SMASH!
MAIL ORDERS PROMPTLY FILLED
Evgs. $4.80, 4.20, 3.60, 3., 2.40, 1.80, 1.20. Reg. Mats. Wed. & Sat.: $3.60, 3., 2.40, 1.80, 1.20
48TH ST. THEATRE, East of Broadway
Holiday Mat. New Year's Day, Tues., Jan. 1st

"GREAT GOOD FUN."—Kerr, Herald Tribune
Katharine CORNELL
Brian AHERNE Grace GEORGE
in SOMERSET MAUGHAM'S Comedy
THE CONSTANT WIFE
with John EMERY
Staged by GUTHRIE McCLINTIC
NATIONAL Thea. 41st St. W. of B'way. PE. 6-8220
Evgs. 8:40. Mon. thru Thurs. $4.80-1.80. Fri. & Sat. $6-1.80. Mats. Wed. & Sat. 2:40, $3.60-1.20 Tax Incl.

SPECIAL HOLIDAY Perf. Next SUN. Eve. Seats Now
"An Irresistible Comedy" Chapman, NEWS
THE PLAYWRIGHTS' COMPANY presents
JESSICA TANDY HUME CRONYN
in The JOSE FERRER Production
of JAN de HARTOG'S Comedy
THE FOURPOSTER
BARRYMORE Theatre, W. 47th St. CI 6-0390
Evgs. 8:40—$4.80 to 1.20. New Year's Eve $6.00 to 2.40. Mats. Wed. & Sat. 2:40—$3.60 to 1.20. Tax Inc.

"ORIGINAL & BEAUTIFUL."—Atkinson, Times
GERTRUDE LAWRENCE in
THE KING AND I
Music by Richard Rodgers
Book and Lyrics by Oscar Hammerstein 2nd
A stamped, self-addressed envelope MUST be enclosed with mail order
ST. JAMES Theatre, 44th St. West of B'way
Evgs. at 8:25. Matinees WED. and SAT. at 2:25

RESUMES TUESDAY EVG.
MATS. THIS WEEK: Wed., Thurs. & Sat.
ALDRICH & MYERS
with Julius Fleischmann present
BARBARA BEL GEDDES DONALD COOK BARRY NELSON
in OTTO PREMINGER'S PRODUCTION
THE MOON IS BLUE
A New Comedy by F. HUGH HERBERT
HENRY MILLER's Theatre, 124 W. 43rd St.

"TAUT, TENSE, TERRIFIC!"-Sullivan, News
THE NUMBER A Thrilling Melodrama
Dane CLARK—Martha SCOTT
with ANTHONY ROSS — JENNIE GOLDSTEIN
BILTMORE, W. 47 St. Evgs. 8:40. Mats. Wed. & Sat.

MAIL ORDERS NOW
OPENS TUES. EVE., JAN. 15
JOSÉ FERRER JUDITH EVELYN
in
THE SHRIKE
A New Play by JOSEPH KRAMM
Produced and Directed by MR. FERRER
Associate Producer, MILTON BARON
Open'g Night: $7.20, 4.80, 3.60, 2.40. Mon. thru Thurs. Eves.: $4.80, 4.20, 3.60, 2.40, 1.80. Fri. & Sat. Eves.: $6.00, 4.80, 3.60, 2.40, 1.80. First Mat. Thurs., Jan. 17; Mats. Thereafter Wed. & Sat.: $3.60, 3.00, 2.40, 1.80, 1.20. Tax Incl.
CORT THEATRE, 140 West 48th Street

Beg. WED. 8:15 P.M. thru Sun., Jan. 6 SEATS NOW
The N. Y. CITY THEATRE COMPANY
Maurice EVANS Kent SMITH
Mildred DUNNOCK Diana LYNN
in MAX FABER'S Adaptation of
THE WILD DUCK
by HENRIK IBSEN
with Philip Loeb, David Lewis, Nan McFarland
Directed by MORTON DA COSTA
Jan. 9 thru 20: "ANNA CHRISTIE"
Jan. 23 thru Feb. 3: "COME OF AGE"
N. Y. CITY CENTER, 131 West 55th St.
Prices: Evs Incl. Sun. $3.00, 2.40, 1.80, 1.20. Mats. Sat. & Sun. $2.40, 1.80, 1.50, 1.20. No Perf. Jan. 14, 28

"COMPLETELY HILARIOUS"-Atkinson, Times
"A FAST & FUNNY SHOW"-Chapman, News
PHIL SILVERS
in the "SMASH HIT MUSICAL"-Danton Walker
TOP BANANA
MAIL ORDERS PROMPTLY FILLED
Mon. thru Thur. Evgs.: $6.60, $6, $4.80, $3.60, 3., 2.40. Fri. & Sat. Evgs.: $7.20, $6, 4.80, 3.60, 3., 2.40. Reg. Mats. Wed. & Sat.: $3.60, 3., 2.40, 1.80
All Prices Incl. Tax Holiday Matinees Jan. 1 & Feb. 12
WINTER GARDEN, B'way & 50th St. Eves. 8:30

"Enormously enjoyable, full of wit, humor and splendor."—Atkinson, Times
BERT LAHR—DOLORES GRAY
IN THE HILARIOUS NEW MUSICAL
TWO ON THE AISLE
MAIL ORDERS PROMPTLY FILLED
Evgs. 8:30: $6.00, 4.80, 4.20, 3.60, 3.00, 2.40
Reg. Wed. Mats.: $3.60, 3.00, 2.40, 1.80, 1.20; Sat. Mat.: $4.20, 3.60, 3.00, 2.40, 1.80 (Tax Incl.)
MARK HELLINGER Thea. B'way at 51st St.
Holiday Mat. New Year's Day, Tues., Jan. 1st

ONLY MAIL ORDERS
FILLED NOW
Box-Office will not open until early in Feb.
16 WEEKS ONLY! Beginning Wed. February 13
THE THEATRE GUILD presents
REX HARRISON LILLI PALMER
in
VENUS OBSERVED
by CHRISTOPHER FRY
Directed by
LAURENCE OLIVIER
Production designed by ROGER FURSE
Evgs. (Exc. Op'g) Mon. thru Thurs. Orch. $4.80 Mezz. $4.20 & 3.60. Balc. $3, 2.40, 1.80. Fri. & Sat. Orch. $6, Mezz. $4.80, 4.20. Balc. $3.60, 3., 2.40, 1.80. Mat. Thurs. Orch. $4.20, Mezz. $3.60, 3., Balc. $2.40, 1.80, 1.20. Mat. Sat. Orch. $4.80. Mezz. $4.20, 3.60, Balc. $3., 2.40, 1.80. All Taxes Included
Please enclose stamped, self-addressed envelope with check or money order specifying 3 alternate dates
ORDERS MUST BE MADE OUT TO
Treasurer "VENUS OBSERVED"
CENTURY Theatre, 7th Avenue & 59th St.

TICKETS NOW!
Hollywood Ice Revue
WORLD OLYMPIC CHAMPION
BARBARA ANN SCOTT
and Company of 200
Jan. 17 Thru Feb. 6
except Jan. 25-26-27
Mats. Sats. & Suns. Jan. 19-20—Feb. 2-3
Children ½ Price Sat. Mats.
Res. $1.50, 2, 3, 4, 5, 6 (tax incl.)
MAIL ORDERS PROMPTLY FILLED
Only Ice Show in Garden this year
MADISON SQ. GARDEN

Advertisement page from the *New York Herald Tribune*, 23.12.51. One flop amid the successes.

Two designs.

Left: Vivien Leigh's first act costume by Roger Furse for *The Skin of Our Teeth.*

Below: Front cloth by Roland Pym for *Oranges and Lemons.*

Above left: Alec Clunes in *The Lady's Not for Burning.*
Above right: Yvonne Arnaud in *The Circle.*
Below: Men Without Shadows. Alan Tilvern, Sidney James, Philip Leaver,
Hector MacGregor, Lyn Evans, Mary Morris (Aubrey Woods on the floor).

Jeannetta Cochrane's everlasting costumes.

Left: Love for Love
(Rosalie Crutchley far right).

Right: The Relapse.
Cyril Ritchard surrounded:
Jessie Evans and Paul Scofield
are amused.

Below: The Rehearsal.
Walter Plinge, Lockwood West,
Diana Churchill, Maggie Smith,
Robert Hardy, Alan Badel,
Phyllis Calvert.

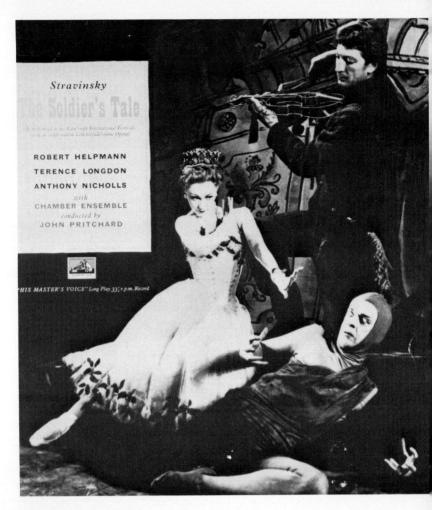

The Soldier's Tale.
Libretto by C. F. Ramuz,
translation by Michael Flanders
and Kitty Black.

Opposite: Venice Preserv'd

Above left: John Gielgud
and Eileen Herlie

Above right: Paul Scofield
and Pamela Brown

Below: 'Oh Mercy'
David Garrick and Mrs Cibber

Above: Ring Round the Moon.
Daphne Newton, Mona Washbourne, Marie Löhr, William Mervyn, Paul Scofield,
Claire Bloom and assorted flunkeys.

Below: Irma La Douce.
Elizabeth Seal on the table
hailed by Denis Quilley and pals.

Above: Lunch at the Villa Mauresque. Somerset Maugham, Vivienne Byerley, Alan Searle's back and KB. Picasso 'Harlequin gisant' on the wall.

Below: J. B. Priestley at the BBC.

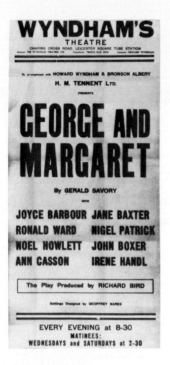

Four H. M. Tennent posters.
Above left: George and Margaret. Above right: The Gielgud Season at the Haymarket.
Below left: the Sartre plays at the Lyric, Hammersmith. *Below right: The Rehearsal* at
the Globe.

running successes and without the creation of a new shop window the normal turn-over of new productions would only provide employment for a handful of artists. It all sounded very exciting. The difficulty was to get it all off the ground. Nobody could find the perfect choice for the opening presentation and every time the directors met the opening date was put back indefinitely. Various plays were on the list – Emlyn Williams had rewritten *Spring, 1600* which John Gielgud had directed originally, but nobody wanted to open with a revival: Maxwell Anderson's *Winterset* was a possibility and there was a new translation of *The Trojan Women* which Murray wanted to do with Marie Ney. After years of frenzied activity at the Globe, sitting doing nothing in the Apollo was an appalling prospect and in the midst of this indecision, Binkie announced that the John Gielgud tour of India for ENSA would have to be cancelled as he didn't have time to organise it.

"But John has promised to go," I cried. "You can't let him break his word."

"In that case you'd better organise it yourself," he replied, and I spent the next few weeks happily seeing that John fulfilled his engagement and corresponding with Colonel Jack Hawkins, at that time the ENSA representative in India. Finding a cast who wanted to go on tour for six or eight weeks wasn't easy as the newly discharged actors weren't anxious to go abroad again after their foreign service and we were making rather slow progress. One morning the phone rang. It was Barbara Lott, calling from Birmingham where she was playing Ann Whitefield in *Man and Superman*.

"There's a wonderful young actor down here," she said. "You simply must see him. His name is Paul Scofield." So I made an appointment for Paul to come up to the Apollo to meet John at once. John was apologetic.

"I can only offer you Guildenstern and Osric," he told the shy young man with the deeply lined face.

"Well, you see," said Paul. "I don't think I can accept because Barry Jackson has offered me Henry V and Hamlet next season at Stratford."

Finally the opening date for the Lyric was set for October, with a new play by Rhonda Keane, a friend of Murray's, and a press party at the Savoy Hotel launched the new undertaking.

"If we want to succeed," said Murray, "we've got to be independent of HMT. We must have our own scenic studios, printers, publicists and staff. If we don't, every time our interests clash with Tennent's, we'll be pushed to one side." And so the Company of Four built up its own organisation, independent of the spider's web of activities spinning so intricately round the Globe offices.

In connection with his highly successful organisation in Salisbury, Murray had collected among other people Hubert Gurschner, an Austrian painter-portraitist who had pictures hung at the Tate Gallery and had painted the last portrait from life of T. E. Lawrence. Next came a young man with flaming red hair called Stanley Moore who was just setting up a scenic construction studio, and at Murray's request, Vivienne Byerley was appointed our press representative. "She always did all the work in Dick Clowes' office anyway," said Murray, and she duly moved into the other room in the Apollo suite.

Our opening pattern of success and failure was an almost exact replica of the HMT beginnings. The eleven plays produced between October 1945 and August 1946 were financially disastrous, losing some £12,000 which was enough to frighten off the Glyndebourne connection, their share being taken over by Tennent Plays. In some ways this was a relief, for trying to get three directors (Guthrie withdrew early on) and the administrator to agree on a schedule of plays was hair-raising and established me firmly in the opinion (if I had ever been in any doubt) that far and away the best modus operandi in the theatre is a benevolent dictatorship.

The opening play, *The Shouting Dies*, starring Margaret Johnston and Gerard Heinz, who had been the wonderful Polish airman in *Flare Path*, was greeted as a respectable attempt, and the second presentation was *The Trojan Women* and *The Happy Journey to Trenton and Camden*, Thornton Wilder's loving reproduction of American middle West life done, like *Our Town*, without scenery or props. *Our Town*, which had been such a success in America, flopped disastrously in London with a disappointing performance from the leading lady who was constantly forgetting her lines. After one such disaster, Marc Connolly her fellow star strolled

down to the prompt corner, and drawled: "Why don't you give her real props and let her imagine the words." But *Happy Journey* was a delight and everyone adored it. For *The Trojan Women* Murray had discovered an Irish-Scottish actress, Eileen Herlie, in a production of *The Little Foxes* and had been so impressed that he invited her to play Andromache. She made a sensation in her short scene. After the first night he gave her the script of Cocteau's *L'Aigle à deux têtes* and said it could be hers if she was prepared to wait for the final adaptation. "I'll wait a year," was her reply, and that is almost exactly how things turned out.

The script of *L'Aigle* had arrived in the office just before a Bank Holiday, and as Binkie was keen to read it as soon as possible, I took it home and made a literal version in three days, even managing to type the whole thing twice in order to produce several copies. Everyone was delighted with the play itself, and the search for a "poetic" adaptor was on. Peter Ustinov refused (too busy with his own writing), Caryl Brahms suggested Christopher Fry, then living near Oxford, but nobody else knew anything about him so the job finally went to Ronald Duncan, after I had given an enthusiastic report on his play *This Way to the Tomb* at the Mercury Theatre. Cocteau demanded to see the first act before giving his approval to the translation and Ronnie was despatched to Paris to interview the Master. Unfortunately, like most people at the end of the war, Ronnie had no passport, and as he only had one weekend free for the trip, we had to get him the necessary papers within twenty-four hours. Urgent telephoning established that if he would go in person to the Home Office, armed with the obligatory photographs, the passport could be issued on the spot, and off he went.

As it happened, he had been shooting with the Duke of Portland and had been given a brace of pheasants which he was carrying by the usual string tied round their necks. As Ronnie was on the small side, the tail feathers trailed on the ground and wherever he presented himself, the sight of the birds, to say nothing of their provenance, created a mild sensation. Eventually, having been shuttled in the usual manner from office to office, he emerged with passport and visa and came to spend the night with us before sailing next morning. Having

been away from home for a week, his suitcase was stuffed with dirty shirts, and when I exclaimed that he couldn't possibly go to Paris without a couple of clean ones, he replied airily that it didn't signify – he could easily buy some when he got there!

"Don't be silly," I snapped. "They're just as strictly rationed as we are," and spent the evening washing and ironing his linen. Ronnie returned from Paris with Cocteau's blessing and I kept one of the pheasant tail feathers as a lucky talisman for the play.

In due course I took the final script to Paris for the author's approval, expecting to pick up the designs for the sets from Christian Bérard, the genius who, like Oliver Messel, stood alone in the field of theatrical design, but Cocteau sadly shook his head. Bébé, as everyone called him, was no longer interested in the stage and had declared his intention of becoming a serious painter. I could go and see him if I liked, but it would be a miracle if I could persuade him to change his mind. Bébé was adamant and I left empty-handed. Cocteau then announced that he wanted a new protégé of his to take over, André Beaurepaire, a precious young man who inspired no kind of confidence, but we had to accept Cocteau's wishes and trust to luck to get us out of the commitment if we didn't like the designs. In due course they – and Beaurepaire – arrived. All our worst fears were realised. The young man had come up with some spiky Strawberry-Hill-Gothic which might have been possible in Paris but would clearly not be within the bounds of practicality at Hammersmith. On Murray's instructions I took M Beaurepaire and his drawings to the Globe and watched Binkie dealing with the unwanted offerings. He held them the right way up, then turned them upside down as if puzzled. Finally he said, "I don't understand. Is this the bedroom or the library?" Exit M Beaurepaire.

Some time later he designed a ballet for Covent Garden and disappeared for days on end while everyone from the Opera House searched for him frantically. According to Peter Brook he was found in the Euston Road in a state of euphoria, having fallen in love with the façade of St. Pancras Station. Eventually the sets for the Lyric were designed by Stanley Moore and painted by Hubert Gurschner.

Cocteau had written the play originally for Jean Marais,

"Jeannot", his boy friend for many years. Jeannot had said he wanted a part in which he could listen, cry and fall downstairs, so Cocteau obliged with a first act speech for the Queen Edwige Feuilliere lasting for twenty minutes, which reduced the young man to floods of tears, and at the end of the play he fell down the stairs, after stabbing the Queen in the back as she was reviewing her troops. (Fanfares by Benjamin Britten in the Lyric production.)

James Donald, who had made a huge success in Noël Coward's *Present Laughter*, was the obvious choice for Stanislas, the young man in question who is the image of the assassinated king for whom the Queen remains in mourning. Noel Willman as the sinister chief of police, Jill Esmond, the first Mrs Laurence Olivier, and Murray Macdonald's production helped to create the kind of overnight stardom for Eileen Herlie that is the most exciting event in any theatrical experience. A few days later Alexander Korda gave her an enormous film contract and her picture appeared on the front page of all the national dailies. She was voted actress of the year and engaged to play Gertrude opposite Laurence Olivier in his film of *Hamlet*. *The Eagle Has Two Heads* went on tour and finally moved into the Haymarket, but all that was a year away and after *The Trojan Women* we had a long way to go to establish our success.

The Lyric was set in the middle of a slum area, without the steady support of a residential population which is the norm for a regional theatre, though the market folk came regularly to every first night, sitting on the hard benches of the gallery and yelling their approval of everything they liked. Often a play would appear to have had a tremendous success and we would all be wildly excited until next morning when the critics would come out with scathing or luke-warm notices which effectively killed the business.

Building the programme was a major headache – with our schedule of rehearsal and touring, three plays were being prepared simultaneously all the time and the moment a first night at the Lyric was over, everyone was having to concentrate on future planning, and we never seemed able to get ahead of ourselves.

Of the original list of plays, Maxwell Anderson refused

permission for us to stage *Winterset* on the grounds that we weren't yet successful enough – my own disappointment has been partly obliterated by the satisfaction of knowing that he missed having the play done in London at all – though Allan Davis directed it at the Bristol Old Vic a couple of years later with Jill Balcon, Nigel Stock, Paul Daneman and John Byron in the cast. A reworking of the Romeo and Juliet story it has one line which I have always remembered, spoken over the bodies of the two young people who have been destroyed by senseless prejudice: "Two thousand years and we cannot yet make a world." Forty years on, the sentiment is still equally valid.

Spring 1600 is the story of an aspiring young actress who disguises herself as a boy and runs away from home to join Burbage's company in London. Brahms and Simon presented much the same plot in *No Bed For Bacon* but the English are notoriously allergic to male impersonations except in pantomime, and this second presentation was no more successful than the first, in spite of the presence of Andrew Cruickshank and Jessica Spencer who both went on to become TV stars. This disappointment led Emlyn to remark that the Lyric housed the Company of Four and the Audience of Two.

After an interesting but unsuccessful production of *Death of a Rat*, a play about cancer research by Jan de Hartog (J. B. Priestley's son-in-law, who was later to write the successful two-hander *The Fourposter*), Peter Glenville arrived to direct *The Time of Your Life* by William Saroyan – a play that had won both the New York Drama Critics Award and the Pulitzer Prize in 1939. Presented by the Theatre Guild in New York it had introduced or won stardom for such artists as Gene Kelly, Celeste Holm and William Bendix, and our production was to star Walter Crisham, who had partnered the Hermiones – Baddeley and Gingold – during their famous *Sweet and Low* series of wartime revues – Frederick Valk, and Margaret Johnston. Maggie was married to Al Parker, ex-film director (he made *The Black Pirate* with Douglas Fairbanks Sr.) now a highly successful theatrical agent, and so could be relied on to produce a good American accent. A couple of GIs were also included to provide authenticity (one of them was arrested by two US MP's at the end of a performance for being AWOL: he changed his name to Biff Maguire, and became

quite a success on Broadway).

The wordless part of the Drunk which had attracted rave notices on Broadway could obviously be cast as a "gimmick" and I persuaded Peter to ask his father, Shaun Glenville to do it for us. As we couldn't arrange the billing to give him his proper status, we decided he should appear anonymously and the cast list was completed by "The Drunk". Shaun made his first entrance immediately after the curtain rose, was recognised by the delighted house and got a huge round of applause. The set was designed by Tanya Moiseiwitch, who had worked with Tyrone Guthrie and Peter Glenville at Liverpool, and built by Brunskill. This was an enormous extravagance as far as we were concerned and cost all of £300, about three times our usual budget for a one set play.

Because of his West End engagement in a sinister play by Mary Hayley Bell called *Duet For Two Hands* Peter couldn't be at the first night, but invited me to supper with his parents at the Savoy after the performance. After we had eaten he led me on to the dance floor and commanded, "Now tell me every-thing from the beginning. The curtain went up, my father made his entrance and there was a round . . ." He cut short my eager continuation of the story by stopping dead in the middle of a turn. "But you dance beautifully," he said in tones of the deepest astonishment. I suppose my reputation for efficiency had precluded anyone from thinking I might possess the odd social talent as well.

We danced until it was time to go down to Fleet Street and buy the first editions as they came hot off the press – they were not enthusiastic for the play but lyrical about the cast and for the first time the box office telephones began to ring and taxi-drivers were able to find their way to the theatre unprompted.

By this time letters were pouring into the Apollo office from artists of all kinds, in addition to the streams of discharged actors who climbed the four flights of stairs to leave their names and addresses for future reference. I talked to them all when Murray wasn't there, and made lists of possible casts, but when the supply became unmanageable, we arranged for mass auditions – usually at the Globe Theatre – giving everyone time to perform a piece of his or her choice. We sat

through endless renderings of St. Joan's post-coronation speech, and more Henrys rushed into the breach than I would care to remember, but a tremendous amount of talent was discovered and used in subsequent productions.

Actor friends told me how they hated this system of auditioning, but I always maintained that you could assess the quality of a performer by the manner in which he walked on to the stage, took in instinctively where to stand and even before he opened his mouth, impressed you with his personality. Miriam Karlin was discovered at one of these cattle markets, as the actors called them, and once when a young actress, Eve Mortimer, auditioned, her cues were provided by her husband, a young man who was so outstanding that I was sent to enquire his name. Unfortunately he was still in the Forces and so was unavailable – his name was Michael Hordern, but Eve got the part and Michael promised to contact us as soon as he was free.

While she waited for the script of *The Eagle* Eileen Herlie agreed to appear in a delightful comedy, *The Thracian Horses*, a version of the Alcestis legend by the American dramatist Maurice Valency. The sets and costumes were by David Ffolkes, a gentle creature who had survived the years of horror involved in building the railway of death in Burma. He told me how they would be set to carrying long bamboo poles from their base two miles into the jungle and back, all day long, existing on a bowl of rice and very little else. His weight had gone down to six stone, and perhaps he owed his survival to his powers of concentration far more than his physical stamina. On the dreadful tramp he divided the journey into three sections, using self-made landmarks, and thought about London, Paris or New York as he covered the ground. He picked up his career again after the war and was divinely happy with a charming wife and a beautiful flat. He died one evening after dinner, sitting at table, just after he had told his wife how happy he was, ceasing perhaps not quite at midnight, but certainly without pain – a lovely way to go. But the play was no more successful than the Lunts' *Amphitryon*, and proved Binkie's point about the British public – they just aren't interested in recreations of Greek legends.

Although the next production, *Tomorrow's Child*, by John

Coates, with Nigel Patrick and Sheila Sim, was successful enough to go on Tour after the Hammersmith run, and Guthrie's production of the Sean O'Casey *Red Roses for Me* also helped to establish the theatre, it was Alec Guinness' adaptation of *The Brothers Karamazov*, directed by Peter Brook, which really pleased the critics. This was the first time I had worked with Peter, though I had been sent to see his production of Cocteau's Oedipus story at the Boltons the previous year, and we had become good friends. He had originally come into our lives while he was still up at Oxford when he wrote to John Gielgud asking permission to film his production of *A Sentimental Journey* in the *Love for Love* set.

After coming down, he had produced a couple of Arts Council tours, and now he began an association with the firm which was to continue over the next twenty years.

John Gielgud was appearing in an adaptation of *Crime and Punishment* at the Piccadilly, with Edith Evans and all the lavish trappings of the usual Tennent presentation, but it was our Dostoievsky, with scenery that had only cost £80, that won the critics' praise. With a cast including Frederick Valk, James Donald, Alec himself, Ernest Milton and Pierre Lefevre we felt we were able to stand any comparisons. Although we were still not making money, the quality of our offerings was beginning to be acknowledged and this was confirmed when the next comedy, a revival of Tom Robertson's *Caste* became our first West End transfer (to the Duke of York's) beating *The Eagle* by a narrow margin.

Peter Ashmore, who had run the Oxford Playhouse successfully during the war, had suggested the play to Murray and by this time it was felt we could depart from the policy of new plays. The company included Elliot Mason, who had appeared in several of Emlyn Williams' plays, Brenda Bruce, everyone's favourite soubrette since her unforgettable Mabel Crum in *While The Sun Shines*, and Bill Owen, in those days known as Bill Rowbotham. Brenda and Bill were physically perfectly suited, though she eventually married Clement McCallin, who lent his dashing good looks to the soldier hero. Leslie Bridgewater wrote a delightful tinkling tune for the ballet sequence, and I paid £5 for a marvellous Victorian music box that played the right sort of lullaby. When the production

closed I "won" the box, and sold it for £200 some years later when I needed the money to refurbish a bathroom.

Paul Scofield had completed his first triumphant season at Stratford and was going to have a few weeks off before rejoining the company. I persuaded him to take on the part of Captain Hawtree, the hero's friend, and he duly appeared at the first reading. Unfortunately he then realised that it was going to be quite mad to spend what was meant to be a holiday playing in yet another production and asked us to release him from the contract. Fortunately Peter Ashmore's cousin, Frith Banbury, was available to take over, and chalked up a very amusing performance.

Everything about *Caste* seemed to work and it had a successful run at the Duke of York's Theatre after the Lyric run. A baby features in the last act and in performances a very convincing doll wore a beautiful Victorian robe and cap but for the photo call I wanted the real thing. Gabrielle Blunt who had appeared in *The Happy Journey* had recently had a son, Paul, so I "borrowed" him, dressed him in the linen and lace, and his picture, taken by Angus McBean, shows the three actresses gazing at him with the gooey expression that always appears on female faces in similar conditions.

Although *The Eagle* was a financial success and the transfer of *Caste* proved that the Lyric was a viable proposition, Murray felt that he couldn't continue as Administrator. He had originally contracted to produce four plays a year and argued very reasonably that as it took three months to prepare, rehearse and bring in a play, he really didn't have time for the office work as well. We discussed this at length and reviewed a likely list of successors. Murray was firm.

"If we want the Lyric to succeed," he said, "we've got to involve Binkie. Without him the whole undertaking will collapse. I think we should suggest he appoint John Perry."

Glyndebourne had long withdrawn from the venture, Tony Guthrie was too busy with the Old Vic, and Norman Higgins was amenable to any suggestion, so Murray took his views to Binkie and the decision was made.

This meant something of a change for me, as I was never on the same terms with John as I had been with Murray. The feeling behind the relationship always seemed to be that I was

still the shorthand-typist I had originally been. If there was a magic circle I was never allowed inside it, but the fun of working at Hammersmith more than made up for any feelings of inferiority.

Murray's stratagem worked. Binkie naturally supported the venture as long as John was interested and the Company of Four went on to become one of the most important artistic forces in London.

Chapter **XIII**

Existentialism and austerity seemed to hit a tired postwar London at approximately the same time, but while we all understood what the latter meant – five shilling meals in restaurants with no bread and butter, utility clothes cut on simple lines with minimal yardage and no luxury fabrics – nobody knew what the French philosophy was about and hardly anybody could pronounce it. However, we were all aware that the High Priest of this new religion was a writer called Jean-Paul Sartre, that he pontificated from a café on the Left Bank in Paris, ably seconded by the beautiful Simone de Beauvoir who while she may not have actually burnt her bra was the leading advocate of Women's Lib. and a highly articulate priestess. But if nobody could read or understand the philosophy, the plays were a different matter and immediately accessible to a delighted public.

I first saw *The Flies*, Sartre's version of the Orestes legend, produced by a drama group at London University. It gave an insight into what the German Occupation had meant to the non-collaborating French – even a wineglass carrying the feeling of contamination – but it was *Huis clos* that caused the greatest sensation as soon as the script became available. Jean-Louis Barrault wanted to bring it to the Lyric, Hammersmith, but the Lesbian element in the drama brought a total ban from the Lord Chamberlain's office (even in French), and it was left to Peter Brook to produce it at the Arts Theatre Club, with Alec Guinness, Betty Ann Davies and Beatrix Lehmann in the cast. The floor waiter was played by Donald Pleasance, a rising young actor Peter had discovered at an audition and used in *The Brothers Karamazov*, and he was incredibly sinister in the part. *Vicious Circle, In Camera* or *No Exit* were the various titles given to translations of the play, but it was the first, in a version by Joan Swinstead and Marjorie Gabain that Peter elected to use. Sartre and Simone de Beauvoir came over

to see the play and Peter arranged the customary lunch at the Savoy to which I was invited. Tremendous good will was generated even though conversation was considerably restricted owing to Sartre's almost total lack of English and the actors' almost non-existent French. So when two more Sartre plays became available, it was natural that they should be offered to Peter and equally natural that they should be produced at the Lyric, Hammersmith.

Huis clos had originally been accompanied by another one-acter called *La Putain respectueuse* with a leading part written for Sartre's current heart-throb and vaguely based on the Scotsboro' Boys case, when two negroes were accused of raping two white prostitutes in a box car. The fact that the Sartre version couldn't actually have happened because American trains don't have closed compartments, didn't affect the drama. The play was an immediate success but, with no Lord Chamberlain to protect their morals, the French public itself raised such an outcry that the offending word was deleted and the title appeared as *La P . . . respectueuse*, which made translation very difficult. Not only could one not use a four-letter word to approximate the same effect (very few members of the theatre-going public at that time would have known what the initial stood for), so as the French title is a paradox, we compromised and called it *The Respectable Prostitute*.

To complete the double bill, Sartre's agent and publisher, Louis Nagel (best-known nowadays as the publisher of the Guides Nagel), supplied another play in two acts, *Morts sans sepulture*, which painted a grim picture of the civil war conditions maintaining between the Resistance fighters and the local para-military organisation known as the militia. Once more the problem of translation was debated, until one day John Perry suggested that I should make a literal version, and after that he and I could collaborate on the final text. "After all," he said, "we're both authors", and so I set to work.

Sartre's dialogue is so vivid and his characterisation so strong that making a translation was like putting one of those dry Japanese flowers in water and watching it spring to life. When the scripts were finished, John Perry declared they needed no revision and could be produced as they stood.

Perhaps this was the greatest moment of my life for I realised that I had managed to convey in English exactly what the original author had meant, without any adaptation or rejigging of the situation in order to make it acceptable in translation.

Mary Morris, with her dark, fierce beauty, was to be the girl in the Resistance play and Betty Ann Davies was the obvious choice for the good-hearted prostitute, though as nature hadn't endowed her over-generously she had to wear rubber "falsies", and very temperamental they proved to be. Synthetic foam had not then been invented and the rubber cups used to crack when David Markham as the amorous senator's son hurled himself on top of Betty Ann as she lay back on the bed. The rest of the cast were chosen from Irish, Scottish or Welsh actors, creating a wonderfully Celtic atmosphere, while David's English quality as the Resistance leader pointed up the contrast with the rest of the group. As a pacifist he found the play very disturbing and refused to appear in it when the production went on tour at the end of the Lyric run.

Alan Badel was one of the understudies and walk-ons and helped to devise the torture scenes that were such a feature of the Resistance play. Listening to the screams of the victims off-stage was such a harrowing experience that nightly faintings and "fits of the overcomings" as my mother called them, occurred at every performance, keeping the St John's Ambulance volunteers busy. The record count was five faintings in the stalls and dress circle and one epileptic fit in the gallery. The young boy was Aubrey Woods, then a lanky teenager, who had made his name in the film of *Oliver Twist* with Alec Guinness, and at the last minute we included a South African actor who had arrived with a letter of introduction from Gwen Ffrangçon-Davies. We could only offer him a small part but he was content to begin with anything. When the Angus McBean pictures arrived, Peter looked at the results and remarked, "That man is going to be a film star – look at the way his face comes off the paper." The actor in question was Sidney James and he went on to star in all those *Carry On* films and TV productions until his recent untimely death.

For some forgotten reason the plays opened in Bangor instead of one of our more usual venues and in the course of the

all-night dress rehearsal the sleeping citizens were wakened by the crash of rifle fire as "Sergeant" Badel directed the stage managers and understudies in a ragged volley that he assured Peter would sound like a machine-gun. By the time the police arrived, in answer to furious protests, the rehearsal was over and Peter assured them that there would be no repetition of such matutinal alarms.

The first night at the Lyric brought its own quota of drama and was accompanied by one of the torrential downpours that make London feel as if it were built within shouting distance of the Equator. I had arranged to hire a car to take my mother home after the performance and then take me on to a party which was being given by Sartre's London agent, Jan van Loewen. During the first interval, after the worst of the torture scenes, I enquired anxiously if my mother was not too upset? "I'm all right," she answered. "I keep telling myself it's only Johnny Byron." (Perhaps I should explain that while temporarily homeless, having let his flat to Caryl Brahms, Johnny had stayed with us and alienated my mother's affections by using TCP in his mouth wash, a smell she found impossible to stomach.)

At the end of a triumphant evening, with Rita Hayworth, Sartre and Simone de Beauvoir among the celebrities, the rain was still sheeting down and finding Peter Brook's mother stranded in the foyer, I suggested my hired car should take her and my mother home and then return for John Byron, Caryl and me. Unfortunately the Brooks lived in St John's Wood and it was some time before the car returned and we three were able to join the party. Everyone else had finished eating, so it was suggested that we should skip the introductions and settle down to the delicious food in the dining-room, where we were joined by Sartre, Nagel, Simone de Beauvoir and an unknown gentleman who sat quietly in the corner while we embarked on an excited babble of English and French. Occasionally, for courtesy's sake, someone would address a remark to the silent one, who would murmur something appropriate but never volunteered any contribution. Next morning when I telephoned Jan to thank him for the party I asked the question we had all debated.

"Who was the silent man in the corner?"

"Rita Hayworth's detective," he replied, and roared with laughter at my description of our efforts to draw him into conversation.

The double bill didn't get a West End transfer, but toured with great success to all manner of strange places, while *The Prostitute* had many successful revivals, including a music-hall production and a brief season with Oscar Wilde's *Salome* at the St Martin's Theatre.

Sartre and Simone de Beauvoir attended a press reception at the Gargoyle Club to welcome them to London and arrived so late that everyone was afraid they had met with an accident. They explained their absence by saying they had been revisiting the places in London where they had been happy.

"Where was that?" asked the press.

"Clapham Common et l'Eléphant et Castle," replied the philosopher.

When asked if he had noticed many changes since his previous visit he replied, "Oui. Les amoureux dans les parcs," referring to the interlaced couples that had begun to appear unashamedly on the grass. I quickly contradicted him. "Ce ne sont pas des amoureux," I cried. "Ce sont des Américains." Even in 1946 our girls would do anything for a pair of nylons.

In staging *Morts sans sepulture* which I called *Men Without Shadows* from a nostalgic poem I discovered when we were searching for a title, Peter had decided to make a revolutionary change. The first scene takes place in an attic, the second – the torture scene – in a schoolroom, the third in the attic and the last back in the schoolroom. Peter argued that the second change of scene would interrupt the tension building up to the final dénouement, when the leader has been released and the rest of the group, having resisted all efforts to make them betray him, are waiting for the next move by the militiamen. Finally they are told they are free to go, but moments after they leave, a volley of shots underlines where the real betrayal has taken place. Peter decided to play the last two scenes in the attic without a break, without consulting the author. On the first night we waited apprehensively for Sartre's and Nagel's comments but neither of them raised any objection. The only reaction was from Nagel who kept inviting me to spend the weekend with him at Brown's Hotel. This reduced me to

helpless giggles as I couldn't imagine a dirty weekend amid all that respectability, but at least it meant we didn't have to justify the cuts and alterations.

The Sartre double bill was followed by the biggest money-maker the Company of Four had had to date, an intimate revue, *Tuppence Coloured*, devised and directed by Laurier Lister. As an ex-serviceman, Laurier had played a small part in Peter's production of *The Brothers Karamazov*, but hadn't worked in the theatre for nearly two years and was getting bored with nothing to do. Before the war he had worked almost continuously for HMT and had then done his war service with the RAF. Discovering he was a theatrical, his commanding officer had suggested he should provide some entertainment, and Laurier had produced some highly successful intimate revues, copied from those produced by the Farjeon régime at the Little Theatre and Norman Marshall at the Ambassadors. As his wartime efforts had been so popular, Laurier began to plan a high-brow revue with the material written by a combination of tried experts and promising newcomers, starring Max Adrian and Joyce Grenfell. Laurier brought his ideas to John Perry and the resulting creation was put into rehearsal in July and opened at Hammersmith in September.

After the gloom and nerve-racking horrors of the Sartre plays, the revue burst on the audience in an explosion of laughter and talents. Looking at the programme it seems impossible that Laurier could have collected such authors, writers and composers as Michael Flanders and Donald Swann, Sandy Wilson, Christopher Fry, H. F. Ellis, Geoffrey Wright and Richard Addinsell all under one roof. There was even a Japanese Noh play produced by Peter Brook and danced by a ballerina who had been with the Ballets Jooss, and a front cloth designed by the cartoonist Emett. This was the artist's first experience in the theatre and when he went to Stanley's studio to see the work in progress he was so amazed to find it had been faithfully copied that he signed his name on the finished cloth – probably the only instance of a genuine signature appearing on a piece of scenery.

In his Diaries, Noël Coward rather patronisingly described this first revue as amateurish, but I think he was deceived by

the freshness and originality of the entertainment, for neither the public nor the critics shared his views. The revue played to packed houses at the Lyric and transferred to the Globe where it ran for 273 performances. John Perry told Laurier that the show had not only recouped all the losses of the first two years' trading at Hammersmith, but had made a handsome profit as well, so naturally plans were made for a successor to be mounted the following year.

Once again Max Adrian and Elisabeth Welsh starred but this time accompanied by Diana Churchill – described by Emlyn Williams as "the worry with the fringe on top". Diana had been successfully paired with her husband Barry K. Barnes in all kinds of comedies and drama, Liz Welch could turn her hand to almost anything, and Arthur Macrae wrote a wonderful piece for them in which they guyed the current habit of serving matinée teas in the theatre, the rattling of teacups being a notorious actors' bugbear. In the sketch the actors drank tea, or ate ice cream as they continued the dialogue – Liz had a piece of sandpaper stuck at the bottom of her ice cream cup which provided a particularly grating comment as she sang a "mad song" with the refrain "Oh, down-a-down derry, alas and poor Tom, Oh, down-a-down derry, oh Derry and Tom." The passing of that famous emporium in Kensington High Street perhaps makes the line less accessible to a modern audience, but it brought the house down at Hammersmith.

The original cast of *Tuppence Coloured* had been chosen mostly from known performers, but for the sequel, *Oranges and Lemons*, so many people were clamouring to get in on the act that endless auditions had to be held. Laurier brought Rose Hill in from Sadler's Wells Opera to sing a Wagnerian aria by Anthony Hopkins, and Denis Martin from the Players Theatre lent his charming tenor to a delightful ballad, 'The Youth of the Heart', which proved to be Sidney Carter's first major success as a composer. *Oranges and Lemons* transferred to the Globe but only ran for three months, which was disappointing, but the real disappointment was that after an unfortunate contretemps Laurier quarrelled with John Perry, and the rest of his revues, *Airs on a Shoestring* and others, were produced at the Royal Court Theatre, or elsewhere.

Tuppence Coloured was followed by the discovery of a new English playwright, Wynyard Browne, who was brought into the fold by Frith Banbury, who was equally at home directing and acting. This play, *Dark Summer*, was a perfect choice for the Lyric, as it had one set and five characters – a necessary economy after the extravagances of the revue before its money-making capacities were established. Dealing with the love of an unattractive Austrian woman for a young Englishman who has been blinded in the war, the play provided a wonderful role for Joan Miller (wife to Peter Coates who subsequently acquired a sort of back-handed fame by being relieved of the job of directing *The Mousetrap*). During the auditions held for the other parts, the choice for the young man was whittled down to the last two, my own favourite being Patrick Macnee who had created a sensation in a production of *The White Devil*, starring Robert Helpmann and Margaret Rawlings. James Agate had singled him out by saying that the way he spoke his one line, "Madam, this is not true," was the most arresting moment in the play. Pat had served in No. 1 Flotilla of MT boats, operating under the command of Peter Scott, and we had taken one of our Sunday shows to Felixstowe when he was stationed there. Unfortunately the decision went against him and my only consolation was that the actor finally chosen faded completely from the scene while Pat became a world famous TV star in *The Avengers*.

One of the striking moments of the play occurs when Gisela, the drab Austrian, knowing the young man's eyesight has been restored, tries to make herself beautiful for him by putting on a glamorous dress. Nothing seemed quite right until rummaging round an old clothes shop in Brighton I found a red and gold jersey dress which was exactly right. I think it cost all of a pound, but it was the perfect garment. That junk shop yielded endless treasures when last-minute purchases were required, including a pair of soft kid shoes for Eileen Herlie to wear in *The Eagle* which, sprayed silver, provided the answer to the classic problem of the tight new shoes which would have killed her performance.

We had been approached by a Dutch impresario who wanted us to bring a play to Holland and *Dark Summer* seemed

the ideal choice. A week's tour was booked, the scenery and costumes duly packed and shipped, but we were assured that all the furniture and props would be available in each of the theatres we visited. In the event this proved entirely untrue – the Germans had raided all the stores and removed every single item that they could possibly carry away, down to the last spoon and fork, and we were reduced to borrowing from the various hotels and boarding houses where we stayed.

The next block-buster was a revival, Tony Quayle's production of *The Relapse*, with Cyril Ritchard, Madge Elliott, Esmond Knight, Paul Scofield, Jessie Evans, Richard Wordsworth and a host of new and old favourites. The *Love for Love* costumes were refurbished, Jeannetta Cochrane made new headdresses and added servants' and trades people's clothes from Simmons' and Berman's stock. Tony asked me to take notes for him during the dress rehearsal and we sat alone in the circle for my first experience of the entire play. I laughed till I cried, and fortunately Tony was laughing so much himself that he didn't notice the almost complete absence of note-taking. Cyril's comedy technique was such that he could convey the exaggerated character of Lord Foppington without guying it, which made it all the funnier, and Jessie Evans' wicked eye-rolling and innocent lechery provided a superb accompaniment. The play's transfer to the Phoenix Theatre made it a worthy successor to the original Gielgud production of *Love for Love*.

A couple of undistinguished offerings followed, although Richard Burton returned to the fold and understudied in *Castle Anna*, adapted by John Perry from a novel by Elizabeth Bowen, and there was a workmanlike production of *Dandy Dick*, which Tennent's had staged in 1945 with Sydney Howard. Unfortunately the star had died unexpectedly and the production had been abandoned. And then there was a new landmark when we were allowed to produce Arthur Miller's *All my Sons*, as it was felt that this anti-war play would be given a better reception at the Lyric, than if it were plunged immediately into the West End. Nobody seemed the right choice for the director until one day a man called Warren Jenkins arrived in the office and asked to be considered for any future productions. In the course of conversation he men-

tioned that he had seen the Miller play in America, and on the strength of this experience he was given the job. It proved to be his very first assignment, but fortunately he was very talented and went on to run the theatres at Coventry and Bristol. Stanley Moore designed a fascinating set and Joseph Calleia and Margalo Gilmore provided authentic American interpretations which the rest of the cast lived up to very satisfactorily. The press and public loved the play and it transferred happily to the Globe for a respectable run. Needless to say all the later Miller plays were produced by the Tennent office, without a Lyric try-out, but then with stars like Paul Muni and Vivien Leigh what else could we expect?

Chapter **XIV**

After the success of the double bill it was only natural that we should have expected Peter Brook to produce the next Sartre play to arrive, the political melodrama called *Les Mains sales* in Paris, a title almost impossible to translate. We called it *Filthy Fingers* until I remembered that its original title in France had been *Crime passionnel* and decided we should use that in London. Translating titles is one of the problems of theatrical metamorphosis, and my own theory is that if you can't translate the title, you won't have a success with the play. I don't mean you have to use a literal version, since obviously *Ring Round the Moon* (*L'Invitation au château*) is a better selling title than *Invitation to the Castle*, but *The Little Hut* works in any language and *Bobosse* should have put anybody off from the beginning.

By the time we were able to schedule *Crime Passionnel*, Peter Brook had been snapped up by Covent Garden and was deeply immersed in matters operatic, so Peter Glenville was the perfect substitute for the job. We had wanted Michael Gough to play the cadaverous young hero, but unfortunately he was busy filming, so Alan Badel was the next in line for the part. Alan was just ending an engagement opposite Mai Zetterling in the stage version of *Frenzy*, and the Henry Sherek management kindly released him before the end of the run. Rehearsals began with Roger Livesey and Joyce Redman, but within a few days Roger issued an ultimatum – "Either Badel goes or I do" – and I had to face up to Alan and say he wasn't wanted after all. Telling an actor he has been fired is probably the worst experience any manager has to go through, and I always had to console myself by remembering how much pleasure is involved in telling someone they *have* got a part.

If you worked with Peter Glenville you had to accept the fact that he would always fire at least one actor in the course of the first fortnight's rehearsal – it was a sort of theatrical tic.

Perhaps his finest effort came in Terence Rattigan's *Adventure Story* when he fired Richard Burton, who had been engaged to play Hephaestion opposite Paul Scofield. But sacking Alan did have its compensations: Michael Gough had just finished his filming and was able to settle down and learn the part with only a fortnight to go.

Perhaps because they all had red hair, a kind of magic grew up between the three leads – actors call it chemistry, which is perhaps as good a word as any, but if it were anything so scientific, it should be possible to analyse and repeat the formula. As it is, it defies all human agencies, and if it doesn't happen, nothing can be done to create it. When it works, the stage lights up, the audiences are electrified and the entire production bursts into a firework display of emotion and experience shared. In this case the play was an instant success with audiences and critics, and the final accolade came when, at a party held at Binkie's house in honour of the French cast who had come over on July 14th (their holiday night) to see the production, I arrived in time to hear Noël Coward declare "It's the best produced, best acted and best translated play I've ever seen." A transfer was obviously on the cards but to my horror even after all the enthusiasm, Roger Livesey handed in his notice as he had been offered a film with Myrna Loy. Even though Basil Sydney, one of our most prestigious actors, was available to take over, the play lost its initial momentum and only ran for a few weeks at the Garrick.

This was the play that brought me into touch with Gabriel Pascal, the flamboyant Hungarian who was responsible for the Bernard Shaw films, *Pygmalion, Major Barbara* and *Androcles and the Lion*. Legend has it that he went to see Shaw and asked for the film rights of his plays when he only had sixpence in his pocket, and Shaw was so charmed with his personality and temerity that he had immediately made a deal. Somehow Pascal had acquired the English language rights to *Les Mains sales* so Binkie had had to negotiate a contract with him in order to stage the play. Pascal was only prepared to offer the English rights, reserving the American market for a separate deal, and demanded the outrageous royalty of 15 per cent though this would include his own profit.

Pascal came into the office a couple of times to carry on the

negotiations and every time there would be a phone call for him from some exotic country. One such call came through when I was in the room. It was from Italy. "Pronto," he said into the receiver. "But I have sent the sound track of *Pygmalion* to Spain and it is lost." We fully expected a phone call for him on his next visit to say the sound track had been found, as Morrie maintained it was merely his secretary calling from his own office with an imaginary message to impress his audience.

At the last minute, with the contract actually on Binkie's desk, Pascal made a final effort.

"Seventeen and a half per cent," he pleaded.

"Fifteen per cent," replied Binkie, initialling the first page.

"Seventeen and a half per cent" said Pascal.

"Fifteen per cent" said Binkie, turning the page and initialling the next until the deal was completed.

Unfortunately Pascal's greed made the running of the transfer very expensive and as the summer of 1948 was a hot one, the audiences didn't justify any extension of the play's run, but it was successfully produced by every repertory theatre in the country and made quite a lot of money in Australia. Pascal sold the American rights to Jean Dalrymple, a lovely lady who made a huge career on Broadway and later became a good friend of mine. She arranged for a new translation to be made by a film scriptwriter called Daniel Tarradash. The result was a disaster, and the play had no kind of success on Broadway. However, later Jean moved into television and returned to my script when she wanted to record the play. By this time Sartre and Nagel had quarrelled violently and were engaged in various law suits involving the payment of royalties, including a film deal made over *La P . . . respectueuse*. Once again another version had been used in America, and the translator, Eva Wolas, sued Sartre on the grounds that she was about to conclude a film deal in Hollywood (a likely tale) when she discovered the French rights had been sold on a world-wide basis.

As a result, all Sartre's earnings in America were frozen and the television production of *Crime Passionnel* seemed a good way of getting some of his money out of the country. I signed the contract on behalf of Jean Dalrymple, Sartre and myself,

and the money was sent to me so I could transfer Sartre's share to France. Eventually even this escape route was blocked, but the accumulated royalties enabled the lawyers to pay off the Wolas claim and at last the restrictions were lifted and all Sartre's books and plays were available again in America. Unfortunately for me, this somewhat devious manoeuvre was seen as a betrayal of Sartre's interests and our literary relations came to an end, but I have always been proud of my association with the early plays and can claim that I have translated the works of three Nobel Prize winners – even though Sartre turned his down.

The Lyric Theatre operation had been promptly joined by a whole series of "try-out" theatres forming what would now be called the fringe of the West End, though the policy at Hammersmith of a four-week tour and a four-week run meant that both author and actors would have sufficient reward for their four weeks' rehearsals. All the theatres had the same aim – to find interesting new plays and possibly stage revivals that the West End wouldn't touch owing to their limited appeal or high cost of production. Equity rates of payment for the actors could be minimal and union rates for stage hands were paid on a lower scale. In fact most theatres operated without any stage crews at all, and the work was done by the stage managers, who were engaged under a different contract calling for "any number of performances and Sunday work as and when required".

In addition to Hammersmith, the two most prestigious venues were the Arts Theatre Club near Leicester Square, where Alec Clunes staged both classics and modern plays, and the Embassy in Swiss Cottage, operated by Anthony Hawtrey, a cousin of John Gielgud's on the wrong side of the blanket. (John used to refer to him as his bastard cousin, and apparently Mrs Gielgud was the only member of the family who would receive Hawtrey's mother after her "fall".) The Embassy now houses a leading drama school, with the auditorium cut in half and the rest of the building very much altered.

Most of these fringe theatres have disappeared, along with the long list of London's "lost" nineteenth-century theatres, but most had their moments of glamour and thrill of discover-

ing new talents. The Lindsey, in Palace Gardens Terrace, now replaced by a block of flats, known as the "tinsy" for obvious reasons, produced a notorious piece, *Pick-up Girl*, an American play by Elsa Shelley, which had been banned by the Lord Chamberlain. It was so successful that a licence was granted on the grounds that the play carried a moral and transferred to the West End. It was even honoured by a visit from Queen Mary, an inveterate theatregoer who according to George V's A.D.C. enjoyed a racy story as much as anyone. The Torch Theatre, where the modern Berkeley Hotel stands, was also known as the Torture because of the extreme discomfort of its seating arrangements; William Douglas Home's early plays, *Now Barabbas* and *The Thistle and the Rose* were both staged at the Boltons Theatre; the Chepstow was in what is now an antique arcade off Portobello Road; and the "Q" Theatre at the north end of Kew Bridge, perhaps the most successful of all, now transformed into a pub, was run by the indefatigable Jack de Leon, whose policy was to present any West End play he could lay his hands on and produce it with any actors he could find who had been in the London cast. He could then advertise that it was "straight from" whatever theatre had housed it, giving the impression that his customers would be able to see the same production for a fraction of normal theatre prices. In fairness he also had an incredible talent for picking promising newcomers, and just as most of today's stars appeared for the Company of Four at one time or another, so most of them had appeared for Jack as well before our company came into existence.

These theatres also operated Sunday clubs, a device intended to defeat the rules and regulations laid down by the Lord Chamberlain. For the present permissive society it is probably hard to grasp that at one time every word spoken on any stage in the land had to be passed by the official whose function descended in direct line from Queen Elizabeth I's Master of the Revels who commanded Shakespeare. From music-hall acts to grand opera, His Lordship licensed the spoken or sung word to ensure that nothing untoward would sully the ears of the Great British Public, or any piece of business be represented that could be construed as shocking or blasphemous.

The Act calling this function into being had been passed in the reign of Queen Anne (who, if you remember, is dead) and was intended primarily to prevent satirists and such from sending up political figures or making fun of the monarch. It also barred the representation of the Deity on the stage, resulting in one or two funny changes. For instance, while it was possible to present God in the mediaeval miracle plays because they predated the act, the famous American negro play, *Green Pastures*, which featured God as 'De Lawd', could not be licensed for stage performance in England, though the film was allowed in and has even been shown on television; in *The Marvellous Story of St Bernard*, the figure of God had to be changed to that of the Virgin Mary, a fine splitting of theosophical hairs.

We had some odd encounters with the Lord Chamberlain over one or two of the plays at Hammersmith. Once a script had been submitted, if any objections were raised by a team of anonymous readers, a dignified letter arrived from St. James's Palace requesting that such words, gestures or business should be removed, and the licence when issued carried this prohibition in full. I have one covering my translation of Sartre's *Le Diable et le bon dieu* which passes the script provided the word "cobblers" is removed from Page 11. Four letter words, of course, were never used – and so never submitted – and swearing had to be kept to the minimum: you might be allowed two or three "bloody's" or a few "blasts" but the name of the Deity must not be invoked too often and "Jesus" was practically forbidden. One Irish play we submitted – called eventually *Galway Handicap*, was full of the richest Gaelic phrases and expressions, but overall as clean as a whistle, so we were considerably startled to receive a long list of required deletions, practically all of them relating to the excision of "Jesus". Not remembering any such blasphemous invocations I suddenly realised that the reader had conscientiously counted the number of times the characters said "Joseph, Mary and Jesus," and pointed out that to confine the prayers to Our Saviour's parents – or rather His mother and stepfather – would be downright upsetting to the faithful. The deletions were all religiously reinstated.

In a Tennessee Williams play, *Summer and Smoke*, a Mexican

girl referring to her father declared "Papa would grunt like a pig to show his passion". The blue pencil struck and the line was supposed to go. I rang up the office, quoted the line in my best Roedean tones and then using a Dolores del Rio accent, gave an imitation of how it would sound in performance. The ban was lifted.

On the whole the Lord Chamberlain was very understanding and usually responded to pleading. After the *Point of Departure* try-out week at Brighton, several old ladies wrote to complain about the love scene played between Dirk Bogarde and Mai Zetterling in the hotel bedroom. I was summoned to the Palace and ushered into the Presence.

"Before we start, Colonel Gwatkin," I said. "May I congratulate you on your promotion?"

When we got round to discussing the letter he admitted that the scene had been passed because the stage directions required the young couple to be lying on top of the bed fully dressed. In performance Mai had discarded her black tunic and was wearing a white *broderie anglaise* slip which was perfectly modest, not to say virginal.

"Oh, very well," said his military lordship. "But tell Mr Bogarde to keep his hands off the upper part of Miss Zetterling's body."

However, if you wanted to stage something really outrageous and knew that in no circumstances would the licence be given, the solution was to produce the play through a theatre club. As the Lord's Day Observance Society forbade the opening of theatres and places of entertainment on a Sunday, this was a way of circumventing their prohibition as well, and several small theatres formed clubs for the dual purpose. The originator of this brilliant manoeuvre was J. T. Grein who founded his Independent Theatre Club in 1891 with the express purpose of staging *Ghosts*, which had come under the Lord Chamberlain's prohibition. A secondary benefit of the Sunday Club was to enable members of the profession who were working themselves to see a play on their night off, but it is doubtful if many artists really did give up their one free evening unless it was to see something quite outstanding. The drawback, of course, was that all theatre staff (though not the actors) had to be paid double time for

working on the Sabbath. Although we began the Lyric with a Sunday opening policy, it was abandoned very early on in the operation and the theatre was only used on Sundays for the occasional poetry recital.

Eventually Tennent's founded a special club theatre of their own, operating from the Comedy Theatre, to stage a clutch of plays that had been banned: *Tea and Sympathy*, as being too overtly sexual, though any modern audience would probably find it about as sexy as *Little Lord Fauntleroy; A View from the Bridge*, Arthur Miller's savage play about illegal Italian immigrants, which included hints of homosexuality, and *Cat on a Hot Tin Roof*, which was considered to be even more outrageous than *Streetcar*. Members of the public paid a nominal sum for club membership – the only proviso being that you had to have been a club member for forty eight hours before you could buy a theatre ticket, a regulation which was honoured considerably more in the breach than in the observance. Finally, under pressure from the public and critics, notably Kenneth Tynan, in 1968 it was decided that theatre censorship should be abolished; authors were free to deal with whatever subject they pleased in whatever language they felt was appropriate.

Chapter XV

It was while we were preparing John Perry's adaptation of *Castle Anna* that I contacted Charles Mozley and asked if he would be interested in designing the posters for Hammersmith. Charles had been the official poster artist for Ealing Films and London was adorned with a wonderful black and yellow design he had done for the Pauline Goddard-Michael Wilding production of *An Ideal Husband*. Charles proved to be an enchanting person, and prepared to work for the peanuts which was all anybody was ever paid for contributing to the Company of Four. He agreed to produce two lithograph designs, one for the double crown and one for the folio bills (anything larger had to be created in ordinary letterpress, notably for the provincial try-outs), the only stipulation being that he would never submit a design. If he was given the lay-out for the names and a rough outline of the plot, he would go ahead and draw directly on to copper plates. He promised he would never use more than two colours to keep the costs down and created a series of outstanding works of theatrical memorabilia in the Daumier-Bickerstaff Brothers tradition of which we were immensely proud. However, not seeing proofs led to an embarrassing mistake on my part – I misspelt the "*Passionnel*" of the Sartre title, leaving out one of the "n"s, and have had the greatest difficulty in dissuading anyone even now from repeating the error. When the play transferred to the West End and Charles had to change Roger Livesey's name to Basil Sydney, he was able to put in the second "n", but it spoilt what was otherwise a very interesting design.

Sadly the extra cost of the printing was one of the items where economies could be made and eventually Charles was thanked and told his services were no longer required.

Refusing to go back to the plain black and scarlet on white of the Tennent printing (the original Gladys Calthrop lay-out had long been discarded), I got Mr Jackson of Claridge, Lewis and Jordan to create a lino-cut surround for our printing –

cribbed shamelessly from the current Covent Garden design which looked as though the information was framed in a house curtain. By using different colours for each production we created variety and also established continuity – the printers enjoying the challenge when asked for a blue to match John Gielgud's eyes or a Guy Fawkes grey for the Tennessee Williams *Summer and Smoke*.

Although Binkie wasn't one to splash out on paid advertising – the press office slogan according to some was "no news is good news" – he did agree that in war-time, with everyone using tubes in preference to above-ground travel, the escalators were an excellent means of calling the public's attention to the attractions presented by the firm, and the advertising agent was instructed to acquire any vacant space that became available. The result was a long line of Tennent posters which the public could study on their way up or down; and as the printing was uniform in lay-out and colouring it made a highly effective pattern. When conditions returned to normal, London Transport wanted to increase the charges for these prime sites by an incredible amount, and as a result of this, to him, unreasonable demand, Binkie got the other impresarios to join a boycott on advertising on tubes and buses, a ban that has only recently been lifted. I doubt if any impresario will ever again wrest control of the escalator positions from the current advertisers.

One folio bill from every production was framed and sent to the Tennent office, where they lined the walls and later overflowed all over the theatre; we copied the same system and had framed folios hung at the Lyric. Sadly when the Tennent lease came to an end, somebody broke the frames and used the posters to make a collage on one wall of the bar, with the result that no complete set of posters can now be assembled. However, a few duplicates came to light for the retrospective exhibition mounted to mark the opening of the renovated theatre and eventually found their way into the Mander and Mitchenson collection. Fortunately they included the superb poster Charles had designed for *An English Summer*, the rewritten version of Ronald Adam's play about the fighter squadron during the Battle of Britain which had already had a try-out as *Fighters Calling*.

Another marvellous Mozley design was for Flora Robson in a revival of *Captain Brassbound's Conversion*, in which she had previously appeared at the Theatre Royal, Windsor. No one could be a better Lady Cicely than Flora, and Richard Leech provided her with very excellent support. I was enormously jealous of my mother who had actually seen Ellen Terry in the original production. The one thing she most remembered was the lady silently darning the captain's coat, an action which Shaw describes as lasting as long as the actress can hold the audience's attention.

Again in a huge cast it is fun to remember small parts played by young actors who went on to fame and fortune, among them Michael Cacoyannis who became a successful film director in his native Greece and rivalled Peter Brook in his bold approach to the classics.

After *Oranges and Lemons* there was a further link with Flora when we staged *The Damask Cheek* by John van Druten and Lloyd Morris, a piece she had created on Broadway, but for which she felt she was now too old. Jane Baxter, the adorable Frankie of the original *George and Margaret* cast was a worthy successor, and Claire Bloom's name appears in small print – she was just beginning to make her mark on the stage.

But it was the next play, *Dark of the Moon*, which was my favourite among the year's productions. The script had been sent to us by Aubrey Blackburn, Peter Brook's agent, and he and I (Peter, I mean, not the agent) went to see an end of term production of it at RADA. Peter felt it couldn't be done unless we could use three of the Americans from the RADA cast – William Sylvester as the Witch Boy, Craddock Monroe as a marvellous Preacher and Gaylord Cavallero (what a name!), who knew all the hillbilly songs and could play the mouth organ. (Bill later went to Hollywood and turned up in films, notably as the scientist in *2001*.) Casting was the greatest possible fun. Peter wanted the witches to provide a contrast to Sheila Burrell, who was playing Barbara Allen. Two splendid specimens showed up, dark-haired Mary Laura Wood, and Sandra Dorne, whose waist-length blonde hair twirled most fetchingly round her shapely person as she demonstrated her dancing ability. Peter had the witches hanging round the scenery in every possible position – Mary Laura had a double-

jointed back which gave her an unfair advantage when it came to lying upside down, but Sandra was determined not to be outdone and, even though she was terrified of heights, insisted on repeating the manoeuvre with a stage hand hanging on to her legs out of sight at the foot of the ladder. Most of the cast were Welsh or Irish – Joan Young, Huw Pryce, Gerald Lawson (Wilfrid's brother) and a couple of Canadians, so that the effect was quite un-English. Stanley and Hubert designed fantastic sets under Peter's guidance: the first scene with a huge rock that could be trundled on and turned round to become Barbara Allen's cabin. The village store had all its props hanging from the ceiling and back wall and the entire thing unfolded and flew out of the way at the end of the scene. This was the first time I saw "black light" (UV) used in a play – the green stone "that shined in the dark" being a piece of cotton wound round a Woolworth ring that glowed with an uncanny brilliance while the rest of the lights were dimmed.

That was the odd thing about Peter. At his age (he was twenty-four) he couldn't possibly have learned everything he knew from practical experience – he had just read everything there was to read and could offer advice to every department because somewhere in his encyclopaedic memory he had stored up some suitable reference. Caryl Brahms described him as looking like a "malicious cherub", and the glee with which he would offer solutions when experienced technicians declared that what he wanted was impossible was a constant joy. In fairness, I must say, nobody at Hammersmith ever tried to frustrate Peter's wishes – everyone was far too devoted to him and anxious to serve his incredible genius. Peter once declared that if he ever had his own theatre he would entrust the casting to nobody but me – sadly when the time came I wasn't available to remind him of this intention.

The two American authors arrived in time for the try-out in Brighton and proved to be immensely attractive young men. Howard Richardson was dark and cadaverous, William Berney fair and bouncing. They were both entranced with the production. We asked them to pick out the Americans among the cast and they chose our three RADA recruits insisting they were the only English actors around!

One big scene in the play is a prayer meeting and for years

afterwards whenever any of our productions appeared in Brighton the stage crew would chant "Get down on your knees", this being the revivalist Preacher's catch-word. During the course of the meeting, the congregation decides that only if she can be possessed by a human can Barbara Allen be delivered from the spell cast by the Witch Boy. Peter pulled no punches in directing this scene to the limit of its potential. To the resulting angry letters and accusations of blasphemy, Peter replied blandly that the whole thing was perfectly innocent – it all took place in the open air. However, the protesters were silenced when the play scored such a success that a transfer was immediately arranged.

Only two theatres were available: the Strand, which is enormous and we felt would drown the play, and the Ambassadors, which was really too small. Choosing as we thought the lesser of two evils, we settled for the Ambassadors. The scenery had to be cut down, and on the first night, when the opening gauze was lifted, the smoke that filled the stage and that had provided such an eerie effect at Hammersmith, poured over the stalls and virtually blacked out the first five minutes of the play. Rather than face a recurrence, we cut the smoke for the rest of the run, but the play didn't survive the change of venue and only chalked up a scant hundred performances.

But if questions were being asked about rape scenes at Hammersmith, a much more serious row was being cooked up in connection with the affairs of the controlling company behind the Upper Circle of the Globe Theatre. Tennent Plays Ltd had for some time been subject to tax demands from the Inland Revenue on the grounds that in spite of the "non-profit-making" terms of its incorporation, the company was liable for income tax. Mr Gwatkin, Harry Tennent's faithful legal adviser, in drawing up the aims of the company had made them as wide-ranging as possible, with the result that it seemed that if Tennent Plays Ltd wanted to operate a dance hall they could – something which clearly could not come within the definition of "educational or partly educational". Eventually an amount equivalent to some £50,000 had to be paid over. In addition, some of the more costly West End productions hadn't been doing too well: the first London

showing of *The Glass Menagerie* with Helen Hayes making a rare appearance, Edith Evans and Godfrey Tearle in *Antony and Cleopatra*, and Eileen Herlie in *Medea*, in an American translation by Robinson Jeffers, had all failed to find public support and the situation demanded drastic measures. Tennent Plays Ltd, was wound up and a new company, Tennent Productions Ltd, assumed the non-profit-making mantle of the defunct organisation. In spite of all these arrangements, such a fascinating bone was not going to be left ungnawed for long.

Binkie decided to hand over Daphne du Maurier's latest play, *September Tide* to the new company and, as it was to star Gertrude Lawrence, use this surefire money-spinner to recoup the fortunes of the so-called educational part of the empire. Entertainment Tax was being charged at 33.3 per cent of the box office takings – in other words, one-third of every penny paid by the public was never received by the management. The figures speak for themselves. Had the play been presented by HMT Ltd that firm would have acquired a net gain of £18,829.9s.1d. (I'm mad about the accuracy of the figures supplied.) By foregoing this very attractive return on their investment, the net gain to the non-profit-making company was £39,578.16s.0d. No capital had been subscribed in order to mount the play, since this was found out of the funds of the new company, which operated under a set of rules which guaranteed that there would be no loophole through which the tax man could creep. As a safety measure Binkie accepted a loan of £5,000 from the Arts Council, the only time he was given anything approaching a subsidy, but within twelve months this loan was repaid and no call was made on it at the time or at any moment in the future.

The non-profit-making funds received a further boost when John Gielgud's production of *The Heiress*, starring Ralph Richardson and Peggy Ashcroft, opened at the Haymarket. James Donald provided the masculine heart-throb element in the play and his understudy was the young and obviously talented Donald Sinden, whose story is fully documented in his own inimitable autobiography. In addition, John decided to appear in Christopher Fry's verse play, *The Lady's Not For Burning*, which I had seen at the Arts Theatre Club with Alec

Clunes in the lead, since Alec had commissioned Kit to write a play for him, and had produced the result with enormous success. Seeing it with Alec I wrote to John: "I cried all the time because it wasn't your voice that was speaking the lines". When this opinion was shared by other people, John decided to do the play, Alec nobly relinquishing the part on the grounds that it was in the author's best interests that he should do so. Oliver Messel's set and costumes, Claire Bloom's beauty, Richard Burton's youthful magnetism, all contributed to a smash-hit and a run of 38 weeks which had to be terminated owing to John's prior commitment to take part in the 1950 Stratford-upon-Avon Festival. Alec maintained that in giving up the part he had performed the most self-sacrificing action of his artistic career; many people remember the original production with affection, thinking the Gielgud touch too lyrical for what was essentially a rugged mercenary, but the play established the Fry reputation and remains a landmark in modern verse drama, followed later by the T. S. Eliot plays presented by Henry Sherek.

Meanwhile, back at the Lyric, a romantic costume drama followed the hillbilly atmosphere of *Dark of the Moon* when Judy Campbell appeared in a piece adapted by Margaret Webster, called *Royal Highness*. This dealt with one of those dark areas of Austrian royal life when any archduke whose wife had given him cause for jealousy could have her clapped into an isolated Schloss or, as in this case, a mental home. It made splendid television a few years later, but didn't rate a transfer, though the cast and production were excellent. It was left to the next production, *Love in Albania*, to continue the story of successes and build up the number of transfers. Written by Eric Linklater, this starred Peter Ustinov, who also directed, with Brenda Bruce, Peter Jones and Robin Bailey as the rest of the lunatic cast. Brenda had to play the cello in the course of the action and did it herself, instead of having it faked by some off-stage expert, since the sound was meant to be excruciating. It was. The play transferred to the St. James's Theatre, since pulled down, which I remember chiefly because the stage hands' loo was the smelliest I have ever known and made all the ground-floor dressing-rooms stink to high heaven, with a combination of cracked drains and beery urine.

Love in Albania ran long enough for it to be followed at the same theatre by one of our most prestigious productions, *The Seagull*, directed by Irene Hentschel, with Isabel Jeans and Ian Hunter as the senior and Paul Scofield and Mai Zetterling as the young lovers. I suppose everyone has a favourite production of every classic – this was definitely mine of that haunting play, and it is hard to imagine it ever being given a better ensemble. Isabel was a fascinating choice for Arkadina. An exquisitely beautiful woman, she had an elegance that was almost Parisian to supplement her English upper-class aura, and the very fact that she was not normally considered to be a "classical" actress gave her performance an added reality. She had another outstanding quality that almost amounted to genius – her stage clothes remained immaculate no matter how long the run, where other ladies seemed to need two sets of everything as no cleaner could remove the layers of grime between one performance and the next. Philip Stainton was the lovable old uncle – Nuna Davey – Nicholas Hannen . . . it's like making up an ideal team to field in a World Cup event. It was my first introduction to Mai, and her professionalism and approach to acting were enormously impressive, though it was to be a twelvemonth before she worked for us again. As if to crown the year, Christmas saw one of our most successful attractions and one that has probably had a longer career than anything else we presented.

During the 1949 Aldeburgh Season, Benjamin Britten's *Let's Make an Opera* had scored an instantaneous success. The manager at that time was Elizabeth Sweeting who had worked for us at the Lyric in all kinds of different capacities. She had been a stage-struck student of Dadie Rylands at Cambridge, and it was he who suggested she gained practical experience: when she left us she worked at Glyndebourne before proceeding to Aldeburgh and eventually running the Playhouse at Oxford. Liz answered a telephone enquiry with the news that the company would very much like to come to London; the venture moved in to the Lyric on 15 November for an eight-week season and repeated its success the two following Christmasses. Even the bus conductors serving the Hammersmith area were whistling the audience songs and the rafters rang every night with the crashing choruses enthusiastically rehear-

sed under the baton of Norman del Mar. *The Little Sweep*, the opera performed in the second half, provided Flanders and Swann with a wonderful line codding Britten's style: "Please don't send him up again", but this was never given in public and enjoyed by only the select few invited to the studio where the boys created their sensational songs.

But the bone that had been worried over the previous year was dug up again when questions were asked in the House of Commons seeking to clarify the situation with regard to the plays running at London theatres that were exempt from Entertainments Duty under Section 8 of the Finance Act, 1946. Sir Stafford Cripps, the Chancellor of the Exchequer, known for his austerity budgets ("We wish you a merry crippsmas") answered a Mr Wilson Harris with a list that included six Tennent Productions, *Death of a Salesman*, *The Heiress*, *The Lady's Not For Burning*, *The Seagull*, *A Streetcar Named Desire* and *Treasure Hunt*. Worrying to get at the meat, Mr Harris pursued his bone and asked if the Right Hon. and Learned Gentleman was really satisfied that all these plays needed the substantial financial assistance which he was giving them.

Sir S. was satisfied.

After a couple of ineffectual nips from other MP hounds, Mr Wilson Harris asked: "In regard to *Streetcar*, if it gives rise to *An Autobus Named Salacity* or *An Aeroplane Named Lascivious*, will the Right Hon. and Learned Gentleman claim that this is really cultural education and say that we can now withdraw from UNESCO?"

Sir S. replied that he should not like to forecast the cultural values of plays which had not yet been written.

But did the matter rest there? It did not. For further thrilling instalments, read on.

On Tuesday, 6 December 1949, Binkie, Mr Gwatkin and Willie Gillespie were summoned to appear before a Select Committee on Estimates of the House of Commons to answer various questions raised as a result of a Memorandum from the Theatre Managers' Association dated 10 November. The enquiry was ostensibly directed at the workings of the Arts Council, but as far as the Tennent angle was concerned, it related to the different productions running under the non-

profit-making aegis and the "commercial" presentations by H. M. Tennent Ltd. In spite of an exchange running to 172 Q's and A's, no form of blame could be attached to the existing set-up, nor could the Hon. Members find anything to carp at in the way the productions were divided between the two organisations. Binkie declared that the sum of £20,000 annually was required to be available to meet the running costs of the Lyric, Hammersmith, and explained how the initial capital, after the disastrous income tax decision had gone against Tennent Plays Ltd, had been recovered by the generosity of the directors in agreeing to hand over the rights in *September Tide* to Tennent Productions Ltd.

Questioned as to whether the play could in the widest sense be described as educational, Mr Gwatkin produced the classic reply that seeing Miss Gertrude Lawrence performing on the stage was an education in itself, comparing her to Sarah Bernhardt in a flight of fancy which probably even Harold Hobson wouldn't have attempted. Asked if the termination of the phrase "in association with the Arts Council" would have any effect on business, Binkie admitted that by now it was the Tennent name that the public might recognise as its guarantee of quality (especially on those underground posters), since there were other companies operating with this slogan as part of their presentation, and quality was not a necessary adjunct of the Arts Council Association.

What surprised the Hon. Gentlemen was the fact that the non-profit-making presentations at that time outnumbered the profit making in the ratio of six to three, and if it is assumed that forty theatres in London were available at any one time, Tennent's under their two hats controlled a good 25 per cent of the available houses. Once again Binkie affirmed that he had nothing to do with bricks and mortar, nor had he lists of artists under permanent contract – everyone was engaged on an ad hoc basis. He reaffirmed that when American or European authors chose to have their plays presented by one or other of his companies it was entirely because they knew they would receive the highest possible quality treatment. Everyone combined to condemn the existence of Entertainment Tax and once again it was spelt out that actors received no increase of salary from the tax-free situation.

I'm only sorry that I wasn't a fly on the wall to see the innocent expression on Binkie's face while he answered any questions put directly to him. He left much of the talking to Mr Gwatkin as Chairman of the two companies, and to Mr Gillespie as chief accountant – they were all surprisingly vague when figures were called for, and merely concentrated on the educational side and the value attached to the encouragement of new writers and actors.

Much play was made between the relative duties of the Arts Council and the Customs and Excise, also on the way various plays might or might not be described as educational, or partly educational. This distinction had been made originally by the Arts Council themselves, who had appointed three so-called experts who immediately became known as the Three Blind Mice. Their ridiculous assessment of scripts had brought the whole question into disrepute, resulting in the system being changed and exemption being granted to companies rather than individual plays. Mr Frederick Willey, the chairman of the Select Committee, weighed in with some curious questions – would *The Rivals* be considered educational if it were written today, or *The Importance of Being Earnest*? Nothing was changed as a result of this enquiry and the final word rested with Mr Gwatkin who, quoting Sir Francis Bacon said: "Success brings reward but jealousy withal". A very good note on which to conclude the proceedings, which seem to have been prompted by the other theatre managers anxious to cut down the Tennent influence by every means at their disposal.

However, there was a coda. Obviously deeply embarrassed at having to admit that not only were 25 per cent of all London theatres occupied by plays presented under the aegis of the Arts Council, but most of them were showing a profit, late in 1950 the directors of the Arts Council lunched on oyster soup and other goodies at the Carlton, after which they repaired to St. James's Square and terminated their association with Tennent Productions, casting it out, in Charles Landstone's words, with bell, book and candle. It can safely be assumed that no other company receiving their support will ever again be castigated for the heinous offence of making money.

To all the critics of Binkie's methods and the acrimonious

condemnation of the stranglehold he exercised over the London theatres, there is always only one reply. If he could do it, why couldn't anyone else?

Chapter **XVI**

One Saturday in November the morning post contained no letters of any interest and only one script. This proved to be a new version of *Beauty and the Beast*, with a covering letter. "As there are only seven characters, I thought this might be suitable for production at the Lyric for Christmas. The sets and costumes have been designed by Joan Jefferson Farjeon" (who had done the set for *Tomorrow's Child*). I opened the script and began to read.

Stage directions: period, 1500 and 1800, more or less . . . a wizard, a baby dragon, a black cock that lays a magic egg at midnight, a lie-detector. I couldn't put it down. When I had finished, I turned back to the first page, found the author's telephone number and rang him up.

"We can't do your play at Hammersmith," I said, "because we've just arranged to present *Let's Make an Opera* but if you'll trust it to me, I'll put it on myself, though I can't tell you how or where."

We then arranged to meet for tea at the SF Café – a popular spot in Denman Street, much frequented by the poorer members of the theatrical community. So began my association with Nicholas Stuart Gray.

Nicky was an intriguing figure. Medium height, with unruly fair hair, small hands and feet, he had an infectious smile, a warm personality and enormous enthusiasm. Later I discovered that until well into his teens he had believed he was a girl, and had gone to acting school in that capacity. The sexual adjustment had been a traumatic experience, for the one thing in life he wanted was a family, but he found consolation in writing books and plays for children; and in the company of innumerable generations of cats.

He had been a colleague of both Paul Scofield and Joy Parker (Mrs Scofield), and indeed all his plays were written for his two friends. Paul never did appear in any of them, but Joy

created several of the leading roles, and very lovely she was in them too.

I knew the Mercury Theatre was dark and arranged to take the play round to Ashley Dukes. When I rang him to ask what he thought of it, he said that although he liked what he had read so far, he couldn't afford to put it on and so wouldn't bother to finish it.

"But I don't want you to put it on," I retorted. "I'm going to do that. All we need is the theatre."

"In that case you'd better come round and we'll talk terms." Ashley was more than generous. We could have the theatre for £8 a week, but he would keep the bar and cloakroom takings. He would present the play through his company, the Mercury Players, thus meeting all statutory requirements and saving me a lot of headaches, and he made the stage available for us in the evenings so we could build the sets and rehearse.

I suggested Mary Morris should have a go at production, as she had recently been teaching at a drama school, but as she was rehearsing for a play at "Q" and would only be able to work with us in the evenings, we had to embark on an extraordinary timetable. All day we got on with our various jobs, and at six would congregate at the Mercury, where we rehearsed until midnight. Ashley would usually wander in around eleven, having dined at the Garrick Club, produce a half-bottle of wine for me from his superb cellar, and general encouragement for everybody else. The scenery, mostly cut out from three-ply, was mounted on free-standing bases made of plaster of Paris, bound together with everybody's laddered stockings, and painted by Joan Jefferson Farjeon. Costumes were made by anyone who could sew – my contribution being the girls' Victorian pantaloons and petticoats, while Joan's mother sewed several yards of fur-fabric round the edge of Beauty's cloak. The Beast's mask and paws came from Theatre Zoo, and magic roses, self-pouring goblets and the lie-detector were created by a host of willing hands.

We opened on 15 December (to get the pre-Christmas notices), and my mother came to the first night. When Ashley was introduced she thanked him for being so kind to her child.

"I had nothing to do with it," replied Ashley. "She asked me if I would do her play. I said no, but she said yes, so what

could I do?"

The cast we finally assembled included Carol Marsh as Beauty, with John Byron as the Beast, while Huw Pryce was the perfect Wizard. Mikey, the baby dragon, was Hector Macgregor's son, Barry (Hector having been one of the torture victims in the Sartre play), and as we couldn't afford an understudy, but had a healthy respect for the suddenness with which children could fall victims to seasonal disorders, a friend's child called Nicholas Palmer learned the part and stood by. Nicholas became a highly successful script writer and never did become an actor, but I like to think his writing success was founded on that early and formative experience.

The first night was a triumph and the notices ecstatic. George Fearon, a leading London press agent, had agreed to do our publicity in return for a bottle of whisky and had done a great job getting the national boys to the play, so with high hopes of a financial success I departed for a Christmas week-end in the country. After the holiday I telephoned to ask how the returns had been, expecting to hear that packed houses had resulted from the auspicious opening but was met with news of total disaster. Audiences just hadn't appeared, and we held the record for the lowest box office return ever taken at the Mercury – three shillings and one penny i.e. one three-and sixpenny ticket sold, less five pence Entertainment Tax. In agony I rang George and told him of our plight. Nobly our press representative rose to the occasion. He contacted Beverley Baxter, the highly influential critic of the *Evening Standard* and although he had 'flu, "Bax" got out of bed and came to the show, bringing a ten-year old companion. Next day he devoted half a page of enthusiasm to the production and the box office telephone began to ring. A week later we had the "house full" notice out, and the situation was saved. The production cost me £200, but it was an entirely joyous and unforgettable experience.

The following year, Paul Clift, who had been Basil Dean's partner, helped to put the play on at the Westminster Theatre. By this time I had discovered that Nicky really wanted to play the lead himself, and as John Byron wasn't available, we were faced with a ticklish situation. Although a brilliant writer, Nicky's physical appearance was against him, and with his

light-weight voice, there might be difficulty in hearing him through the mask. My personal choice was Alan Badel, and when Alan proved triumphantly at an audition that he would be the perfect Beast, it was left to me to break the bad news to Nicky. A compromise was reached when we invited him to direct the play and this became a formula that was used in subsequent years.

Paul Clift used to say he could never really forgive me for getting him involved in *Beauty*. His small daughters insisted that he read the entire play through to them as a bedtime story every night for a year.

Nicky's achievements brought him worldwide fame. The plays were produced all over England every Christmas, translated into endless languages and seen in every country of the Commonwealth. Barry Jackson mounted one every year for seasons of anything up to twelve weeks and declared that the Birmingham Rep. was able to operate entirely on the profits made by the Nicholas Stuart Gray plays. But we never managed to make money in London.

There were two schools of thought about plays for children. One (ours) was that they should be brought to the theatre as an exciting experience so that they could discover the magic of scenery and lighting, and live contact with actors, the effect of the darkened auditorium and the glow of the footlights on the house curtain. The other school believed in taking the theatre to the classroom and making it a shared experience with improvisation and the minimum of stage effects. In an impoverished climate this latter theory naturally carried away the bulk of the money available in grants from the GLC, the only body that was able to help, as the Arts Council was precluded from financing anything to do with children. The GLC's annual budget for drama was £2,000, which was mostly spent on special matinées of Shakespeare at the Old Vic. We didn't want 'O' level schoolchildren – we wanted them from six upwards – so we either had to finance the productions ourselves, or put on three performances at a time in venues like the Rudolf Steiner Hall for £150, which was all that Joe Hodgkinson of the GLC could scrape up for our benefit. Scenery was pushed on hand-carts to save money, and costumes continued to be made by whoever had a sewing-

machine or nimble fingers.

Beauty was followed by *The Princess and the Swineherd*, marked by a superb performance as the prince in disguise by Tony Britton. Out of an audition of two hundred little girls we found the perfect Siesta of Spain when a deep-voiced blonde capped the lines spoken by her two colleagues . . . "the rose", . . . "the nightingale", . . . with "the relief", a full octave lower. Her name was Diane Cilento, and as it turned out, she had worked with the authors of *Dark of the Moon* at the Barter Theatre in America, where admission could be bought with a few eggs or half a pound of butter.

I had been in America when Nicky and Joan formed themselves into a non-profit making organisation called the London Children's Theatre, but the following Christmas I was back in the team, and once more Ashley welcomed us at the Mercury for a production of *The Swineherd*. Tennent's were producing *An Ideal Husband* and Binkie wanted Cecil Trouncer for a small part which he didn't want to play. His way of getting out of the dilemma was to ask for an enormous salary, which Binkie wouldn't pay, so I knew he was available. I rang him and asked if he would play the Emperor?

"Of course I will if I like the part," he replied, so I hurried down the King's Road to leave the script on his doorstep.

A day or two later I met John Perry. "I hear you've got Cecil Trouncer," he remarked. "How much are you paying him? Eight pounds a week?"

"No," I replied proudly, "Ten."

I was immensely thrilled when Nicky dedicated the published version of the play to me, "For Kitty, who believes in magic," the first of three books with similar dedications: they all hold pride of place on my bookshelves. It was wonderful too to be in charge and make the decisions, saying "I want" instead of "Don't you think it would be a good idea if". Three years later, my salary having doubled, I was bold enough to try a much wider canvas, and for *The Marvellous Story of Puss in Boots* we took the Fortune Theatre and embarked on an ambitious production. B. J. Simmons agreed to make the costumes "new for hire" to Joan's designs, Reggie Woolley of the Players Theatre, whose Christmas pantomimes always included a sensational transformation scene,

agreed to do the sets, which were built by Brunskill's, though Joan did the painting herself. Once again the problem of who would play the lead cast a shadow over the proceedings and once more Nicky had to be frustrated, the part of Puss being created unforgettably by John Stratton. Joy Parker was delicate and withdrawn as the spellbound Princess, and David King-Wood, Andrew Faulds and Patrick Troughton, later the second Dr. Who, featured in the original cast list. In subsequent productions actors of the calibre of Alan Judd, Alan McNaughtan and William Gaunt appeared for us, including a whole host of moppets of both sexes. Nicky felt that if a child were included in the cast the children in the audience would identify with him and find the other characters more accessible. Some of the remarks we collected showed the extent to which we succeeded.

At a performance at the Rudolf Steiner Hall in the East End, a ten year old arriving late looked at the stage and remarked, "Oh, look. Technicolor."

At the Theatre Royal, Stratford, East, where we staged *Puss*, a small figure peered over the top of the box office, laid down his one shilling and sixpence and said: "Same again, please."

"Have you seen it already?" asked the amazed booking lady.

"Free times," replied the Cockney patron, and departed blissfully to his fourth experience in the gallery.

Sadly the fashion for Nicky's plays changed, and although he continued to write his personal versions of fairy tales, my own involvement came to an end with *Puss*. Nicky turned to writing books and short stories, and was as successful in this medium as he had been in the theatre, winning all kinds of awards and becoming a best seller as well as a favourite with the children's departments in all the lending libraries. His eyesight began to fail, and ill-health overtook him at the same time, but he retained his indomitable spirit to the end. Just before his death I went to see him in Cowes where he had gone to live with his sister Winnie, and it was Nicky who held my hand and comforted me as he talked with all his old enthusiasm.

In his version of *The Emperor's Nightingale*, Joy Parker had

played Kwang Lin, who in Chinese mythology is the Goddess of Mercy as well as the Goddess of Death. I only hope that when the end came, Nicky was released from all his pain and suffering by a figure as gracious and compassionate as the vision created so unforgettably by his life-long friend.

PALACE COURT

Chapter **XVII**

Although Vivien Leigh appeared for the firm on many occasions, adored Binkie and took his advice on every possible subject, including the advantages or otherwise of having a baby, Laurence Olivier only joined the team on two occasions, first when he directed Vivien in *The Skin of Our Teeth*, the Thornton Wilder allegory of the story of mankind, in which Vivien played Sabina the maid. She pinned her hair up with a toothbrush and used her Scarlett O'Hara accent with tremendous éclat, but the play didn't have any real success in London. Olivier's second production, *A Streetcar Named Desire*, was a different story altogether.

After the New York excitement over the play, which in addition to the Pulitzer Prize and the Drama Critics Circle Award had also been given the Donaldson Award, thirteen London managements were bidding for the rights, including Olivier, who suggested he should direct the play for the Old Vic as a vehicle for Vivien. In her book, *A Private View*, Irene Selznick, Louis B. Mayer's daughter and ex-wife of David O. Selznick, tells the story of the London presentation. She consulted Harold Freedman, then one of the most important theatrical agents in New York and subsequently a good friend of mine (breakfast at the Savoy), who filled her in on the various personalities. Harold gave Binkie a good reference and Irene sailed for London with an open mind to choose her associate.

She was met at Waterloo by what she describes as an immaculate young man with an air of anonymity who introduced himself as Hugh Beaumont. At first she couldn't believe anyone so important would come in person on such a mission but, when she was convinced, she allowed him to dismiss the car that had come to meet her and drive her to Claridge's in his own. They spent the evening together and before they parted the deal was made. Tennent's would present *Streetcar*. He then

suggested she might like to come to his office and sit in on his day-to-day running of the organisation, as she was still very inexperienced in managerial terms, an offer she accepted; we all became familiar with her elegant presence in Binkie's office. Perhaps another management might have used different methods and got the same results, but when it came to charm, Binkie knew he could beat any three of his rivals with one hand tied behind his back. Or even both.

Years later, when I was in New York for the production of one of my translations, I was invited to a party by the authors of *The Heiress*, Ruth and Augustus Goetz. Everyone present was a celebrity of one sort or another, when suddenly the *frisson* that runs through such gatherings when a super-star makes his or her entrance heralded the arrival of Irene. She is very tall, and on that occasion was wearing an absurd little boater perched on top of her head, with a single rose on a long flexible stalk rising above the crown. The rose nodded as she moved around and the buzz of conversation intensified wherever she passed. Finding myself standing beside my host I murmured to him admiringly, "Irene is the most wonderful woman I know." "Irene is not a woman," he retorted. "She's a force a' nature."

In Binkie she found a kindred spirit and their association was among the most rewarding he ever knew. Periodically rumours would fly that Irene wanted to marry him – and perhaps if he had been an American they would have done just that. As it was, they remained friends and associates over many successful productions, including *The Chalk Garden* with Edith Evans and Peggy Ashcroft, and *Bell, Book and Candle* with Rex Harrison and Lilli Palmer.

Meanwhile at the Lyric, to mark the opening of 1950, John Gielgud agreed to direct Christopher Fry's play about St. Cuthman, *The Boy With the Cart* and combine it with the famous Barrie curtain raiser, *Shall We Join the Ladies?* This was usually done at charity matinées as it provided parts for plenty of stars, male and female, but in our case it was used for its original purpose and the same artists followed on in the Fry play.

Free of his film commitments, Richard Burton played the young saint, with Mary Jerrold, a marvellous veteran, as his

mother. John set the play in modern dress to make the appeal more immediate and the effect was electrifying. Burton brought an almost mediaeval beauty shot through with spiritual power to the part and staggered everyone who saw him – including the top-ranking film star Stewart Granger, who went round to the dressing-room (one for each sex) to congratulate him and make an appointment in Hollywood as he was sure that was where Burton would end up.

The double bill was followed by C. E. Webber's *Man of the World*, the only time Kenneth Tynan worked for us as a director. It had been staged at the Phoenix on a Sunday night, using the set and lighting for *Death of a Salesman* – the Americans were just beginning to introduce their batteries of lanterns hung "in view" all over the stage and auditorium, superseding the old fashioned idea that lighting sources should always be invisible. The play was sufficiently praised by the press to warrant a production at the Lyric and Roger Livesey and his wife Ursula Jeans agreed to appear.

The piece was one of those backward-in-time sagas with the cast starting as old age pensioners and growing younger all through the action – in this case, spread over three acts. For the juvenile, Ursula suggested a newcomer, a girl she had seen at an Air Force concert at Tangmere, with ash blonde hair and a sexy curvaceous figure. Her stage name was Diana Dors, which bore no relation to the one on her birth certificate. Apparently when her father, a respectable butcher in Swindon, was approached in connection with the change he roared, "What's wrong with Fluck?"

In spite of paternal outrage, Dors it became and very fetching she was when she appeared at an audition to read for the part. In the event she was as hard-working as anyone and the Hammersmith stage hands took absolutely no notice of the famous legs parading below a man's pyjama jacket which was Ken's idea of a sexy outfit. Reece Pemberton designed the elaborate sets and as always with this particular artist, the drawings were very late in reaching the studio. The finale featured a mass of wrought iron and the effect was achieved by painting the design on canvas flats and then cutting away the unpainted areas with razor blades. Obviously this required no particular skill and was a job that could be left to the last

moment. We opened at Stratford-upon-Avon and while everyone else was busy with more technical matters I took over the razor blade and sawed away for hours in the intervals of making cups of coffee and soup for the team who were working through the night. At about 4 a.m. I was moving around with yet another trayful when I met the Master Carpenter – a divine character called Tom who wore canvas shoes slit open in a fetching pattern to liberate his corns and bunions. He gave me a dazzling smile.

"Do you think we're winning, miss?" he enquired, as he accepted a steaming mug.

I wonder whether many stage hands nowadays would produce that kind of humour or if they would be more concerned with reminding the management that they were now switching over to double-double-overtime? Peter Brook came to see the play at Hammersmith and picked out a young man who emerged from the "swimming pool" wearing bathing trunks and wielding a towel.

"Who's that?" he hissed in the darkness.

"Lionel Jeffries," I replied. That's all it takes to show talent.

Years later I exercised the same sort of perception when I wanted a young man for *Puss in Boots*. The underclad figure who had carried the on-stage end of Achilles' tent at Stratford-upon-Avon and posed immobile for a few moments had caught my eye. On enquiry he proved to be Donald Pickering, and he has gone on to enjoy an appreciable theatrical success ever since. Talent spotting of that kind was one of the things I most enjoyed and I suppose ranks with the sultan's choice from his otherwise anonymous harem – in his case of course he could always throw the lady back if he didn't like what she had to deliver (preferably into the Bosphorus) – but once you found you were right and the talent was there it was a wonderfully satisfying feeling.

True to the usual pattern, *Man of the World*, which hadn't been a success, was followed by one of our most profitable undertakings, *The Holly and the Ivy*, a new play by Wynyard Browne, a Norwich-born dramatist who had been discovered by Frith Banbury (of *Caste* fame). Wynyard's family went back into the mists of time (one of his ancestors was a famous

medical figure) and the play was in the finest traditions of the English family drama, enjoying the same kind of success that *Dear Octopus* had had a decade or more earlier. Set in a middle-class household at Christmas time, it was given a perfect interpretation by Jane Baxter, supported by two formidable actresses – Margaret Halstan and Maureen Delaney – who squabbled like alley cats as they jockeyed for position. The young brother was played by Bryan Forbes who was to go on to become a film director and TV tycoon and who had already done yeoman service in *Fighters Calling* and other productions.

A minor tragedy occurred very early on in the run when Frith cast Cecil Ramage as the beloved uncle in the play. Cecil had been one of the handsomest men of his time and with his beautiful wife, Cathleen Nesbitt (Rupert Brooke's beloved), had enjoyed much commercial success. Sadly he had taken to the bottle and been away for many years, but Frith felt he had now recovered completely and could be trusted to make a come-back in what was a delightful and very suitable role. Unfortunately this trust proved to be misplaced and poor Cecil succumbed once more to temptation and had to be replaced by Patrick Waddington, another dashingly handsome veteran, who had appeared as Prince Hal in George Robey's version of *Henry IV* at His Majesty's. Patrick had formed part of a singing trio with Virginia McKenna's mother which provided the cabaret at the Mayfair Hotel for many years, and he went on to become the director of the Actors' Orphanage, until an appalling motorbike accident cut short his career. The play transferred to the Duchess Theatre where it ran for 413 performances and proved a boon to repertory and amateur companies for years afterwards. I think it's one of the pieces I would most like to see revived.

The rest of the spring programme was made up of plays by new writers, Rachel Grieve and C. P. Snow, whose *View Over the Park* starred John McCallum and Googie Withers. This was yet another of those cure-for-cancer-shots-in-the-dark but it was nice to have such a distinguished writer among us, even if he didn't know too much about stage technique. We also had visits from the Bristol Old Vic with Allan Davis' production of *Tartuffe* – by now he was the Administrator at Bristol and making a great reputation as a director, with a

highly successful pantomime to his credit as well as the classics that made up the rest of the programme. The English Opera Company presented Britten's version of *The Beggar's Opera*, first with a marvellous huge Canadian baritone, Bruce Boyce, and subsequently with the part re-written for Peter Pears. A revival of *The Old Ladies* didn't quite have the same impact as the original production with Edith Evans, but toured successful after the Hammersmith run.

The highlight of the year came for me with the production of Anouilh's *Eurydice*. During our theatre going days as schoolgirls in Paris, Guégué had taken us to a tiny theatre in Montmartre to see a new play starring Pierre Fresnay, with whom we were all in love as a result of his performances in the Pagnol trilogy. The new offering was also intriguing because it starred Hélène Perdrière, a juvenile who had recently left the Comédie Française where we had seen her in a variety of classical parts. The new play, *L'Hermine*, dealt with the torments of a penniless young man in love with the granddaughter of a rich old harpy who was making her life intolerable. Finally the young couple decide to murder the grandmother, but as soon as the deed is done, the young girl finds she can't bear to touch the young man and in the subsequent reaction to this body-blow, in a staggering *coup de théâtre*, the young man blurts out his guilt to the policeman who has until then been unable to shake his alibi. Once the war was over, Jan van Loewen produced a nap hand of plays by France's most currently successful writers, and to my amazement I discovered that the list was headed by the author of the Fresnay vehicle, Jean Anouilh.

By now the plays had been published, and the author had grouped them into volumes of comedies and dramas, which he called either "black" or "rose-coloured". Most of the early ones had been written for the husband and wife team of Georges and Ludmilla Pitöeff – the legendary pair who were the French equivalent of the Lunts, so there were alternating leading roles for the man or the girl, and a regular pattern of parts, obviously written for the permanent members of the Pitöeff company – the elderly eccentrics, male and female, the pure young girl, the high-minded penniless young man, and the butler-cum-companion figure, flanked by the female com-

panion-cum-governess. Another factor the plays seemed to have in common were marvellous first acts, with a general falling off as if the author had grown tired of his chosen subject, and they all appeared to be very French in feeling.

I fell in love with *Eurydice*, and for my own pleasure made a translation as I was confident somebody would produce it. With their anti-Greek classic policy, the firm turned it down, and I then had the bright idea of sending it to the BBC. David Peel was exactly right for the young man and he gave the script to Raymond Raikes, then the leading BBC drama director, who also fell in love with the play and made an excellent radio adaptation. On 14 May we had a triumphant transmission and the following morning every management in London seemed to be clamouring for the rights. At this point Tennent's stepped in and claimed first refusal, so the play was scheduled for the Lyric, Hammersmith.

Mai Zetterling had just announced that she was about to produce another Anouilh play, *La Sauvage* but when I remarked to John Perry that *Eurydice* was infinitely better, he suggested I should send her my translation with the idea of her appearing in it at Hammersmith. To my great joy she agreed at once – Peter Brook was to direct, and we all decided Dirk Bogarde would be the perfect foil to Mai's blonde beauty. The script went to the film studio where he was currently engaged and again the answer was yes – the only snag being the length of time we would have to wait for both stars to become available.

Dr Jan van Loewen, the agent for all these plays, was a newcomer to the theatrical scene. A brilliant lawyer and musician, born Hanns Loewenstein in Berlin, he changed his name to the more Rembrandtish version after the war, even appearing under that name in the character section of *Spotlight*, though I have no direct record of any film or stage work that he did. However, he soon entered the literary field, and as the English representation of the French Société des Auteurs was up for grabs, tried to get himself appointed as their agent. French authors are obliged by law to belong to the Société in France, where their royalties are fixed and collected on an official basis, but they are free to employ agents for

outside work and overseas productions. Many choose to have personal managers, but a fair number leave all translation rights to the Société, so it is important that their representatives abroad should be persons of the highest standing. They didn't feel that the newly established Doctor measured up to this requirement, so he took the problem to Spencer Curtis Brown, then the head of the largest literary and dramatic agency in London – twice the size of its nearest rival. The Curtis Brown list included such luminaries as Queen Marie of Roumania, Somerset Maugham, Hammond Innes and Daphne du Maurier to name, as they say, but a few, and of course they were perfectly acceptable to the moguls in the Rue Blanche, who agreed at once to the joint representation. Van Loewen proved to have an incredible facility for juggling international finance, and was able to extract vast sums of accumulated royalties from countries that had blocked the authors' earnings during and after the war while exchange control was still very tight, and his genius in these matters was of infinite value to his growing list of authors.

With his attractive red-headed wife, Elizabeth, van Loewen soon became a popular host on the London scene, entertaining first in his flat off Westbourne Grove, and later at a charming house in Angmering or his villa in the South of France. He also brought a beautiful house in Victoria Road, Kensington, before the property boom took off. "Bricks and mortar can't lose," he said, "and London property is grotesquely undervalued at the moment."

How right he was, and he was equally shrewd in his wooing of authors. Before he retired he numbered both Rattigan and Coward among his clients and of course administered the Anouilh boom throughout.

While we were waiting for Dirk and Mai to become available, another Anouilh play (like Ayckbourn, he turned them out on an annual basis) L'Invitation au chateau appeared, and was immediately bought by HMT. I produced my usual literal translation, but while everyone had been very complimentary about Eurydice, a more poetical approach was felt to be essential for the fragile beauty of the Chateau dialogue. Christopher Fry was the obvious choice to make the adaptation, but he was busy with his new play, Venus Observed,

which had been commissioned for the Oliviers, and couldn't take on anything else. I reworked my translation, Peter Brook had a go, but somehow nothing seemed satisfactory. Christopher was working to a deadline and we were still racking our brains when I heard through the grapevine that he was stuck at the end of the second act with no prospect of meeting his dates and the Oliviers had decided to produce another play.

I wrote to Kit, imploring him to reconsider the *Chateau* situation – I offered to do his typing, filing, cooking, cleaning – anything to get him to make the translation. Over the luncheon table he agreed to set to work with Peter, and the final result, *Ring Round The Moon*, made theatrical history. Oliver Messel designed a wrought-iron conservatory for the play, the first time metal had been used for stage construction, and the cast, led by Margaret Rutherford and Cecil Trouncer, introduced Claire Bloom to an adoring public with Audrey Fildes as the imperious Diana and Paul Scofield unforgettable in the twin roles of Hugo and Frederick. Just what he did to alter his personality was perfectly undetectable, but nobody was ever in any doubt as to which twin he was representing when he came on stage. Richard Wattis and Marjorie Stewart danced an incredible tango, and Richard Addinsell's music added the right touch to the Edwardian atmosphere.

Everything seemed set for Peter to repeat this success with *Eurydice* but when the time came he said he wanted to talk to me. He seemed very serious when he arrived at the flat, and we crossed the road into Kensington Gardens and sat down on the grass while he explained that he felt he couldn't go ahead with the production. He had been in love with one girl when the play had first been discussed and the whole production seemed bound up with her personality. Now the affair was over, he was in love with somebody else, and he felt he couldn't go back to what now seemed a closed chapter. As if to add to my personal distress, a large Alsatian dog passed at that moment and lifting his leg, peed on the very attractive black leather bag I had propped up on the grass beside me.

Once again the Peters were switched. Peter Ashmore came in to fill the vacancy and Stanley Moore and Hubert Gurschner designed the very attractive and unusual sets. Casting sessions combined looking for new people with some firm

ideas as to who should be engaged – to all Peter's suggestions I replied that only two actors would be right for the sinister hotel waiter and the bullying theatrical manager – Peter Moffatt and Erich Pohlmann.

"What happens if I don't like them?" wailed Peter.

"You will," I assured him, and of course he did.

Erich had appeared as an anonymous musketeer in the Ralph Richardson *Cyrano* and I had been so impressed by his personality that I had investigated his possibilities. Unable to work in the theatre during the war as an enemy alien, he had become a chef and had only been allowed to resume his profession with the cessation of hostilities. Filmgoers will remember him as the original Menace in the James Bond films, with the beautiful white cat on his lap, but he was a considerable classic actor, a fine bridge player and the most adorable of men. His performance in *Eurydice* remains one of my favourite memories.

The name of his character produced a curious incident. One day after the play had opened, I received a letter signed Edmund Dulac, saying that the famous illustrator was upset to learn that his name was being used by the villain in the Anouilh play and asking if we would be prepared to alter it? I wrote to Anouilh, pointing out that Dulac had illustrated so many of my favourite children's books that I felt almost as though I had been contacted by a Brother Grimm, and that it would be enormously appreciated if the author would make the change. Anouilh graciously agreed, and for the rest of the run the name was altered to Molac, but with the death of the charming artist, the name reverted to the original.

With Binkie's dislike of Greek classics there was no question of using the original title, and we racked our brains for weeks until one night in a telephone conversation with Peter I said "that might make a good point of departure . . ." and the title was found.

The chemistry between Mai and Dirk flamed into the most perfect fusion and on the first night at Hammersmith it seemed as though everyone in the audience was enjoying a good cry. Mai herself was so overcome that during the last scene Dirk found his espadrilles were soaking wet with her tears and set to work to console her under cover of the dialogue. A transfer

172

was immediately arranged, we opened at the Duke of York's Theatre on Boxing Day and when Queen Mary was among the visitors who came to enjoy it, we felt sure we were set for a long run. But once again any translation of mine seemed doomed to disaster and after only six weeks in London Dirk was ordered to leave the cast on medical grounds. He handed me this bombshell in his dressing-room on a Friday night. Apparently unmoved, I accepted the news as an act of God, remarking, "Oh well, I suppose people do have babies," and went off to telephone Binkie from the Salisbury (the Edwardian pub in St. Martin's Lane, much frequented by theatricals), accompanied by Tony Forwood, Dirk's great friend and personal manager. We were completely clueless as to who we might approach to follow Dirk, but God seemed to provide the answer, for as we opened the door, who should be on his way to the Gents in the basement but Peter Finch.

"After him!" I yelled to Tony and by the time they emerged from the depths the affair was concluded. Peter had just signed a contract to appear as the Sheriff of Nottingham in the Disney film of *Robin Hood*, but had a six weeks gap which he was quite prepared to fill at the theatre. Being a quick study, he took to the part immediately and in no time at all he was ready to open. Seeing him in the dark blue shirt and slacks Dirk had worn I realised they would never do. "Fling the whole lot in a bucket of bleach," I ordered and the resulting washed-out material exactly matched Peter's eyes. He changed his hair-style too, at my suggestion, and indeed wore it in the same manner for the rest of his life. Dirk came back to the cast at the end of his medical treatment, but somehow the original impetus had been spent and the play only ran for twenty-two weeks.

Fortunately that wasn't the end of the story. The Theatre Guild, which had provided HMT with one of its biggest successes in *Oklahoma!* decided to buy the American rights and produce the play for Dorothy Maguire who had become a film star after a promising career on Broadway. "She's worth eighty thousand dollars advance at the Box Office," pronounced Lawrence Langner, the head of the Theatre Guild, and everything seemed set for success when Richard Burton was cast to play opposite her. We were also allowed to take Hugh Griffith to repeat his triumph as the father – rolling those

enormous goosegog eyes in all directions and stealing every scene in which he appeared. Noel Willman already had an American Equity card and so could appear as Monsieur Henri, but everyone else in the cast had to be American. John Perry gave me two months leave of absence to help with the casting and see the play's opening (I received my full salary but had to find my own fare and expenses while I was in New York), but I would have agreed to any terms just to have the chance to work on Broadway.

The flight was fascinating – sixteen hours in the air, with real beds to sleep in and a stewardess to wake you with coffee and orange juice (which I promptly spilt all over my pyjamas). We ran into a storm over the Atlantic and had to make a huge detour to Iceland where we refuelled, and next morning we were several hours behind schedule. By this time I had discovered that my fellow passengers included Ivy Benson, the famous band leader, and the managing director of Goya perfumes. Everyone was very interested in the Broadway production and promised to come and see it if they were around when it opened.

Peter Ashmore had already reached New York and had taken up residence at Park Chambers, a set of service flats which were convenient to the theatres and very reasonable in price and together we sallied forth to meet the press at the welcoming cocktail party the Guild had arranged to announce the show, and to meet our new leading lady.

Chapter XVIII

Like Tennent's in England, the Theatre Guild was a long-established American institution. Founded in 1918, it had been part of the revolution that had helped to liberate the American theatre from the hackneyed formulas of the nineteenth century. In his book, the distinguished critic Norman Nadel comments that while this revolution was going on many people resented the Guild, just as so many London managements resented HMT – the feelings aroused being identical, though possibly for different reasons. The Guild came into existence to try and raise standards of production and literary content above the blatant commercialism represented by Klaw and Erlanger and the brothers Shubert. In my time the two former had disappeared but the others remained as a formidable force, controlling nearly all the Broadway bricks and mortar, maintaining the theatres with a minimum of modernisation, cramped backstage conditions and total disregard for the comfort of stage hands or actors. The current gibe in 1950 was "What are the three things wrong with the Broadway theatre today?" The answer was "the Shubert brothers and syphilis."

It was this attitude which the Theatre Guild set out to change, the original group of six consisting of university drama graduates Helen Westley and Philip Moeller, while three of the others, Theresa Helburn, Lee Simonson (the designer) and Maurice Wertheim had studied at the George Pierce Baker '47 Workshop at Harvard. This intellectualism was balanced by Lawrence Langner, the only one of the six not originally an American. Born in Swansea (did he and Binkie get on so well because they were fellow Welshmen?) he was stage struck from the age of ten when he first began playing with a toy theatre. Subsequently he worked very briefly as a junior clerk in a theatrical agency and then as a novice for a patent office. Eventually at the age of twenty he went to New

York as technical assistant for his firm, specialising in patent law, working with inventors such as Charles F. Kettering who had just designed the automobile self-starter and it was his royalties from this invention and others that formed the foundation of the Langner fortune.

As early as 1914, together with a group of like-minded enthusiasts, Lawrence had founded the group that was to be known as the Washington Square Players, with a manifesto proclaiming its determination to produce plays of artistic merit, and a subscription scheme designed to keep the price of tickets at 50 cents. These were to be two of the legacies the Theatre Guild inherited – play quality and the subscription plan. Eventually the Guild extended their organisation to cover every major city in America – theatre buffs could take out a subscription "blind", knowing that the four or five attractions for which they had paid in advance would have the high quality the Guild guaranteed and this system continued for over fifty years. The roll-call of Guild productions, like the Tennent playbills, represents all that was best in the American theatre and no name of major importance is missing from their list of achievements. Lawrence was a devotee of Bernard Shaw and presented most of his plays for the first time on Broadway while European authors ignored by the "commercial managers", such as Tolstoy, Strindberg, Molnar, Georges Courteline, André Obey and Karel Čapek were included in their earliest seasons.

By 1922 American names were beginning to appear: Elmer Rice, Sidney Howard, and Rodgers and Hart, with a show called *The Garrick Gaieties* sandwiched between productions of *Caesar and Cleopatra* and *Arms and the Man*. (How I wish I could have seen Alfred Lunt as Bluntschli). Romney Brent was the juvenile in the musical – later to be the first person to sing 'Mad Dogs and Englishmen' in a Coward revue in London. The Lunts became the Guild's reigning stars, though a polite fiction maintained that they didn't subscribe to the star system and everyone in the company was equal. In 1984 it is tempting to remark with Orwell that this may have been the intention but some were obviously more equal than others.

A reciprocal agreement between HMT and the Guild provided an exciting cultural exchange across the Atlantic and

Binkie's charm ensured that Terry Helburn and Armina Marshall (Mrs Langner) remained perfectly happy with the arrangement. The first Tennent-Theatre Guild partnership dated from 1936 when Dodie Smith's *Call it A Day* was produced on Broadway with Gladys Cooper and Philip Merivale repeating the London success of Owen Nares and Fay Compton. *Amphitryon 38* was also originally presented under their aegis, though John C. Wilson had co-presented the play with HMT in London.

By this time American authors included Philip Barry, whose play, *The Philadelphia Story* introduced the young Katherine Hepburn, as well as William Saroyan, Maxwell Anderson and Tennessee Williams, whose first play, *Battle of Angels*, which appeared in 1941, never made the Great White Way, though in a rewritten version it eventually arrived under the title of *Orpheus Descending*. Like all successful managements, the Guild had their ups and downs and they were trying to ride a very severe down in 1942 when the classic turning point arrived. A play called *Green Grow the Lilacs* by Lynn Riggs was tried out on tour and provided the basis for a new musical, the team responsible being Richard Rodgers and Oscar Hammerstein II. Legends about this production abound – how they couldn't find backers for the show and Alfred Drake and other members of the future cast climbed stairs and rapped on doors, forcing potential moneybags to listen to the songs – imagine being asked to listen to 'Surrey with a Fringe on Top', 'People Will Say We're in Love' and 'The Farmer and The Cowman Must Be Friends' sung by that magical baritone at point-blank range. Finally most of the backing was scratched together, but Lawrence had to make up the end money out of his own purse, thus acquiring a sizeable chunk of what was to become the greatest money-spinner of the decade. The opening number was unsatisfactory and Rodgers wrestled for two weeks with an idea that finally resulted in a suitable melody. Hammerstein was out of town and Dick sang him the tune over the phone.

"I'll call you back," promised the lyricist and two hours later kept his word.

"Oh what a beautiful morning," he carolled and the day was saved.

The publicist tells how at the very last moment the title was changed and *Oklahoma* was picked as the substitute. All the printing had to be redrawn, press releases altered and after two sleepless nights the poor man was just settling down to a well-earned nap when the phone shrilled.

"Put an exclamation mark at the end," ordered Langner, and everything had to be done again.

The London first night fell on 30 April, my birthday, which explains why Binkie had to allow me to buy two dress circle tickets although the public demand could have sold the house out several times over. At that time advance albums of stage shows were unknown – we were still using 78 acetates, and managements believed in keeping everything under wraps until the first night, so it was extraordinary to be sitting in the theatre and hearing that overture for the first time – like being in a similar situation for *The Magic Flute* – and by the end the audience was beginning to cheer. Then the curtain rose on an empty stage, with 'Aunt Ella' sitting centre with her milk churn and only the brilliant backcloth to close the vista. From what sounded like a distance of several miles a splendid baritone burst into 'Oh What A Beautiful Morning' and Harold Keel erupted on to the stage. (Modern audiences will know him better under his later name of Howard Keel and recognise him as Miss Ellie's elderly admirer in *Dallas*.) Song after song followed, each more wildly applauded than the last, but the Guild had decreed 'no encores' and the rule was obeyed. After the opening of the second half, when the square dance appeared for the first time on a London stage, the audience went mad and refused to stop applauding until "Aunt Ella" seized the gun from the Sheriff's holster and fired a shot in the air. In the resulting silence she spoke her line, "And now let's get on with the auction," and the show was able to continue. At the end there must have been twenty minutes of encores and for the first time we saw formation grouping and changing for each number – previously the cast of a show would merely keep their curtain call positions and sing where they stood.

Everyone connected with the show had a special affection for *Oklahoma!* Some people stayed in the cast for four or five years, considering it a privilege to be allowed to appear in it,

and tour after tour continued long after the end of the Broadway and London runs. It was all the more exciting because it was so wonderful to have Drury Lane back in commission with a smash-hit, as the first post-war offering, Noël Coward's *Pacific 1860* had been a horrid flob in spite of introducing Mary Martin to London. Fortunately she returned later in one of her greatest triumphs and washed that man right out of her hair for as long as she was prepared to stay in the cast of *South Pacific*.

New York was a revelation after the austerities of post-war London. (Periodically we would wonder if we had actually won the war.) We had however joined in one revolution when Christian Dior rebelled against the simplistic lines of current fashion and burst into a joyous swirl of godets and circular skirts – dropping hemlines by anything up to fourteen inches so that the more extreme fashions descended to just above the ankle and *guêpières* clinched in slender waists to emphasise the hour-glass line that hadn't been seen since the heyday of the Gibson Girls. But we were still severely restricted as to food and the lavishness of New York restaurants took the visitors' breath away.

My first Saturday night I was taken out by a chum, Peter Forster, who had been "lent" to me by his girl friend in London and he ordered the dinner, waiting as he said afterwards to register my expression when the huge portion of roast beef was put in front of me.

"What am I supposed to do with this?" I wailed.

"Just like everyone else – eat two mouthfuls out of the centre and leave the rest."

I couldn't believe such waste. The restaurants didn't even have pig buckets to collect the remains, and any dish that left the kitchen was promptly junked, no matter that it might not even have been touched by the diner.

On the way home Peter stopped at a news vendor's kiosk.

"Here you are," he said and pressed fifteen pounds of newsprint into my arms. "I wanted to be the first to give you a New York Sunday Times." How many acres of forest had gone into that edition I couldn't guess, but it was on a par with the rest of American extravagance that nobody seemed to mind.

Alas, nobody seemed to mind about Orpheus and his love-lorn search for Eurydice either. The title had had to be changed as another American play, *Point of No Return*, had just opened with Henry Fonda and it was felt that our London title would cause confusion. After a lot of cabling and no agreement I arrived to find it was now called *Legend of Lovers*, and the poster showed Orpheus fiddling away in a café, whereas on stage it was an accordian since Peter felt it provided a much more identifiable French sound. From then on, nothing seemed to go right. Burton and Griffith quarrelled violently in Welsh over the heads of the director and designer: Dorothy Maguire proved to have considerably less expertise than Mai had brought to the part, and although Burton did all he could to help her, in rehearsal it became evident that the girl led every one of their dialogues and if she didn't set the right pace there was nothing he could do to correct it.

The Guild had refused to have Mai on the grounds that her name would mean nothing in America – how did newcomers ever make their mark, I wondered? (The answer was provided by a young lady called Audrey Hepburn, who appeared as an unknown in *Gigi* and the following morning had her name put above the title, much to Cathleen Nesbitt's rage and fury – but that was another story and another management.)

The final scene change provided another battle. Lawrence Langner felt the action should be continuous and wanted to have the father's big speech used as a transition scene while the set was moved into position. Hughie flatly refused to do this and when asked to arbitrate Peter disappeared – taking to his bed, his usual habit whenever a crisis developed. No matter what we tried the play just didn't repeat the London success – no American could possibly identify with a philosophy that preached death was better than life, with or without Eurydice, and we closed after an ignominious two weeks. Ironically enough, the other Guild offering *Venus Observed*, starring Rex Harrison and Lilli Palmer, whose booking had opened on the same day as ours, chalked up far more than the $80,000 advance Lawrence had predicted for us and went on to become the hit of the season.

While New York is a wonderful place to visit, working in it for a long period and particularly when all the hard work

culminates in disaster, was a very different matter. Television had just burst on an astonished world in a big way and every bar had its lights dimmed so the customers could goggle at a miniscule box tucked away in a corner. All conversation was silenced, and if you wanted a swift gin to perk you up, you could only choke it down in an atmosphere resembling a period of national mourning and flee into the great outdoors as quickly as you could. There was none of the friendliness and camaraderie of my usual drinking haunts in London – I always felt that if you started crying into your gin in a pub the landlord would have you upstairs in his private snug inside nothing flat while his wife brewed you a nice cuppa and invited you to tell them your woes – if you cried into your gin in a New York bar nobody would pay the slightest attention, except perhaps to push their own drink away from yours to avoid any adulteration of the contents. So it was with huge relief that I finally flew back to London on New Year's Eve. When the captain announced that it was now midnight, I kissed the man beside me (he turned out to be the head of the Harvard Business School) and resumed my activities at the Lyric.

The feature of our presentation that had received universal acclaim were the beautiful sets designed by Eldon Elder, the Guild's newest and youngest protégé, an absolutely delightful theatre buff. We became great friends and while he has continued to enjoy a highly successful career, our friendship has proved equally enduring, proving once again that no experience can possibly be all bad.

1950 brought two outstanding successes for the commercial side of the Tennent Empire. Elsie Beyer had been "lent" to Laurence Olivier for his 1948 tour of Australia with the Royal Shakespeare Company, and her place at the Globe had been taken by William (Bill) Conway – an enchanting person who brought a new atmosphere of calm to the over-charged emotional set-up which John Perry's arrival had created – and life was considerably eased in consequence. It was to him therefore that I reported excitedly after the Easter break.

The previous night, 10 April, the Repertory Players had

tried out a piece called *Seagulls over Sorrento*, in which Anthony Viccars, a particular chum, was playing the wife-stealer who only appears in the last act. As the Monday was a Bank Holiday I had gone to tea with David Evans and Hazel Terry in Bayswater to meet up with Patrick and Barbara Macnee, together with young Rupert their first born, then about two years old. In the course of the afternoon the skies had opened, and in the resulting downpour there was no way of getting Barbara and Rupert back to World's End where they lived. Not a taxi was visible and even the Daimler Hire cars were all bespoke, so by the time the storm eased and Pat had collected a solitary cab from the street, there was nothing for it but to take mother and child home first and then go on to the theatre. We arrived during the first interval and found ourselves sitting behind Kathleen Harrison. Turning round she declared, "This play will run for a year," and we proceeded to share her opinion over the next two acts. Owing to the bad weather – and perhaps the holiday – only one other management was represented at the showing, George and Alfred Black (no relation), just setting up in management and very anxious to snap up this obvious money-spinner. However, once I had reported to Bill Conway with all the details of the evening's success, he pulled the same argument that had applied to *George and Margaret*, claimed that the script had gone from the Globe to the Repertory Players and pre-empted the Black management's offer. In the end, a compromise was reached and the play was presented as a joint offering, opening at the Apollo in June where it clocked up 1551 performances.

Basil Lord had played the lead on the Monday night and I was furious when I discovered that Ronald Shiner would be taking over. The two artists had worked together before when Basil had first understudied and then taken over from Ronnie in *Worm's Eye View* which had filled the Whitehall for years. However, honour was satisfied because eventually Basil took over the part and toured in it for months afterwards. Ronnie was a marvellously generous person and specialised in giving parties that catered for all tastes – champagne and lobster for the gourmets and jellied eels for the stage hands and fellow devotees of this Cockney delicacy – he ran a pub called the Black Boy and was much beloved by customers and fellow

artists alike. It is always sad to remember those far-off days and register the mortality rate. The cast included Bernard Lee and William Hartnell – the former becoming James Bond's boss in so many films and the latter the original Dr Who. The part my friend had played was taken by David Langford, who happily is still with us, partnered by Gordon Jackson – the two of them meeting again over many episodes of *Upstairs, Downstairs*.

Tennent's other smash-hit was a French attraction, *The Little Hut* by André Roussin, which introduced Nancy Mitford to the theatre scene. The play had already run for three years in Paris before Binkie decided to do it after reading the usual literal translation I provided, though of course Nancy didn't need any help from me. As the play was subsequently filmed with Stewart Granger, David Niven and Ava Gardner, presumably a fair number of people will remember the plot – a husband and wife cast away on a tropical island with the husband's best friend who is also the wife's lover. The lover is directed to the little hut while the married couple share the larger one until the lover revolts and insists on restoring what had always been the status quo in England. The plot is complicated by the arrival of a Noble Savage, who in the original was a black man, but in the interests of obtaining the Lord Chamberlain's Licence, the part was changed to a Scandinavian, heavily suntanned and played with great éclat by Geoffrey Toone. "He does an awful lot of weight-lifting," said John Perry, "and loves showing off his physique."

Whatever the reason, Geoffrey was superb in the part, completing the roll-call of Robert Morley, David Tomlinson and Joan Tetzel. The lady was a friend of Robert's and was engaged at his suggestion. She was inordinately pretty but a typically "difficult" star, driving the wardrobe mistress crazy with her likes and dislikes, though as she only had one dress, designed by Balmain, which grew more and more tattered as the evening wore on, scope for such histrionics was strictly limited. When the play was revived Geraldine MacEwen played the part, and at my suggestion the Noble Savage was rewritten to be played by a black man, but the choice of actor wasn't too happy and they'd have done better to stick to the Mitford solution.

So with Eileen Herlie back at the Haymarket in *The Second Mrs Tanqueray*, Emlyn Williams in *Accolade* at the Aldwych and Terry Rattigan's *Who Is Sylvia?* at the Criterion, the Tennent stable chalked up a memorable list of successes for the new decade.

Chapter **XIX**

At the start of 1951, while the Lyric was housing various visiting companies, a bitter-sweet decision had robbed us of an interesting new writer.

For some time I had been corresponding with an actor/ dramatist, John Whiting, then working at the York Repertory Theatre, who had been sending us his plays. His odd quirkiness of phrase and obviously original mind were indications of a considerable talent, and eventually after letters of encouragement had gone back with each script, the latest to arrive, *A Penny For a Song* seemed to hit exactly the right note and it was passed on to Peter Brook. Peter, of course, adored it and the next I heard was that it was to be produced at the Haymarket with a star-studded cast, a set designed by Oliver Messel with a fire-engine created by Emett, and Virginia McKenna making her début in town. Unfortunately it fell as flat as the proverbial pancake and nearly put paid to John's writing career.

Whether the play would have pleased critics and public better if it had been presented at Hammersmith without all the razzmatazz, nobody will ever know, but of course I was firmly of the opinion that if we had put it on there, without the star names that seemed to promise so much, the critics would have "discovered" the author and the play might have made a better impact. This theory was put to the test a few months later when John's second play, *Saint's Day* was produced at the Arts Theatre Club. Audiences just didn't materialise in spite of glowing tributes in the press from all the top artists in the business, but in it John had created the original Angry Young Man, predating John Osborne by several years, and displaying much of the violence and passion that was found later in John Arden's *Sergeant Musgrave's Dance*.

1951 was of course Festival of Britain year and our own contribution to this celebration of the centenary of Prince Albert's Great Exhibition was a revue that concentrated on

various topical themes. The opening calypso exhorted all
concerned to "come to Britain for holidays," and included a
reference to a famous classic painist:

> . . . Eileen Joyce,
> She can really be a lot of fun
> Playing six concertos for the price of one.

Noël Coward's reference to the Festival's organiser was
reasonably prophetic:

> . . . and if it turns out all right
> Knight Gerald Barry.

The revue marked William Chappell's début as a director.
An ex-ballet dancer who had trained with Marie Rambert (he
created the Gemini dance in *Horoscope* with Margot Fonteyn
and Michael Soames for the Sadler's Wells Ballet), Billy
seemed able to turn his hand to anything, designing the dresses
for *Point of Departure*, writing a biography of Margot Fonteyn
and filling the monkey skin in a brief appearance at the end of
The Little Hut. He was very much a favourite with everyone,
and the new revue was as successful as the earlier ones had been
under Laurier's direction. It also broke the pattern of Hammersmith planning by running from the end of May to the end
of September before transferring to the Globe, which meant I
was allowed to spend the whole of June in the South of France
– the longest holiday of my working life – and revelled in that
magic atmosphere with brandy at 25s. a litre, and no building
boom to ruin the coastline and fill the corniche roads with
motor cars.

Through my French connections I could always arrange for
money over and above the legal travel allowance, and I
pioneered the villa holiday by renting a house for three months
and then letting the place, a fortnight at a time, to anyone else
who wanted to use it. Our first experience had been in a tiny
house in St. Paul de Vence for which I paid seven pounds a
month. This was found for me by Georges Wakhevitch, the
French designer who had been used by Peter Glenville for
Terry Rattigan's *Adventure Story*. The first of Georges' designs
to be seen in London was a ballet danced by Jean Babilée, *Le
Jeune Homme et La Mort*, in which a marvellously ingenious set

began as a Montmartre attic, and then folded into a tent-like shape which disappeared into the flies to reveal the roofs of Paris over which the young man was led by the young girl representing the figure of Death. Georges came over to London to stay in our flat while he painted the most wonderful designs in gouache in the kitchen where any mess could more readily be removed. He calmly pointed out that if any design wasn't accepted he could easily wash it off the specially prepared surface, and responded to my horrified protests by giving me one of the condemned designs and signing it "Merry Christmas".

The second villa had been recommended by my new friend Louis Nagel and was a much larger, modern construction at Roquebrune, high on the hillside, overlooking the bay of Menton, and we could watch the lights of the Italian riviera from our terrace, below the dancing pinpoints of the fireflies, and the nearer lights of the French coastline. For the first time in my life I tanned a deep golden brown, fell in love, and drove over the coastal routes and mountains in a two-seater Mercedes. The third villa was in the Californie district of Cannes, overlooking Aly Khan's villa where he was married to Rita Hayworth in the maternity wedding dress designed by Dior. Wonderful holidays when we seemed to be permanently drunk on atmosphere, brandy and sun – and the most expensive rent was £30 a month.

The revue was followed by another Fry double bill – *Thor With Angels* and *A Phoenix Too Frequent*, directed by Michael MacOwan, later principal of LAMDA where the theatre has now been renamed in his memory. *Thor* was an "early Briton" play with George Cole and Dorothy Tutin as the juveniles – Tutin already showing signs of the star quality she has proved so frequently since. The play opened in a thick fog, and contains one of my favourite Fry lines: "A push in the lucky direction we're leaning towards," while George appeared again in the second piece opposite Diana Churchill and Jessie Evans. Paul Scofield had created the part at the Arts Theatre Club and I had always felt he was too much the officer type for the simple soldier who finds the lady starving herself to death in her husband's tomb. George had always appeared in Cockney or "wide boy" parts and was amazed when I

suggested he should don Roman tunic and armour. For fun I chose the gaudiest and most elaborate outfit that Berman's could supply and when George sheepishly appeared at the dress parade there was a shout of admiration.

"George! You've got the most wonderful legs!" and he went on to enjoy himself hugely.

Emlyn Williams created his Charles Dickens readings that autumn, for which Angus McBean designed a montage picture for the poster combining a profile of Dickens with a portrait of Emlyn. His considerable feat of memory was instantly acclaimed and thirty years later, Emlyn is still repeating his success. In making their apologia for the activities of the non-profit-making side of the Tennent Empire, the fact that Emlyn had created his Dickens readings at Hammersmith was produced as one of the proudest feathers in the firm's cap – nobody could complain that the offerings consisted wholly of foreign imports and outmoded revivals.

The year closed with our first presentation of a play by Tennessee Williams, *Summer and Smoke*. Peter Glenville was to direct and we had been given an outline of the plot before the script arrived. It was handed in by Tennessee's current boy friend and everyone was amazed. The play bore no resemblance to the one we had been led to expect and was a rambling exercise that read like the first draft of a bad translation. Fortunately this odd concoction turned out to be another play altogether, *The Nightingale of the Delta*, and in due course the right script arrived and starring Margaret Johnston and William Sylvester transferred to the Duke of York's. Tennessee asked us to book him a room at a hotel with a swimming pool as he did all his thinking under water. We compromised by getting him temporary membership of the RAC Club – if his fellow swimmers had known what was being churned up in the depths below they would probably have leapt from the water in alarm for fear of contact with this intellectual Jaws.

At the beginning of February I spent a joyous week in Paris where Jan van Loewen introduced me to several French authors, among them Henri de Montherlant, who astonished me by offering neither coffee nor a drink when we called at his flat. His plays were enjoying the same kind of success with the French intellectuals as T. S. Eliot was to experience in

London. *Le Maître de Santiago* was the one I liked best and it was eventually done in London in a translation by Jonathan Griffin. We also took in the only play Simenon ever wrote, *La Neige était sale* and the newest Anouilh offering, *La Répétition* (*The Rehearsal*), with which I promptly fell in love. Making the translation was a joy though the play didn't appear in London for another ten years.

The Paris production, starring Jean-Louis Barrault, Madeleine Renaud and Jean Servais, a dynamic and powerful character actor who created Sartre's *Kean* as well as his *Le Diable et le bon Dieu*, had the most lovely settings and costumes by Denis Malclès, the artist who had succeeded to the Béraud mantle. The play opens with one of Anouilh's stunning stage tricks – the characters are in 18th-century costume, the set appropriate for a Marivaux comedy when suddenly the Countess lights up a cigarette and we discover that they are rehearsing an amateur production. As the action progresses the initial elegance and posturing gradually give way to naked passion and the real nature of the characters is revealed – Malclès underlined this by stripping off the period frills and ruffles from the ladies' dresses until they were left with what could pass as modern ballgowns. The two main roles were declared to be playable only by Gielgud and Olivier and the play languished for years under option while endeavours were made to bring those two stars together. Finally the contract ran out and John Hale embarked on a passionate crusade to get the rights for Bristol. By this time George Devine was firmly installed at the Royal Court Theatre and sent for me.

"You know there's another version being offered," he said, "I don't like it at all, but yours isn't quite right either. Why don't you get one of your Curtis Brown authors to help you rewrite the Marivaux scenes?"

I immediately thought of Pamela Hansford Johnson, who had recently published an excellent study on Proust, and was exactly the right person to approach. She agreed at once and we set to work on a very happy collaboration. She and her husband, C. P. Snow, were living in Cromwell Road at the time, with a huge double desk built along one wall of their study where they worked side by side at a matched pair of typewriters. Occasionally Charles would look in on our

189

conferences and suggest a word or phrase and the result pleased everyone. John took the two scripts to Binkie, made him sit down and listen while John read comparative passages out loud to convince him that our version was infinitely superior and in the event this was the one that was used.

We opened in Bristol to rave reviews and who could wonder, with a cast headed by Robert Hardy and Alan Badel, with Maggie Smith as superlative in her role as Mai had been all those years ago as Eurydice. The play transferred to London and had an unusual career, opening at the Globe and then in turn moving to the Queen's, the Apollo, and back to the Globe. Every time we moved, of course, additional advertising had to announce the fact and each time the business improved, so we chalked up just under a year's run. The American rights were bought by David Merrick, and Keith Michell replaced Bob Hardy, with Coral Brown as the Countess and a very lovely Jennifer Hilary as the girl. Peter Coe directed, with costumes by Tony Walton (Julie Andrews' husband) and we had a successful opening at the Royale a year later. But disaster, as always, seemed to follow my translations. At the end of a three months' run that looked set fair to continue, President Kennedy was shot, and the theatres closed for national mourning. When they reopened, the business didn't warrant a transfer and the play closed soon afterwards. I flew to New York for the opening and had one other night free before returning to Manchester where I was working in television.

"You must see *How To Succeed In Business Without Really Trying*," said Lucille Lortel, my hostess at the after theatre supper party at Sardi's.

"You'll never get tickets," said another guest, but Lucille chimed in, "The only man who can get them for you is sitting beside you at the next table."

He was the box office manager for the show, and sure enough he produced two back row gallery seats for me at $4.50 each. I arranged to meet my boy friend (I had one of my own this time, not one borrowed from a friend) and he met me outside the theatre.

"Do you realise you could sell these tickets for a hundred apiece?" he asked me.

"I know," I said. "Let's just sit in them and feel rich."

It turned out that the performance had been sold to one of the garment manufacturing consortiums and the audience sat like dummies throughout what we thought was the best show we had seen for years. Most of the time we were the only couple laughing.

1952 was a vintage year for the Lyric in every sense. The usual Britten Christmas opera season was followed by *The Same Sky*, Yvonne Mitchell's first play, which marked her out as an extremely interesting and promising author – exactly the kind of talent for which the Company of Four had been called into being – and it joined the growing list of transfers with a happy run at the Duke of York's. Frances Hyland, a charming Canadian who went on to great things in her native land played the lead with Thora Hird as her mother. Dirk Bogarde came back to us after that in a revival of *The Vortex* – Michael Gough took over when the play transferred to the Criterion – Dirk not liking long runs and growing more and more apprehensive about working in the theatre. But in terms of acting, the triumph probably came in *Montserrat*, adapted by Lilian Hellman from a French original by Emanuel Roblès, directed by Noel Willman and Nigel Green. The cast list was enough to make theatre buffs drool – Richard Burton, Noel Willman, Joy Parker, Elspeth March, Philip Guard, Esmond Knight – the set was superb and the direction impeccable – the only trouble was the play itself. It deals with a classic situation – the band of random hostages taken off the street and shot one by one in an endeavour to make the hero, Montserrat, reveal the whereabouts of Bolivar. Once the first hostage was shot, it was obvious that all the others would have to die too, and although the details were fascinating all sense of drama and tension was lost. I always maintained that if the other characters had known all along what was behind Montserrat's silence – that he was playing for time to enable Bolivar to escape – we could have seen them reacting, preferring to die rather than betray their leader, or to quote from Sartre's *Men Without Shadows*, they could resist because they had something to hide. Not surprisingly there was no transfer, but the acting remains as a vivid memory when details of other more successful productions have faded.

The early translations from Sartre and Anouilh were treated by the critics as so many original works with only the rarest acknowledgment of the language change. References were made to Sartre's "fluid, symbolic dialogue," "his prose cleaned to the knuckle", "the writing touches the highest level", with only an "immaculately translated" from the Daily Mail to put in my scrapbook. The translation of *Point of Departure* rated a couple of "excellent's" and "lively's" but on the whole the press continued to assess the plays as if the French authors possessed the polyglot talents of the Twelve Apostles and spoke of their "theatrical craft" and "sparkling wit".

The Society of Authors recognised that something ought to be done and formed a Translators Association to try and win recognition for practitioners of the art as creators of a new copyright, sending endless letters to editors and critics to point out that honour should be accorded where honour was due and that a work in translation should always be mentioned as such in reviews, with the appropriate credit.

By the time *The Rehearsal* was produced, the constant hammering at critics and editors had gradually begun to have some effect and almost unanimously the notices referred to the contribution of the English writers. Led by Kenneth Tynan, Philip Hope-Wallace and T. C. Worsley, they reported our work as "excellent", "fresh, lively, idiomatic", "splendid" and "a striking production and an even more striking translation". *The Queen* waxed even more lyrical and declared "the translation is . . . sharp and steely: the glinting exactness of the language seems miraculously Gallic". It was all immensely gratifying, but though the plays in question have continued to earn royalties for their authors all over the world, neither Pamela nor I was ever asked to translate another Anouilh play.

Peter Ashmore staged another Victorian revival – *Trelawny of The Wells* – to launch Barbara Jefford, featuring Lionel Jeffries in another character part. The romantic lead was played by Leslie Howard's son, Ronald, and we also persuaded Shaun Glenville to come and play the old waiter as a music hall turn which was immensely entertaining. At a party to celebrate the play's opening, Peter Glenville invited me to

his parents' flat where our blonde hostess was matched by another equally glamorous figure, Mae West. According to Peter, the first time she had worn the two enormous diamond clips clasping her décolleté that were knocking our eyes out a friend had remarked in shocked tones, "Mae dear, you have now gone *too far*. They're *much* too big!"

"I don't think so, dearie," drawled the famous voice. "They're no bigger than a man's hand."

The next excitement was the arrival of Charles Morgan with the script of his new play, *The River Line*, which Michael MacOwan was to direct. Charles had been the theatre critic of the Times for many years, and had written his first play, *The Flashing Stream* for Godfrey Tearle and Margaret Rawlings. This was one of those inventor/scientist prophetic stories of some magic weapon – a sort of heat-seeking missile – that was being created at a research station in the days before computers. One of the scientists was a woman – Margaret Rawlings – and being married to a playwright himself, Charles knew all about women's lib. *The River Line* was the story of one of the escape routes for Allied prisoners of war, and strictly speaking Charles was breaking the Official Secrets Act by writing about it – though as the war had been over for more than five years it didn't seem too harmful a breach of confidence. Charles was the first Englishman to be elected to the French Academy – the Immortals – the body that honours men (and now women) for literary achievement and he made his speech of acceptance in French, beginning with an elaborately constructed sentence that contained that bugbear of all students, the past imperfect of the subjunctive. There was a hoot of laughter, and when Charles showed his bewilderment, his host explained gracefully that a new Academy should be founded for the preservation of the *imparfait du subjonctive*.

"I shall be the first président," he declared, "and you, my dear Charles, will be the only member."

Charles' beautiful English prose was safely entrusted to Pamela Brown, Paul Scofield, Michael Goodliffe and John Westbrook – a lifelong friend of both the Morgans – and we had the distinction of appearing at the Edinburgh Festival after an opening week in Leeds. By this time I had acquired my first

car, a 1936 Ford 8 that I called Charlie, and I drove up and down to Yorkshire in great style. Charlie had cost £100 new, but by the time I acquired him, second-hand car prices had sky-rocketed and he cost me £150, found out of the biggest fee I have ever collected – $500 for writing a ten-minute two-handed TV sketch for the Kate Smith Hour in New York. This lady was a popular comedienne and had a drama spot on each of her programmes in which special guests would appear. Bill Berney had been asked to provide a sketch for Rex Harrison and Lilli Palmer while I was in New York for *Legend of Lovers*. "I can't write English dialogue," said Bill. "You do it." So I cribbed shamelessly from a Noël Coward one-acter, and turned in a piece about a burglar and a diamond necklace. For some reason Rex and Lilli didn't appear in it, but I was paid anyway, and it was eventually performed by Richard Greene and a lady whose name I have forgotten, but as everyone said I would, I have never forgotten my first car, and was quite glad when Charlie was eventually written off in a head-on collision coming home from Stratford-upon-Avon on a wet Sunday. I could never have borne to sell him to somebody else.

Chapter XX

In the meantime the most exciting season was being planned for the end of the year. John Gielgud's career had been having some curious ups and downs, and at various times when he had been out of work, I had pleaded with Binkie to let him do a play at Hammersmith. But Binkie had been adamant. To appear at the Lyric would have implied that John was slipping and it was better to wait until we were more successful. Now that we were firmly established as the theatre where exciting and top quality productions were always to be seen, the situation was different. John would direct Paul Scofield in *Richard II* (an odd choice for Coronation year surely) then direct and appear in *The Way of the World*, followed by *Venice Preserv'd* (at last) directed by Peter Brook.

It was during the run of *The River Line* that I plucked up courage to ask John Perry for an increase in salary. By this time we had produced fifty-six plays at Hammersmith of which nineteen had transferred and I was still getting £15 a week. The argument in the past had always been that we were losing so much money that I couldn't expect a rise, but with the record of the previous year and the future plans, it seemed only fair that I should get the same amount (£20) as the other heads of department at the Globe. (I didn't know at the time that Binkie never paid himself more than £30.)

When John demurred and seemed unwilling to provide the increase I was goaded into asking a fatal question. What future did I have with the firm? After all, I had been with them for sixteen years and could expect to go on working for at least another twenty or thirty.

"If you mean, will you ever be the Administrator at Hammersmith, I can tell you now that you won't be," was his reply, and in the face of my stunned reaction he added, "I'll talk to Mr Beaumont about your salary. Next morning he told me the firm was prepared to pay me £18. "But," he added, "if

you get the offer of a better job we won't stand in your way."

So it seemed a quite extraordinary coincidence when the phone rang a few weeks later and Jan van Loewen's voice enquired if anybody else could hear us? I assured him that we had no switchboard and he asked, "How would you like to run the drama department of Curtis Brown?" Jan had several times suggested I might like to work for him, but I had never contemplated leaving the firm. Now . . . I told him I might, and he set up a lunch for me with Spencer Curtis Brown.

It would be impossible to imagine anyone who provided more of a contrast to Binkie and his circle than Spencer. Large, sandy haired, and wearing what always seemed to be very tweedy clothes, he had big feet, even bigger shoes, and as I discovered later, was an ardent womaniser. He was also immensely clever. "I used to run the drama department myself," he said. "At one time we had eleven shows on in the West End. If you play your cards correctly, you could control the London theatre. We'll pay you £1000 a year (it sounded much more than £20 a week), against one-third of the turnover of the department and it will be up to you to see how high that figure is." I said I must discuss the offer with Binkie – after all, he would be my most important client – and Spencer readily agreed, giving me a deadline for about a month ahead, as he was due to go to New York and needed a decision before leaving.

I asked Binkie's secretary to arrange a meeting for me but the days went by and I was always told he was too busy. I had to keep stalling Spencer whenever he telephoned. Finally Binkie and John Perry went abroad and I had to make up my mind without getting any advice.

We had an exciting new production at Hammersmith, *The Square Ring*, a play about boxing by the Australian author Ralph Petersen. Warren Jenkins was to direct, and he and I were left to cast it, arrange for the try-out in Brighton and the opening at Hammersmith. The action took place in a seedy dressing-room of a stadium where the various boxing weights were represented, ranging from fly weight (Bill Owen) to heavy (Bill Travers) with Duncan Lamont carrying the main story line as a boxer who had promised his wife not to fight again. Peter Bayliss looked in and out as the stadium manager,

Rex Garner was the cheerful ringside attendant, Ronald Lewis the perfect golden boy type juvenile and George Rose appeared as a punch-drunk old heavy. Bill Travers spent his whole time reading a Mills and Boon type novel and had one memorable line. Looking up from his book he quoted, " 'and there beneath the oasis he kissed her!' Well, what I want to know is where's her oasis?"

Binkie and John Perry appeared in time for the dress rehearsal in Brighton and had no criticism to make except that Bill Travers' hair style was too smart, so he combed it straight forward over his eyes and looked as gormless as he probably felt. Seeing my thunderous expression Binkie said quickly, "I think Kitty wants to speak to me. We'd better meet at the hotel after dinner." Everyone had been sworn to secrecy so I was amazed when Binkie began our interview with "I think I know why you want to talk to me."

"In that case," I said, "you'd better tell me."

"No, no," he said. "You go ahead."

So I told him of Spencer's offer and that I had decided to accept. True to his poker-playing reputation, Binkie never batted an eyelid.

"You'll be quite excellent in the job," he said, and I could have hit him. The rest of the conversation was about ways and means – John Wright's Marionettes were coming to the Lyric during November, and the Ballet Rambert were booked in afterwards, giving everyone plenty of time to prepare for the Gielgud season.

"I'd like to see the opening of *Richard II*", I said "and leave at the end of the year."

And then I asked the vital question. Was that what he had been expecting to hear? Binkie had the grace to laugh.

"I thought you were going to. ask me for some money for your children's theatre," he said, and for once acknowledged he had been really wrong.

Preparing for the Gielgud season was the high point of those eight years of hard work. The *Richard II* sets and costumes were by Loudon Sainthill, an adorable Australian with a stutter who produced designs based on mediaeval manuscripts, with a gold cycloroma and brilliant clear colours. Paul was to be supported by Herbert Lomas, Eric Porter and Paul

Daneman, with Joy playing his queen and John Whiting as the herald who calls the combatants into the lists.

One morning the phone rang and Loudon's voice said, "K-K-Kitty – I was supposed to c-c-come and s-s-see you this morning but last n-n-night I went to s-s-see *The Tales of Hoffman* and this morning I've – got a black eye."

Even now I think the violence of the colours in that Pressburger and Powell film might have the same effect on a sensitive retina. Inspired by the gold cyclorama I designed a poster for the play showing Richard's white hart badge on a gold background with Paul's name above the title supported by the author, director and designer in black letter press. As no block could be made to print an area as large as a double crown or folio bill the printers declared it couldn't be done, but I had just seen the new Sanderson's wallpaper catalogue in which they featured gold and silver paper, so we bought rolls of the former, cut it to size and silk-screened a tracing of the white hart from the back of the Wilton diptych on this opulent background. The poster stood out like a beacon in the library windows and I still maintain it is the best advertisement for the play that has ever been created.

In the event the production was disappointing – John Gielgud admitted that he had tried to make everybody copy what he had done himself and he chivvied poor Paul Daneman into stitches by trying to make him age twenty years when he was still very inexperienced. The real triumph of the season was reserved for *Venice Preserv'd* with Leslie Hurry's magnificent designs and Peter Brook's imaginative direction.

The day of my departure drew ever nearer and the freezing sensation in my toes barely melted when John Perry remarked that they hadn't been able to think of my successor yet – it was a heart-warming compliment even if not exactly intended as such. Eventually they offered the job to Diana Plunkett who had been the house manager at the Lyric since the departure of Lovat Fraser. She at least could be relied on to carry out the job with the minimum of fuss. On the verge of being happily married to Charles Zwar, she would have no ambitions to force the bosses into activities they would rather not undertake.

Binkie's parting gift was a bright orange woollen shawl

from Balmain's which Ginette Spanier had allowed him to buy at a cut price. After sixteen years of devoted service it didn't really seem to be enough, but in fairness I have to say that, once Ginette had allowed me to exchange it for a black one, it proved a very elegant and serviceable additon to my wardrobe and after thirty years is still going strong.

The first day in a new office is very similar to the first day at a new school – pleasant or unpleasant as the case may be. The first day at 6, Henrietta Street was very much like the move from the Globe to the Apollo and every bit as dirty and traumatic.

Spencer maintained that while Americans believed plushy set-ups impressed their clients, they were far more impressed by English offices if they were dark and musty, which they described as being full of atmosphere and Dickensian charm. My new office was the ultimate in this form of thinking especially as it had been left unoccupied for about six months. Up two flights of linoleum-covered brass-edged stairs, it had been partitioned off a much larger room and was more like a narrow corridor. Taking up a good third of the space was a huge chair in front of a roll-top desk of the same vintage as the one I had left behind at the Apollo. It had belonged to the founding father, Mr Curtis Brown himself, and the drawers were stuffed with his old diaries, a pair of his spectacles, my predecessor's dirty handkerchiefs and soiled shirts, while the floor was covered with carpet so worn that the original stitching had long since disintegrated and the strips lay like mournful banana skins on the unstained wooden boards. The room was lined with shelves, inches deep in dust, supporting a pile of even dustier scripts that had obviously never been opened since the day they arrived, and the uncurtained windows looking on the foggy street made the place seem even colder than it really was on a cold January day.

My predecessor, Lionel Hale, had had to resign as the result of a nervous breakdown and looking at my bleak surroundings I wondered how long it would take me to go the same way. There was a welcoming telegram from Jan van Loewen (sweet of him) but apart from that there seemed nothing to offer any kind of assurance that I had made the right decision. I

sat in front of that enormous desk and began to drown under a wave of hopelessness. This was obviously not the right mood in which to tackle a new job. Before I could control the West End theatre I had to control myself, so I retired to the loo (no hot water) and had a good cry. The classic remedy worked its usual magic and after borrowing a duster and polish from the post room I set to work to create a new image.

Spencer and the other directors looked in to offer welcoming noises and explain that the room hadn't been done up for me as they thought I would prefer to choose materials and colours for myself. On their instructions I did my shopping at the Army and Navy Stores (my carpet was so much better than anyone else's that when we moved to King Street, Graham Watson, one of the directors, had it fitted in his own room). I bought a set of Victorian custard cups from the nearest junk shop and a bottle of sherry to entertain colleagues and future clients and returned to the top floor very much improved in spirits. A childhood friend who was now a successful Curtis Brown client unexpectedly turned up and took me out to lunch and I began to feel that the new job might prove to be everything Spencer had promised on our first meeting.

To begin with, there was the fun of getting to know my new colleagues and fellow employees.

Like Elsie Beyer, who had wanted to be a nurse, Spencer had had no intention of being an agent but had wanted to be a farmer; the initial frustration seemed to have added a strain of bitterness to both their natures. Elsie had had to give up her nursing training when her father died, and when his elder brother, the heir, was killed in World War I, Spencer had had to accept the inevitable and join the agency business. He took over when his father died and a major crisis erupted with the departure of three of the firm's leading executives, Pearn, Pollinger and Higham, who founded their own agency, taking with them some of Curtis Brown's leading authors. Undeterred, Spencer had soldiered on, reorganising matters so that no similar defection could strike the firm such a body blow again. Each aspect of the business was divided among specialist departments, so that if an author wrote plays, and novels, and film scripts, his interests would be looked after by three different people – which also insured the author's loyalty

for, as sometimes happened, if he or she didn't like any one of the heads of department, they probably had one particular favourite among the others, which guaranteed continued business. Like Binkie, Spencer didn't believe in contracts. "An agent is only any good to an author if they like and trust each other, and even if we did establish formal relationships, there's never any point in keeping an author against his will. A contract can always be torn up." This was his philosophy and he stuck to it.

Besides Spencer, the directors included Juliet O'Hea (the prettiest name in the business, said Cyril Hogg of Samuel French admiringly), and Graham Watson, who both dealt mainly in fiction; films were handled by Hettie Hilton, foreign rights by Molly Waters, short stories and newspaper articles by Dorothy Daly and Peter Janson-Smith. Supplementing my own efforts in the drama department was a formidable gorgon called Gladys M. Day who presided over the repertory bookings and concluded contracts and dispatched scripts to far-flung outposts like Penge and Tonypandy. I was to handle the amateur rights, which meant conferences with Cyril Hogg and later Peter Richards of Evans Brothers, newcomers to the field, who provided healthy competition to the virtual monopoly which the older firm had built up.

The closest link was with the film department, since most plays might prove likely subjects for film sales, but it was also important to keep in touch with the rest of the agency for any new novel might turn out to be dramatisable, and it would be more lucrative if we could suggest the adaptation to one of our own authors, rather than wait for somebody to come and make the offer from outside.

The fiction department had at its disposal the services of several readers, among them Stevie Smith, the poetess ("not waving, but drowning"), and a lady with a Polish name, Zoë Zajdler, who was fiercely Irish in her sympathies, though Spencer said she really came from Liverpool and had only moved to Dublin as a teenager. I was never allowed to use a reader for the plays that flowed in like torrents of dirty washing – as Spencer pointed out, if anything was any good I'd have to read it myself in any case, and you could tell whether a play was readable after the first half-dozen lines. Of

course I knew a lot of this already from my Lyric experience – twelve pages submitted as a five-act tragedy, with fourteen scenes, ranging from the Hanging Gardens of Babylon to the Pyramids by moonlight – they could be looked at, tossed aside and returned within twenty-four hours with a polite note. The time-consumers were the ones that were promising, very promising, or very nearly acceptable, and here you needed time to read carefully, meet the author, decide whether he had the right equipment to alter and improve, or whether the whole thing was a flash in the pan and not worth wasting further effort on. Eventually I took every Wednesday off, and spent the day at home with piles of scripts which could be more easily assessed in the quiet of my own room. (A system which I may say I carried forward into my next job when I went to work for television.)

But to return to No. 6: as the firm had American origins, "old Mr Curtis Brown" had decreed the use of initials for identification, so everyone answered to two or three letters of the alphabet, ranging from SCB to ZZ.

ZZ was an absolutely fascinating person and we became good friends from the very outset – sharing a mutual passion for all things Polish as well as for John Gielgud who, after all, has Polish ancestry. Zoë's Polish husband was either a hero or a shit, depending on who was speaking, Zoë or Spencer, for at the beginning of the war he had taken her home to Poland, or been thrown out of France, whichever version you preferred, and when the Russian invasion came, sent her back to England to write his country's wartime history, while he stayed behind to fight. Fortunately Zoë still had her Irish passport and was able to convince the Nazi authorities that she hated Great Britain and only wanted to get home to a country which shared her opinions, but she had some horrendous experiences on the journey via Scandinavia, was badly wounded in the head, thrown into prison and saved her reason only because she had a pack of patience cards which she found in the pocket of the apron she was wearing when she escaped.

True to her promise, she learned the language in order to read the reports coming out of Poland, though no one could have imagined the terrible experiences she would have to suffer at first hand. In every casualty list she expected to read

her husband's name, and the horrors she described in the two books she published gave her recurring nightmares for the rest of her life. She and Spencer had been lovers and he was always very good to her, eventually buying her a charming house in Stratford-upon-Avon where she was able to enjoy the theatrical world she adored and even provide hospitality for John Gielgud during his seasons there.

Together we discussed theatre and literature by the hour, and it was through her that Beverley Cross joined the firm, first as a novelist and then as one of my play authors – to be known ever after as "one of our babies". One lunchtime he and I discussed the plot of a play for teenagers that could appeal on the same level as *Treasure Island*, and a week later he handed me the result, *The Singing Dolphin*. Eventually it was produced at the Hampstead Theatre Club and found its way into hardback with two other plays he wrote later.

It was all very different from the Globe and the Apollo, and if I missed some of the excitements of the regular cycle of first nights at the Lyric, there were increasing compensations. For the first time I had an expense account, or rather, permission to entertain at the firm's expense. "Take the managements to the Ivy or Boulestin's," said Spencer. "Your established authors can go to Rules or Scott's, but the newcomers and other agents can perfectly well eat at the Nag's Head," naming the pub at the corner of Floral Street opposite the stage door of the Royal Opera House. The pecking order was strictly established even in the matter of food. So my diary began to fill up with luncheon dates (it never seemed to be dinner) and I learned to drink sherry and white wine in the middle of the day without falling asleep in the office afterwards, and began to meet and enjoy the company of a great many managements other than HMT.

Of course, said the wiseacres scornfully, how can you possibly be an agent? You'll send all your plays to Binkie and if he turns them down you'll have to explain to the others that he has already rejected them. So I made my authors a vow. I will never send a play to Binkie, I said, unless you specifically ask me to, and the records speak for themselves. Although HMT features on a couple of contracts, the names of Henry Sherek, Donald Albery, Peter Saunders and Allan Davis, by now a

West End manager, appear far more often and with the first two at least I benefited enormously both in friendship and in business success.

Henry was probably the most amusing of the London impresarios at the time and I doubt if he has found a successor now. Vastly overweight, he was an outsize personality as well as a human colossus. He had been involved in the staging of the cabaret at the Dorchester for many years, served in the war with distinction (he said he had taken part in a cavalry charge at the end of World War I, which I doubt), and had a huge appetite for life as well as for food. Dining with Henry was like watching a Magimix at work, and whenever we went to Paris to see some new play, the opening of his suitcase on the Customs benches would display the odd clean shirt but always a couple of apples or pears. He was a compulsive eater, and equalled in gastronomic feats by his American colleague, Gilbert Miller. The two enormous men could be seen at the Ivy or Écu de France, eating their way steadily through double helpings of everything that was most fattening, and then when the coffee was served, each would reach into a waistcoat pocket and produce a box of Saxin.

Henry adored telling funny stores, which he did extremely well, and also enjoyed taking the mickey out of Gilbert, whose American wife Kitty was also part of the legend.

"Gilbert asked me the other day, 'D'you know what the Prince of Wales calls Kitty?' "

"No."

"Kitty."

On one occasion when the Millers had been departing for New York and had spent the night in their Sussex home, a careless workman having left a ladder lying around, a cat burglar reared it up against Kitty's window and departed with all her jewellery, valued at £75,000. When Henry rang up to commiserate Gilbert replied, "Aw gee, it's the kinda thing that could happen to anyone." Gilbert had presented *Gigi* in New York, and Henry was the sponsor of T. S. Eliot and presented *The Cocktail Party* and *The Confidential Clerk* in Edinburgh and London as well as *Edward, My Son* and other plays by Robert Morley. Henry and his wife Pamela also introduced me to my own eventual heart-throb, but that was a

later exercise.

Donald Albery is about my own age and somehow this made it easy to deal with him, as well as extremely stimulating. The son of Bronson Albery (who had produced John Gielgud's early successes), he was just now setting up in management with his wife Heather Margaret, the Donmar title being an amalgam of their two names, and it was through him that I had my first major break in the agency business at the end of my first year – which always made him very special as far as I was concerned.

I had seen John van Druten's *I Am A Camera* when I was in New York for *Legend of Lovers*, so when the play arrived on my desk with a letter from John's New York agent, Monica McCall, who had been my predecessor some years previously at CB's, saying Donald wanted to buy the rights, it was easy to share his enthusiasm. Dorothy Tutin was appearing in Graham Greene's *The Living Room* in which she had made an enormous success, and was reluctant to switch to such a radically different part as Sally Bowles. At Donald's request I went to see her and described the impact Julie Harris had made and eventually she agreed to do the play with predictable results.

For the first time I had the handling of a package deal which included author, adaptor, designer and director, and when the film rights were bought by an English company, the triumph was complete. Through Spencer's percentage deal I doubled my annual salary out of one-third of the turnover of the department and never dropped below that figure for the rest of my time with the firm.

Chapter XXI

Oddly enough, my first day as an agent coincided with the opening of the HMT presentation of a play by one of our authors, R. C. Sherriff's *The White Carnation*, starring Ralph Richardson. It opened at Brighton and I travelled down to see it, staying at the Royal Crescent Hotel where "everyone" always booked. The managers, Mr and Mrs Taunt, were very theatre minded and didn't care how late supper parties continued or how long discussions went on in the lounge afterwards, so there was always a pleasant and welcoming atmosphere.

The Sherriff play had one of the most stunning introductions imaginable. While the host is saying goodnight to his guests out in the street, the front door of his house suddenly slams and he can't get any reply to his knocking and finally goes round to climb through a window. The set revolves and we see him entering an empty and unfurnished room. Is he a ghost or is the whole thing a dream? Unfortunately the rest of the play didn't measure up to this block-busting five minutes and it was obvious that a great deal of work would have to be done to make it a success. As everything had been settled before my arrival, I wasn't included in any of the discussions and sat miserably in my bedroom knowing that if I had been doing my job correctly I should have been offering constructive criticism and helpful directives. As the play was a flop when it opened it was just as well I didn't get involved and could proceed to form a friendship with Bob Sherriff uncluttered by failure.

Bob never succeeded in writing a success to match his first play, *Journey's End*, but he was unfailingly kind and gentle and developed a passion for archaeology which his friend Mortimer ("Monty") Wheeler satisfied by letting him excavate a "desirable residence" among the Romans-in-Britain finds that Monty himself was researching. The result

was a play antedating Howard Brenton by several decades, but like Rudyard Kipling's centurion, Bob's Romans were happy in their new home, where their families had been settled for generations and were now being forced to flee in the face of the barbarian invasion, leaving behind a young son to join with the Cornish hero, Arthur, in trying to stem the tide of darkness. The woman was a Christian and her husband agreed to convert to her faith as together they went out to face the Long Sunset, which eventually became the title of the play. I am sure Mary Whitehouse would have approved.

It seems incredible that even in 1953 *The Archers* should have been such a popular programme that plans were made to turn it into a stage presentation, as now happens with popular TV series. The adaptation was made by Ted (Lord) Willis in collaboration with the original authors and I became the agent for the deal. (Later Ted performed the same operation on both *Doctor in the House* and *Doctor at Sea*.) After meeting Edward Mason and Geoffrey Webb in Birmingham, I concluded a contract with a newcomer to the managerial scene, Ralph Birch.

This gentleman had arrived unheralded in London, opened an office near Cambridge Circus and inside nothing flat was expanding into the most active of entrepreneurs. Nobody knew very much about his background – there was a coach firm in the North of England of the same name, but he may not have been any relation. Rumour had it that his grandmother supplied him with the ready and whenever he was short, he would be off to her tea table and return triumphantly with a large suitcase stuffed with used five pound notes. Be that as it may, he presented the stage version of the radio show, and almost immediately we ran into trouble. Mr Birch's administrative ability left a very great deal to be desired, and when on top of his other sins of omission he started being careless in the matter of royalty payments, stern warnings were issued pointing out that he was in breach of contract. The money would usually arrive anything up to four or five days late. Eventually "the boys", as the Archer authors were always called, decided they had had enough, and in any event they had now been approached by Jack Hylton, the band-leader turned impresario, who wanted to put the show

on for a summer season in Blackpool. Next time Mr Birch failed to come up with the spondulicks, a carefully worded letter went out from Henrietta Street, terminating his contract. Simultaneously another document arrived at the Hylton office transferring the rights to him and from then on the authors' cheques arrived on time. However, Mr Birch was not a man to lie down under such treatment and promptly sued Curtis Brown for restitution of his marital rights, so to speak, a case which went against him, whereupon he took the matter to the Court of Appeal where I eventually made an appearance.

While all this was going on, I had had to retire to a private room in University College Hospital for some running repairs and was tickled pink to find the room had previously been occupied by Duncan Sandys and a direct line was still installed to 10, Downing Street. I had no occasion to use it, alas, but kept my own phone busy while my secretary appeared every morning with armfuls of scripts and letters, for although painful, my surgery didn't interfere with my capacity for business. My doctor John, afterwards Lord Hunt, arrived late one night to find me surrounded by floral tributes which I had refused to have carried out into the centrally heated corridor.

"I see you don't subscribe to the theory that it's dangerous to keep flowers in your room at night," he marked. "We carried out some tests once and discovered that you'd need two hundred hydrangeas to equal the carbon dioxide output of one night nurse."

However, my medical experiences provided the defending counsel, Mr Cyril Ray, with an excellent opportunity of adding at intervals "Miss Black said . . . Miss Black was in hospital," while he laboured to prove that we had acted incorrectly in terminating Mr Birch's lease of the property. (It's odd that plays can be referred to in the jargon of building societies.) I was amazed when after all the sarcastic implications that ill-health had robbed me of any balanced judgment the learned gentleman approached me in the corridor to enquire solicitously whether I had made a complete recovery. The poor man was barricaded behind an enormous pile of legal tomes as he tried to prove his point until – oh frabjous day – the Master of the Rolls looked over the top of his glasses and

remarked: "Mr Ray, if what you maintain is correct it is to make the law an ass," at which point the whole case collapsed and not surprisingly the matter was settled out of court, though I don't think Mr Birch ever paid any of his legal costs.

I was very disappointed at not being called on to give evidence, but got my wish years later when I became the chief witness in a murder trial – which all goes to show how dangerous wishes can be – the gods may hear you and the result may not be in the least what you want.

With *The Archers* safely under control another international figure was introduced into the office. For some time I had been friends with an ebullient young Australian, Thérèse Denny, who was working for William Collins the publishers, but also doing interviews on her own account for Australian radio. She now introduced me to a best-selling author, Pierre La Mure, whose book and subsequent film, *Moulin Rouge*, was the top earning item on the international market. Pierre was a frustrated playwright, and had dramatised the book, wanting more than anything to see it on the stage. As nobody was going to mount an expensive period piece after the film rights had been sold, the likelihood of this being seen in London was fairly remote, but he had a wide circle of acquaintance, and came up with a lady who ran a company in Italy and saw herself in the role of the glamorous prostitute. Pierre agreed to let her stage the play in the open air during the Venice Biennale, and asked if I could go out with him to assess the possibilities. At this time Curtis Brown were very anxious to acquire Pierre as a client, and I was given permission to go, with instructions to bring him back to London at all costs.

"If I do, will you install hot water in the wash-rooms?" I asked, and the bosses agreed.

Nothing could have been in greater contrast with my first visit to that ravishing city when Dorothy, Vivienne and I had stayed at the cheapest possible *pensione* in a back street – now Pierre and I were booked in at the Daniele, overlooking the Grand Canal, and lunched and dined in all the best restaurants. When the first night came, the rain was falling in torrents and at the last moment the production was shifted to the Fenice – that exquisite eighteenth-century red and gold jewel – and sprays of the new Moulin Rouge rose were flown in from

Holland and passed over to every lady in the audience. Pierre arrived at the theatre in a gondola with Linda Darnell, the Hollywood film star, trailing yards of white pebble crepe and dozens of white foxes. It was a shame that after all the glamour the play was a total disaster, and Pierre and Linda disappeared to her hotel afterwards to offer mutual consolations.

Next morning he rang my room.

"There's no point in staying here, is there?" he said. "Why don't we go to Paris?"

What could be nicer? We took the train, had a day and a night in my favourite city, where we saw Robert Dhéry in *La Plume de Ma Tante*, and Pierre told me he had written a song which he very much wanted to have published.

"Then you must come to London," I urged, "and we'll take it along to Teddy Holmes of Chappell's."

Which is how a song by Pierre La Mure figures on the list of Curtis Brown properties for 1953, and the CB lavatories were provided with hot water. Alec McCowen eventually appeared in a production of *Moulin Rouge* at Bromley but it did nothing to advance his career and it was many years before *Hadrian VII* established him as one of our most interesting actors.

In spite of the agency activities, I managed to continue translating, just as I had done while working full-time at the Lyric. Norman Marshall, whose book *The Other Theatre*, gives a detailed description of the smaller London theatres of this period, was now in charge of the New Watergate, a small theatre club in Villiers Street, where he produced my version of *The Snow Was Black*, Simenon's only play. The cast was headed by John Le Mesurier with Roland Curram as the young murderer and Carol Coombe as his distracted mother. Even the presence of a future leading member of *Dad's Army* and Lord Snowdon's step-mother couldn't make the play a success, but I am indebted to Norman for one piece of theatrical advice. "On a stage as small as this, or the Arts, production doesn't matter. Just see that the actors don't mask each other and let them get on with the lines . . ."

As 1953 was Coronation Year, we finally prevailed on my mother to install a television set in the flat so we could watch the ceremony and subsequent procession. In the event she became just as much of a TV buff as anyone and the BBC's

superb presentation must have chalked up a good many similar converts to the new medium. With our balcony overlooking Kensington Gardens we had a splendid view of the contingents of troops that were quartered all over London as they marched to join the procession or line the streets. Everyone must have their favourite memory – the Polynesians with white jagged skirts and bare feet in sandals, sailors returning with the rain streaming down their faces, streaked with the pipe clay off their hats. My favourite was the flash of the Star of Africa in the centre of the Imperial crown as the returning procession after the luncheon break caught the full glare of the TV spotlights. Once the coach left the Abbey I sprinted across Hyde Park to a position outside the Dorchester in time to see the state coach and the open carriages following with Queen Salote of Tonga grinning delightedly at the crowd and never trying to wipe away the rain which by now was sluicing over her. Legend has it that when asked who the tiny man was sitting opposite her, Noël Coward replied "her lunch", but next to our own beloved monarch there's no question that that massive lady was the prime favourite of the crowd.

The new set came in handy later in the year for my first TV translation/adaptation, *The Public Prosecutor*, a French Revolution affair by the Swiss writer Fritz Hochwaelder, starring Jack Hawkins and Googie Withers (on the front cover of the *TV Times*) with Bill Sylvester as the handsome Tallien. This was one of Sidney Newman's Armchair Theatre presentations and a few weeks before his death the director, Denis Vance, telephoned to say that even after thirty years it was still his favourite production and he would very much like to revive it.

Together with the change of job that year also marked a change in holiday plans. John Boteler, an ex-Fleet Air Arm pilot who had served with my brother Alan, was acting as Public Relations Officer for the chairman of Short Brothers and Harland, Admiral Sir Matthew Slattery. John asked if I would like to go to Paris for them as interpreter during the Salon Aeronautique at Le Bourget, so piling into Charlie, my sturdy little Ford 8, I duly reported at the air show and helped to assemble the stand, distribute literature and entertain any clients who might be interested in buying Seamews, the

amphibious plane Short Bros. were marketing that year. I was also required to stall the fire authorities, as it was suspected that our stand, which had been built in Ireland, wouldn't measure up to French regulations. The *pompiers* arrived and enquired if our hardboard had been fire-proofed.

"Bien sur," I replied. The leading officer produced a box of matches and proceeded to test a sample which immediately burst into flame. To the horror of my fellow employees, who should heave into view at this moment but the Admiral. Everyone expected an explosion as their incompetence was so blatantly exposed, but all he said was "Why doesn't she set fire to his beard?" Fortunately the French also saw the joke and agreed that if we doused the hardboard liberally with fire-proofing solution (fortunately I had tucked the formula into my reticule), they would be prepared to pass the construction.

Even though we were on our feet from nine to nine and pretty well exhausted at the end of the day I managed to take in my usual quota of plays: Obey's *Une fille pour du vent*, *Sud* by Julien Green, *L'Heure éblouissante* with the incomparable Suzanne Flon and *Une fille pour du vent* by André Obey which enabled me to contribute an article on the French theatre to the first edition of *Plays and Players* and later to arrange for John Whiting to translate the Obey play which we called *Sacrifice to the Wind*.

I had drinks with Julien Green one evening and talked to that fascinating Franco-American in the summer dusk in a flat overlooking the Russian Embassy. My attention kept wandering, against my will, for the most ravishing sounds from an unaccompanied violin came floating through the window and next morning I read that David Oistrakh had been giving his first recital outside the USSR. Julien had another anecdote about that Russian garden: apparently he had been intrigued at seeing the ambassador walking up and down, deep in conversation with an anonymous figure, stopping occasionally to make stabbing gestures at the ground and emphasize some important point. The explanation didn't come until the spring when instead of the expected dragon's teeth all the marked sites blossomed into a riot of tulips.

How does a literary agent acquire clients? Obviously the old-boy network is invaluable, especially the Oxbridge con-

nection, but my main fishing ground proved to be actor chums turned writer, with the top earner among them already in the Curtis Brown stable. Harry Tennent always referred to him as "the third son of the Earl of Home" which was of course true, but it amused Harry that he should be employed as a mere juvenile by his social inferiors. William Douglas Home appeared in several Tennent productions, invariably getting engaged to his fellow juvenile and flitting off to the next one at the end of the run until he found his ideal partner in Rachel Brand. He was never able to persuade Binkie to put on one of his plays, not even *The Secretary Bird*, but he had already had several successes including *Now Barabbas* based on his wartime experience of being court martialled for refusing to obey an order. One of my predecessors in office had been Archibald Batty, a genial character actor of the Colonel Pickering type who was a shrewd judge of scripts and an admirable play doctor. He had helped William with numerous drafts and shaped untidy plots or tightened up construction with tremendous success. My first experience of this came when William gave me an early version of *The Reluctant Debutante*, in which he featured his own father-in-law, somewhat in the manner that Charlotte Bingham used her father in *Coronet Among the Weeds*. William's dialogue was brilliant and witty, but the plot line was giving him trouble. The girl in the play disappears for several hours with a new beau and when she eventually returns the question is did they or didn't they? William had written both endings and asked my opinion. Memories of *Flare Path*.

"You've written a family comedy, haven't you?" I demanded.

"Of course," said William, balancing his umbrella on top of his head.

"Then you've got to keep the party clean or Terry Rattigan's Aunt Edna won't like it," I replied. The maiden was allowed to keep her virginity.

Anna Massey created a debutante as pure as the driven snow and made one great leap into stardom while William coined a fortune from the stage and film rights, as well as providing wonderful parts for Wilfrid Hyde-White and the incomparable Celia Johnson.

213

Because the firm had been in existence for so long their list included most of the leading authors and playwrights of the past half-century. Of the senior citizens, Somerset Maugham was probably the most lucrative; hardly a week went by without some document having to be despatched to Cap Ferrat for his signature. This provided a very pleasant addition to the attractions of our South of France holidays, for he would invariably ask me to lunch at the Villa Mauresque and include Vivienne Byerley in the invitation.

In the summer of 1954, *Illustrated*, a popular magazine (Every Wednesday Fourpence), was doing a spread on the villa and its inhabitants and they considered it would be very suitable to show Maugham and his secretary Alan Searle entertaining a couple of women. When the article appeared they didn't use our picture, probably because we weren't celebrities, but they did send me a copy and it's fun to identify the painting behind our host's head as a "blue period" Picasso which was sold for £80,000. Other pictures in the dining-room included a male nude which was a standard "catch" – no guest could identify the artist except Kenneth Clark, who correctly ascribed it to Toulouse-Lautrec. Apparently it had been the artist's favourite painting and he had kept it in his own study as his family hated it. I wonder what became of it and where it is now?

That first visit Alan showed us all over the villa – the walls lined with the collection formed from Willie's contemporaries – including six Marie Laurencins, and another vast Picasso, which I hated. The window of the study had been bricked up so that Willie wouldn't be distracted by the view and the outside light was filtered through a glass panel which he had acquired from Gauguin's house in Tahiti. Apparently Gauguin had decorated the three panels of the front door with three portraits of his wife – the pigs had licked the paint off one, the children had broken another, and like Lord Elgin with the Parthenon marbles, Maugham had carried out a rescue operation just in time. The latest exhibit at the villa was the Graham Sutherland portrait, executed at about the same time as the Churchill picture which Lady Churchill destroyed. Maugham had had much the same reaction as Churchill and looking at it now in the Tate, it is easy to see why. His face is

bright yellow and his hands look like monkey's claws. He was very proud of his small hands and feet but Sutherland was painting a personality and not creating a photographic likeness.

The food was always absolutely delicious and a great feature was the avocado pears which grew in abundance in the garden. Local chefs continually begged cuttings from the trees which the gardener always willingly supplied for a consideration – omitting to mention that the avocado is a sexy vegetable and needs both male and female elements in order to reproduce. The Maugham household found this excruciatingly funny. There was also a succession of Pekinese who were not allowed in the dining-room during meals but joined us for coffee afterwards when Alan and Willie's cups each carried a special biscuit which the little dogs knew quite well would be supplied.

Maugham had always been one of my literary gods, and it was wonderful to be able to meet him face to face and thank him for the pleasure he had given over the years – the unmatched short stories especially and the brilliant craftsmanship of the plays. Terry Rattigan was also an ardent fan and said he owed so much of his own technique to a study of the master.

Maugham was also responsible for involving me in quite an important piece of inter-office wheeling and dealing. The world TV rights in the short stories had been leased to an American lady who had made him a lot of money, but after a while he had gone off her and was refusing to sign the renewal she was trying to acquire. By the middle fifties English TV was beginning to take off and everyone was pressing for permission to use the Maugham material which was obviously ideal for the small screen. Owing to the quota system whereby American imports were restricted (they still are) it was obvious that nobody was going to sacrifice the chance of buying cheap Westerns for the pleasure of presenting American versions of the Maugham stories – even though Willie introduced each of the programmes himself. Spencer dreamed up a splendid compromise and suggested that the American lady should restrict her world rights to the USA, which after all was the only territory she was interested in,

leaving Maugham free to deal with the rest of the world himself. The original contract had been negotiated jointly with Jan van Loewen but by this time he had fallen out of favour with SCB.

"We don't have to include him in the new deal," said Spencer, and so the new document was drawn up.

When I relayed the gist of the offer to Alan he was positive in his reactions.

"Willie will never sign," he said. "He hates . . ." (naming the American lady), "but you can always come and see him and explain." Off I went to Cap Ferrat, armed with an overnight bag. Alan met me at Nice airport, and we drove up to the villa in time for tea. I explained the situation again in detail and outlined the benefits of allowing the British public to enjoy the Maugham stories on their domestic boxes.

"The peke has just had puppies," said Willie. "Alan will take you to see them and show you the garden." So off we went. When we returned, Willie said, "There's your contract. I've signed it and now you'd better go down to your hotel but do come back for dinner."

Next morning I flew home with the precious document, an armful of carnations for Jean Curtis Brown, and a very lucrative deal for Spencer. Unfortunately it put paid to the long friendship I had enjoyed with Jan van Loewen and I left Curtis Brown before I could enjoy my percentage of the future earnings from the TV contracts.

The annual lunches at the Villa had some amusing repercussions. On one occasion Alan took Viv and me up to his room to powder our noses before lunch and seeing myself in his long mirror I removed the rope of pearls which didn't seem to go with my Horrockses cotton frock. On packing to go home I couldn't find the pearls anywhere and suddenly had a thought. On the next contract dispatched to Alan I scribbled a P.S. "Did I leave my pearls in your bedroom?" and the answer was yes, Kenneth Clark would be returning to London after a stay at the villa and I could collect them from the National Gallery. Soon afterwards I had to write and tell Willie, together with all my other clients, that I was leaving the firm to get married and in his charming letter of congratulation Willie added "I'm not

sure I oughtn't to tell your fiancé that you are the kind of girl who leaves her pearls in another man's bedroom."

Maugham came to London every summer for a short holiday and always had the same suite reserved for him at the Dorchester where he also kept some of his pictures so that he would feel at home in the hotel surroundings. It became traditional for me to join him at lunch and give him a quick guide to the best offerings in the London theatre so that he could make his choice. One year there didn't seem much to recommend but I was enthusiastic about the Oliviers' *Macbeth* at Stratford.

"I'm so glad you liked it," said Willie. "But poor Vivien got such bad notices."

"Don't you believe it," I retorted. "She's the best Lady Macbeth I've ever seen" (this was before Judi Dench). "She's the most beautiful woman in Scotland, people travel miles to spend the week-end at her castle and the only thing wrong with her is that she is so ambitious for her husband that she would willingly chop anybody into pieces if she thought it would further her husband's career." Stuttering slightly, Willie replied, "You have just given a g-g-graphic d-d-description of – my daughter."

His relationship with Lisa was variable, to say the least. He maintained he had been extremely generous to her, and yet they quarrelled violently at the end, when Willie tried to adopt Alan in order to save death duties and other financial commitments. He also told me he had left her the Villa Mauresque in his will. "Do keep it as it is," I urged, having just seen the shabby state of San Michele, made famous by Axel Munthe, but where everything was falling to pieces.

"Not on your life," said Willie. "I've told her to sell it and everything in it as soon as she can."

In point of fact most of the pictures were sold long before his death and there would have been no point in trying to preserve the shell of the house without the decorative contents. He gave his theatrical paintings to the National Theatre, including the Zoffany of David Garrick in *Venice Preserv'd* and founded a travelling scholarship for young writers which seems to have been awarded to every current writer of note, among them

Kingsley Amis, Doris Lessing, Francis King, John Wain and Michael Frayn – how splendid to be able to indulge such generosity and what a wonderful monument to leave behind.

Chapter **XXII**

In the present climate of women's lib. it's quite surprising to look back and remember just how many successful women literary agents there were at that time. Margery Vosper, Joyce Weiner, Helen Gunnis and Dorothea Fassett were leading figures on the London scene, and Paris boasted Marguerite Scialtiel, (christened Grey Daisy by Joyce Carey), who lived in a Colette-like apartment in a crumbling house overlooking the Seine, as well as Denise Tual and Ninon Tallon. Kay Brown, Leah Salisbury, Monica McCall and Audrey Wood dominated the New York scene. Quite why females are so successful is probably hard to say – perhaps women are more temperamentally suited to dealing with private problems as well as literary dilemmas, with methodical minds to register details of contracts and remember anniversaries and celebrations. An agent should be able to handle tax affairs, buy first night presents, suggest titles, offer sympathy when the work isn't going well and above all, be ready to listen. "Remember always," said Spencer, "that while you may have many clients, each author only has one agent and you must never let any of them know that you have anyone you consider more important than they are."

It's also quite useful if you can play golf, as the long hours in the open air provide ample opportunities for discussion and friendly rivalry. William Douglas Home, Bill Darlington, the dramatic critic of the Daily Telegraph and Patrick Gibbs once stood together on the first tee at Liphook realising they had one thing in common – they had all been soundly defeated by me. Good judgment must surely be indicated by an ability to send long irons and tee shots straight down the middle, while no author could possibly put his trust in an agent who was the victim of a bad putting twitch.

Following my success with Chappell's and the Pierre La Mure song, the next move was obviously in the direction of

musicals. CB's had never handled any composers, but Spencer had no objection to my attempting to expand the department in a new direction. *The Boy Friend* had opened at the Players Theatre in 1954 and 'everyone' – including Noël Coward and Princess Margaret – had flocked to see it. At that time it was prefaced by half an hour of "Late Joys" and Binkie in common with everyone else answered my enthusiastic recommendations by saying that yes, it was delightful, but only for a specialised audience. Without the introduction of the Late Joys . . . The run came to an end and still a transfer hadn't been arranged. Meeting Reginald Woolley at the theatre one night I still insisted that the production could make a fortune and Reggie challenged – very well, if you can sell it, you can be our agent.

Nobody would listen. Finally Reggie persuaded Sandy Wilson to add half an hour to the original show, put it on at the Embassy Theatre (now the Central School of Speech Drama) and the following morning every management in town was clamouring to buy it – but I had missed my chance.

My next musical was a trifle more up-market. Robert Helpmann rang to say he was going to perform Stravinsky's *Histoire du soldat* at the Edinburgh Festival with Moira Shearer and two actors from the Old Vic Company, Terence Longden and Anthony Nicholls (they were all appearing in a production of *The Dream*) and would I like to make a new translation? I told him I couldn't write lyrics but he said that was ridiculous. Not wanting to argue, I rang up Michael Flanders who, coincidentally, had just taken part in a concert performance of the published text and thought the music divine but the translation dreadful, and enlisted his help. I produced a literal version, Michael turned it into rhyme based on the Ingoldsby Legends and after thirty years the American copyright has just been extended for another thirty.

The production was by Gunther Rennaert of the Hamburg Opera House, while the musicians (among them Jack Brymer and Jimmy Blades) were directed by Hans Schmidt-Isserstedt, who had known Stravinsky and seen the original production with Georges Pitoëff as the soldier. I travelled up to Edinburgh for the dress rehearsal before the first night, or rather first morning, for the performance was to begin at ten

o'clock. Sitting with the cast over a fish tea they expressed their delight at seeing me, as I would now be able to explain what it was all about, while Bobby complained that he had to deliver a fiendishly difficult four lines against a musical background after a particularly exhausting ballet sequence when he had no breath at all. Terry Longden, who was playing the soldier, also chimed in with a complaint which I cut short by pointing out that at least he didn't have to dance.

"That's what you think," he retorted. "I've got a *pas de deux* with Moira, and then a *pas de trois* with Moira and Bobby . . ."

"You," I said, "have *pas de chance*."

In the event the production was a triumph, HMV made a recording, conducted by John Pritchard (our names on the same label as Stravinsky) and two years later, on 5 June, 1956, there was a concert performance in the Queen Elizabeth Hall at ten-thirty in the evening, conducted by Alexander Gibson, with Michael Flanders himself as the narrator and Ralph Richardson and Peter Ustinov as the soldier and the devil. Even at that late hour the hall was full and they turned away money. John Wright has made a marionette version, which was performed originally in the Purcell Room and there have been performances all over England and America. Unfortunately we don't get any royalties as the French author's heirs refuse to share any of the money with the translators.

When Wolf Mankowitz suggested making a musical out of one of his newest books, *A Kid For Two Farthings*, I took the idea to Peter Brook and Vivian (*Bless the Bride*) Ellis. Vivian too fell in love with the book and immediately saw the possibilities of a Jewish musical (this was long before *Fiddler on the Roof*) and set to work enthusiastically until one afternoon Wolf sprang a bombshell. He had sold the film rights to Carol Reed. I was appalled. After *Moulin Rouge* nobody would touch a play, let alone a musical, without the film rights, and the whole deal fell through, not without a certain flaring of nostrils.

The next attempt was more successful. One of CB's young novelists, Roger Longrigg, worked in an advertising office with Julian More among his colleagues and Julian had written a musical called *Grab Me a Gondola* with Jimmy Gilbert (now

head of light music at the BBC) based on the antics of the starlets during the Venice Film Festival (Diana Dors travelled down the Grand Canal in a gondola wearing a mink bikini). Starring Joan Heal and Denis Quilley, the musical opened at the Theatre Royal, Windsor, and then transferred to the Lyric at the end of November. There were only four chorus girls in addition to Joan and Jane Wenham, each of whom went on to fame and fortune. One of them was thinking seriously of changing her name, but eventually decided to continue to call herself Una Stubbs.

Julian had written another musical, *The Apple and Eve*, with the pianist-composer David Heneker, and when Monty Norman approached David for some cabaret material, Monty suddenly found himself roped into rewriting the musical, and embarked on his own highly successful composing career. When the musical was eventually given a performance, among the invited audience were Wolf Mankowitz and Peter Brook, with the result that when Wolf wanted to write a musical based on Cliff Richards' career, called *Expresso Bongo* and Peter wanted an English version of *Irma La Douce*, the Wolf-David-Julian-Monty team was called into action. Wolf eventually dropped out of the Irma venture, but the others continued on their creative way and the results are still giving pleasure today.

By this time, my mother having died, I had taken up residence in a Victorian house with a forty-foot drawing room. The little piano bought from *Bonnet Over The Windmill* was still doing yeoman service and once slid into position at one end of the room provided the perfect setting for those auditions to backers, stars and impresarios which is so much part of the musical scene. Monty and his wife Diana Coupland would sing all the numbers, with Julian providing a running commentary and David playing manfully throughout the sessions. The Ludwig of Bavaria syndrome was satisfied and I enjoyed those moments of early creativity almost as much as the finished products. J. B. Priestley once remarked, "It's a terrible thing to have a stage-struck agent," but unless you *are* stage-struck you have no business working in the theatre at all.

Priestley had come into the stable as a result of what I was privately beginning to call Kitty's Luck. In an article in George

Bishop's theatrical column on Monday 16 November 1953 in the *Daily Telegraph*, he announced that A. D. Peters, then as now a highly important agent, who had represented all Terence Rattigan's early plays, had decided to give up his drama department. By the time Spencer climbed the stairs to my office with a copy of the article in his hand, I had rung up every one of Peters' authors and invited them to join our firm. The job was all the easier because he had omitted to give them news of his intentions. That was how we acquired Priestley, Dennis Cannan and John Whiting, to name but a few, and the first results were a play by Dennis, *Misery Me!* directed by Alastair Sim, with George Cole in the cast, and a charming Priestley trifle, *Mr Kettle and Mrs Moon*, starring Ralph Richardson, which introduced Wendy Craig to an adoring public.

Jack Priestley had found himself at a dinner party sitting next to Helen Arnold, mother of the MP and then wife to the late Tom Arnold, who had presented most of Ivor Novello's musicals and been a successful stage performer herself. She was pining away from inactivity and Jack suggested she should go into management and present his play. We became good friends into the bargain (she too was a golfer) and I was more than sorry that her taste and judgment for things theatrical were curtailed because her husband didn't like to lose so much of her time – though who could blame him? It was a sad loss when she withdrew from the small group of women producers.

One lady who did have several successful years was Anna Deere Wiman, an American ex-dancer, who I met originally through Bill Berney and Howard Richardson. Her family fortune came from agricultural machinery (nowadays in Norfolk every farm seems to be equipped with John Deere tractors) and her father, Dwight Deere Wiman, had been a highly successful Broadway impresario. Anna's first English offering was *Mountain Fire*, which introduced a very young Julie Andrews, but when she wanted a solid London partner I was able to steer her in the direction of E. P. Clift, who provided her with all the expertise she could possibly want. It was they who eventually presented *The Reluctant Debutante* and when Michael Flanders and Donald Swann appeared at the New

Lindsay on New Year's Eve 1956/57 and were inundated with offers from managements wanting to transfer their superb double act to the West End, I threw in a word for Anna as by this time she had acquired the lease of the Fortune Theatre, and they began their highly successful partnership there.

Unfortunately Anna's weakness was alcohol, and I was shocked out of all self-control when she came to tea to meet my mother and was obviously reeling at four o'clock in the afternoon. The problem continued, sadly, with the result that her managerial career was a relatively short one, but at least she had a few really important notches on her gun for posterity to remember. She was the typical Poor Little Rich Girl, with apparently everything she could wish for – surrounded by attractive young men, a hairdresser in attendance every evening (my dream!) – and yet she never appeared to be really happy. She had a fall which injured her back and kept her in constant pain, but it wasn't only that that kept her drinking. Some people have a demon burning inside them, and Anna's penalty for possessing beauty, riches, talent and brains, was to feed that demon until she burnt herself out in fires of her own creation.

I had been in my new job for just over a year before I did my first deal with Binkie over another Anouilh play. I had just acquired a new author, Penelope Packenham-Walsh – pen name Patricia Moyes – who had already written one play, *A Fiddle at the Wedding*, which Peter Ustinov had directed. Although it had not gone further than a provincial tour, the writing was charming and she had an excellent turn of phrase. Like Penelope Mortimer and Penelope Gilliatt she had worked for *Vogue* at a time when all their staff seemed to be literary geniuses. To date Penny has turned out nineteen or so crime stories which have been translated into dozens of languages but at that time she was badly in need of encouragement. Raymond Raikes wanted a new translation of Anouilh's *Léocadia* for a radio production, and it seemed the ideal solution for Penny to take on the job.

One of Margaret Rutherford's friends heard the first broadcast, told Margaret to listen to the repeat a few days later and Margaret promptly rang Binkie to say she would like to do the play. An astonished Penny was summoned to the office on

Sunday afternoon, confronted with Billy Chappell and Peter Rice, director and designer, and told the play was to open at the Lyric, Hammersmith in three weeks' time.

The result was *Time Remembered*, and it introduced a delightful Mary Ure, supported by Paul Scofield as well as Margaret Rutherford. As I have said, the policy at Hammersmith had been changed and the plays were put on for regular runs. Eventually *Time Remembered* transferred to the New (now the Albery) to be followed at Hammersmith a few weeks later by yet another Anouilh piece, *The Lark*, adapted by Christopher Fry and starring Dorothy Tutin.

There were to be only a couple more productions at the Lyric under the aegis of The Company of Four, and the lease was up at the end of March 1956. At that time there had been 69 productions, of which 23 had transferred, but as the lease would have required a long term renewal, it was felt that the financial commitment was too high. £20,000 annually was needed to cover the almost certain losses, and as the firm's reserves stood at only £20,151 they preferred to call it a day and retire on their laurels. There were other considerations, of course, such as the one-way system round the theatre and parking restrictions making it more and more difficult for audiences to reach the building. (The new Lyric has been resited in the High Street to provide much easier access and of course has vastly improved facilities.)

The most important offering to come out of France wasn't strictly speaking a translation at all, for which I was heartily grateful. I couldn't begin to imagine the difficulties of trying to make an English version of *En Attendant Godot* but fortunately Samuel Beckett made his own and all I had to do was sell it. Peter Glenville was very anxious to buy the rights – he wanted to stage it with Alec Guinness and Ralph Richardson – but Donald Albery was also in the market. Peter pointed out that a director would work untiringly to get a play on if he was going to do it himself – Donald argued that a management could call on the services of half a dozen directors and not have to wait until one individual was free. We compromised with a joint deal and eventually they used another Peter, Hall of that Ilk, who had recently taken over as director of the Arts

Theatre and was very much the latest in the line of boy wonders.

Peter directed the first production with two more namesakes, Bull and Woodthorpe, with Paul Daneman and Timothy Bateson to complete the quartet – I don't remember who played the small boy but it's reasonably certain that he would have been called Peter too. The rest is history. Experienced theatregoers would emerge from the Arts white and shaking, declaring that they hadn't understood a word, the critics praised it unreservedly, the house was sold out every night and the play eventually transferred to the Criterion, giving the BBC announcer a splendid lead on New Year's Eve as he surveyed the crowd.

"Up here," he said, "we're all waiting for 1956 and down there they're all waiting for Godot."

What we were waiting for, though we didn't know it at the time, was the opening of the English Stage Company's lease of the Royal Court Theatre and the play that was to make history, *Look Back in Anger*. George Devine had originally planned to run the theatre in true repertory fashion, changing the programme every night, and adopting the policy which is now common practice at the Barbican and National Theatres. Binkie had always considered this a totally uneconomic system and indeed resigned from the board of the Royal Shakespeare Company when Peter Hall decided to bring the company to London and run a season on similar lines at the Aldwych Theatre. Naturally, nobody could have anticipated the size of the subsidies the Arts Council and other bodies would be able to provide and in the fifties the theatre was still meant to be self supporting.

George opened with three plays, the first being Angus Wilson's *The Mulberry Bush* which had previously been tried out at the Bristol Old Vic with a very young Peter O'Toole in the cast. The Royal Court line up was glamorous enough – Gwen Ffrangçon-Davies, Nigel Davenport and Kenneth Haigh among the names. Nigel Dennis' *Cards of Identity* followed soon afterwards and then Jimmy Porter was introduced to London as the third offering.

After a few weeks George sent for me as Angus' agent and explained that the cost of the repertory policy was proving

prohibitive, and they were no longer in a position to keep all three going: the Osborne piece had one set and five characters, it was obviously the cheapest to keep on, and regretfully the other two would have to be dropped. *Look Back in Anger* ran for a few weeks, and then went on tour, but it wasn't until it returned to the Royal Court after it had been shown on television that it really built into a success. Even so, the real money spinner that saved the English Stage Company from financial disaster was a revival of *The Country Wife* with Lawrence Harvey and Joan Plowright, imitating the success we had had at Hammersmith with *The Relapse*.

Although George's policy was designed to foster new playwrights they were slow to arrive and the myth that untold quantities of brilliant scripts are always waiting for discovery prompted Kenneth Tynan, by now dramatic critic of *The Observer*, to persuade his paper to launch a major play competition in the spring of 1957. The prize was to be the princely sum of £500, and a production at the Royal Court. A panel of judges was set up, consisting of Ken himself, Peter Ustinov, Peter Hall, Alec Guinness and Michael Barry, then head of the BBC drama department. Plays were to be submitted anonymously and had to be on a contemporary theme. About five hundred were expected but over two thousand scripts were received, and an equally anonymous panel of readers weeded out the non-starters and left the main judges with a selection of some twenty odd from which to choose. In the event they were so impressed that they awarded six extra prizes, while about a dozen others rated special mention. A complete list of the titles and a description of the plays' contents appeared in Ken's theatrical column on 6 August, 1957.

The runner-up was a CB author, or rather authors, for the play, *Sit on the Earth* was a joint effort by two American writers Gurney Campbell and Daphne Athas, who had come to us via the ever-faithful Monica McCall. We also represented one of the extra prize-winners, Romilly Cavan. I had had advance news of the winners from Ken (himself a CB author) and his office supplied me with a list of the prize winners, their agents, if they had one, and their telephone numbers if they hadn't. I spent a happy afternoon ringing up all the private

numbers, offering congratulations and inviting any unattached writer to join our stable. Several of them agreed immediately, the most important being N. F. Simpson, a quirky writer whose plays, *A Resounding Tinkle, The Hole* and eventually *One Way Pendulum* were all produced at the Royal Court.

I arranged a cocktail party at my house the following Wednesday to which all the writers were invited to meet each other and the judges – a highly enjoyable piece of diplomacy with which even Spencer expressed himself as satisfied. But in spite of all the publicity, no major talent seemed to emerge. Ironically enough, the first prize went to a play already under contract to H. M. Tennent – *Moon on a Rainbow Shawl*, by the West Indian writer/actor, Errol John, and when it was staged at the Royal Court, acknowledgment had to be made of the cooperation of HMT. So much for the legend that commercial managements are not interested in new writers.

There was a further complication because on the way to a holiday in North Africa where he was joining John Gielgud, John Perry read a play called *Five Finger Exercise* by Peter Shaffer. The two Johns fell in love with the play and it was produced the following year with a brilliant cast headed by Adrianne Allen and Roland Culver, introducing Michael Bryant in his first West End role. The play was withdrawn from the competition, causing quite a few indignant ripples, and one is tempted to say with Churchill at Harrow at the end-of-term ceremony; "I'm so sorry for the prize winners – doomed to failure from the start." Still there were exceptions. Ann Jellicoe, the third laureate, spent some time at the Royal Court as a writer and director, and Gurney Campbell is still creating interesting work, including an exhaustively researched *Gandhi*. The competition launched with such high hopes made singularly little lasting impact on the theatrical scene, but it did add a few more authors to the Curtis Brown list.

The drama department seemed to be ticking over very satisfactorily and I even acquired my first cat to complete my household. She was a Tombola prize at the Opera Ball, an annual event designed to raise money for the English Opera Group, the organisation that had staged all the early Britten

operas. The little kitten sat in a gold florist's basket decorated with a red bow, and I fell in love with her at first sight. She was a fluffy tortoiseshell, though the overall effect was dark brown and black, with only one cream toe on a back foot to provide the third colour. She had green eyes in a small pointed face and looked exactly like Vivien Leigh. Her number wasn't drawn until right at the end of the evening, by which time I had spent a fortune on tickets.

Not knowing the first thing about cats, I began by feeding her all the wrong food which upset her tummy and the appalling results were always deposited in the middle of the kitchen floor to make quite sure that I couldn't miss them. The whole house stank of this unfortunate condition and she obviously gloated over my guilty feelings. Fortunately the local vet provided a cure, and the smell gradually died down, providing an easy barometer, or perhaps olfactometer, to her progress. All this time she had been called "Baby" as no suitable name seemed to present itself until one morning the radio struck up with Maurice Chevalier's favourite song. "Every little breeze seems to whisper Louise . . ."

"Baby," I called excitedly, "you've just got yourself a name." and Louise she became. She grew into the most beautiful cat, with a tail like a fox's brush which she always carried straight up in the air. When she inspected her food, if it was something she didn't like, the tail lay in a straight line on the floor behind her. If it was one of her favourites, she would settle down with an audible sigh and wrap her tail round her crouching body. When I left London I had to give her away – but like Charlie the car, I will never forget the first time I was taken over by a cat.

So with golf trophies on the shelves, and even Spencer admitting that I was beginning to know my job, I might have continued with CB's for the rest of my life, except for a totally unexpected development.

One evening I was told to present myself at an address in Hatton Garden and arrived to find a shabby workroom, filled with an indescribable and faintly familiar smell. Curtly ordered to wait at a table covered with dirty cracked cups and half-empty bottles of milk I sat obediently until I was presented with an object lying on a sheet of pale blue tissue paper. It

was a nine carat diamond, a virgin stone, that had been cut specially for me. The funny smell came from the final stage when the polished stone was boiled in sulphuric acid to clean off the cement in which the facets had been embedded. I was so startled I nearly dropped the paper. It was some days before the completed ring could be fitted on my finger as no jeweller in London had a ready-made setting for such a rock. When it was finally in position the office gave me a farewell party, two very pretty Waterford lamps and an early print of Covent Garden. All the authors were written to and advised that John Barber had agreed to take over my job. Louise and my car were given away and sold, and the household waved me a fond farewell as I departed for a life of luxury and leisure on foreign shores.

And there the chronicle ought to end, except that anyone who has read this far won't be in the least surprised to learn that inside twelve months I was back in the thick of the theatre scene, getting involved in television, pirate radio ships and a murder trial. But, as Scheherazade might say, that is a different story altogether.

Just for the Record

a: Complete chronology of productions by
H. M. Tennent Ltd: 1936–1973

Play	Theatre	Opening date	Number of performances
1936			
The Ante-Room: Kate O'Brien	Queen's	14. 8.36	10
Farewell Performance: Lajos Zilany (adapted by John L. Balderston)	Lyric	10. 9.36	11
Follow Your Saint: Lesley Storm	Tour	2. 9.36	
	Queen's	26. 9.36	
Mademoiselle: Jacques Deval (adapted by Audrey & Waveney Carten)	Wyndham's	15. 9.36	147
Charles the King: Maurice Colbourne	Lyric	9.10.36	179
Heart's Content: W. Chetham Strode	Shaftesbury	23.12.36	84
1937			
Candida: Bernard Shaw	Globe	10. 2.37	101
Retreat from Folly: Amy Kennedy Gould & Eileen Russell	Queen's	24. 2.37	47
George and Margaret: Gerald Savory	Wyndham's	25. 2.37	799
The Constant Wife: Somerset Maugham	Globe	19. 5.37	36
They Came by Night: Barré Lyndon	Globe	7. 7.37	76
Bonnet over the Windmill: Dodie Smith	New	8. 9.37	101
Blondie White: Jeffrey Dell	Globe	13.10.37	
Robert's Wife: St. John Ervine	Globe	29.11.37	606
You Can't Take It with You: George Kaufman & Moss Hart			
1938			
Plan for a Hostess: Thomas Browne	St. Martin's	10. 3.38	161
Operette: Noël Coward	His Majesty's	16. 3.38	133
A Thing Apart: Joyce Carey (Jay Mallory)	Tour		
People of Our Class: St. John Ervine	New	11. 5.38	
Spring Meeting: John Perry/M. J. Farrell	Ambassadors	31. 5.38	311
She Too Was Young: Hilda Vaughan	Wyndham's	16. 8.38	110
Dear Octopus: Dodie Smith	Queen's	14. 9.38	373
1939			
Design for Living: Noël Coward	Haymarket	25. 1.39	203
The Importance of Being Earnest: Oscar Wilde	Globe (matinées only)	31. 1.39	
We at the Crossroads: Rodney Ackland	Globe	7. 3.39	
Sugar Plum: Arthur Macrae	Criterion	15. 3.39	
Rhondda Roundabout: Jack Jones	Globe	31. 5.39	
Hamlet: Shakespeare	Lyceum	28. 6.39	6
The Importance of Being Earnest: Oscar Wilde	Globe	15. 8.39	20
	Tour	16. 9.39	
Second Helping: Ivor Novello	Tour		
All Clear: Revue	Queen's	20.12.39	162
Full House: Ivor Novello	Tour		
1940			
The Light of Heart: Emlyn Williams	Apollo	21. 2.40	126
Cousin Muriel: Clemence Dane	Globe	7. 3.40	

Rebecca: Daphne du Maurier	Queen's	5. 4.40	181
Ladies into Action: Ivor Novello	Lyric	10. 4.40	
I Lived with You: Ivor Novello	Tour		
The Devil's Disciple: Bernard Shaw	Piccadilly	24. 7.40	
Plays and Music (Fumed Oak: Coward & *The Dark Lady of the Sonnets*: Shaw)	Tour		
Thunder Rock: Robert Ardrey	Globe	30. 7.40	
On Approval: Frederick Lonsdale	Haymarket		

1941

Dear Brutus: J. M. Barrie	Globe	20. 1.41	124
No Time for Comedy: Noël Coward	Haymarket	27. 3.41	348
The First Mrs Fraser	Tour		
Blithe Spirit: Noël Coward	Piccadilly & Duchess	2. 7.41	1,997
The Nutmeg Tree: Margery Sharp	Lyric	9.10.41	269
The Morning Star: Emlyn Williams	Globe	10.12.41	474
Old Acquaintance: John van Druten	Apollo	18.12.41	218

1942

The Doctor's Dilemma: Bernard Shaw	Haymarket	4. 3.42	474
Skylark	Duchess	26. 3.42	109
Ducks and Drakes: M. J. Farrell	Tour		
Watch on the Rhine: Lillian Hellman	Aldwych	22. 4.42	673
Macbeth: Shakespeare	Piccadilly	8. 7.42	109
Strangers Road	Tour		
To Dream Again: Ivor Novello	Tour		
Flare Path: Terence Rattigan	Apollo	13. 8.42	670
The Importance of Being Earnest: Oscar Wilde	Phoenix	14.10.42	
The Little Foxes: Lillian Hellman	Piccadilly		

1943

A Month in the Country: Turgenev–Emlyn Williams	St. James's	11. 2.43	313
Heartbreak House: Bernard Shaw	Cambridge	18. 3.43	236
Love for Love: Sir John Vanbrugh	Phoenix	8. 4.43	471
They Came to a City: J. B. Priestley	Globe	21. 4.43	278
Present Laughter: Noël Coward	Haymarket	24. 4.43	43
This Happy Breed: Noël Coward	Haymarket	3. 7.43	43
Landslide: Luchaire-Black & Peel	Westminster	5.10.43	29
There Shall Be No Night: Robert Sherwood	Aldwych	15.12.43	220
While The Sun Shines: Terence Rattigan	Globe	24.12.43	1,154

1944

The Druid's Rest: Emlyn Williams	St. Martin's	26. 1.44	182
Pen Don: Emlyn Williams	Tour		
The Cradle Song: Gregorio & Maria Martinez Sierra	Apollo	27. 1.44	76
Françoise Rosay season	Haymarket		
Staff Dance: Robert Morley	Tour		
Uncle Harry: Thomas Job	??	29. 3.44	122
Crisis in Heaven: Eric Linklater	Lyric	10. 5.44	38
The Last of Summer: Ronald Adam	Phoenix	7. 6.44	19
Ballets Jooss	Haymarket		
Uncle Harry (Revival): Thomas Job	Garrick	7. 9.44	188
John Gielgud season (*A Midsummer Night's Dream, Hamlet, Love for Love, The Circle, The Duchess of Malfi*)	Haymarket	11.10.44	347
I'll See You Again: Ivor Novello	Tour		
Private Lives: Noël Coward	Apollo	1.11.44	716
Another Love Story: Frederick Lonsdale	Phoenix	13.12.44	173
Love in Idleness: Terence Rattigan	Lyric	20.12.44	213

1945

The Years Between: Daphne du Maurier	Wyndham's	10. 1.45	617
The Wind of Heaven: Emlyn Williams	St. James's	12. 4.45	268
The Skin of Our Teeth: Thornton Wilder	Phoenix	16. 5.45	78
Lady Windermere's Fan: Oscar Wilde	Haymarket	21. 8.45	428
Sigh No More: Noël Coward	Piccadilly	22. 8.45	213

A Bell for Adano: Paul Osborn (adapted by John Hersey)	Phoenix	19. 9.45	69
Dandy Dick: Sir Arthur Pinero	Tour		
The Rivals: Sheridan	Criterion	25. 9.45	166

1946

The Guinea-Pig: W. Chetham-Strode	Criterion	19. 2.46	560
A Man about the House: Francis Brett Young (adapted by John Perry)	Piccadilly	27. 2.46	100
A Play for Ronnie	Tour		
Our Town: Thornton Wilder	New	30. 4.46	31
The Winslow Boy: Terence Rattigan	Lyric	23. 5.46	478
Portrait in Black: Ivan Goff & Ben Roberts	Piccadilly	30. 5.46	116
Grand National Night: Dorothy & Campbell Christie	Apollo	12. 6.46	289
Crime and Punishment: Dostoievsky	New & Globe	26. 6.46	160
The Skin of Our Teeth (Revival): Thornton Wilder	Piccadilly	11. 9.46	109
The Gleam: W. Chetham-Strode	Globe	4.12.46	144
Antony and Cleopatra: Shakespeare	Piccadilly	20.12.46	83

1947

Caste: T. W. Robertson	Duke of York's	22. 1.47	
Jane: Somerset Maugham (adapted by S. N. Behrman)	Aldwych	29. 1.47	280
The Eagle Has Two Heads: Cocteau/Ronald Duncan	Haymarket	12. 2.47	170
Othello: Shakespeare	Piccadilly	25. 3.47	22
Candida: Bernard Shaw		26. 3.47	39
Present Laughter: Noël Coward	Haymarket	16. 4.47	328
Oklahoma!	Drury Lane	30. 4.47	1,543
The Play's The Thing: Molnar/Anon	St. James's	24. 5.47	48
Angel: Mary Hayley Bell	Strand	6. 6.47	10
Deep Are The Roots: Arnaud D'Usseau & James Gow	Wyndham's	8. 7.47	135
Trespass: Emlyn Williams	Apollo	16. 7.47	158
Peace in Our Time: Noël Coward	Lyric	22. 7.47	167
Tuppence Coloured: Revue	Globe	15.10.47	273
Dark Summer: Wynyard Browne	St. Martin's	15.12.47	72
Macbeth: Shakespeare	Aldwych	18.12.47	76

1948

The Relapse: Sir John Vanbrugh	Phoenix	28. 1.48	253
I Remember Mama: Kathryn Forbes (adapted by John van Druten)	Aldwych	2. 3.48	62
The Happiest Days of Your Life: John Deighton	Apollo	29. 3.48	604
Traveller's Joy: Arthur Macrae	Criterion	2. 6.48	954
All My Sons: Arthur Miller	Globe	8. 6.48	108
The Glass Menagerie: Tennessee Williams	Haymarket	28. 7.48	109
Crime Passionnel: Sartre/Kitty Black	Garrick	4. 8.48	61
Medea: Euripides	Globe	29. 9.48	61
The Return of the Prodigal: St. John Hankin	Globe	24.11.48	69
September Tide: Daphne du Maurier	Aldwych	16.12.48	267

1949

Oranges and Lemons: Revue	Globe	26. 1.49	117
The Heiress: Henry James/R. & A. Goetz	Haymarket	1. 2.49	644
Adventure Story: Terence Rattigan	St. James's	17. 3.49	114
Dark of the Moon: Richardson/Berney	Ambassadors	12. 4.49	101
The Lady's Not For Burning: Christopher Fry	Globe	11. 5.49	294
Love in Albania: Eric Linklater	St. James's	22. 7.49	142
Death of a Salesman: Arthur Miller	Phoenix	28. 7.49	202
Treasure Hunt: M. J. Farrell & John Perry	Apollo	14. 9.49	358
A Streetcar Named Desire: Tennessee Williams	Aldwych	12.10.49	333
The Seagull: Chekhov	St. James's	15.11.49	62

1950

Ring Round The Moon: Anouilh/Fry	Globe	25. 1.50	682
The Holly and the Ivy: Wynyard Browne	Duchess	10. 5.50	412

Seagulls over Sorrento: Hugh Hastings	Apollo	14. 6.50	1,551
The Little Hut: Roussin/Mitford	Lyric	23. 8.50	1,258
The Second Mrs Tanqueray: Sir Arthur Pinero	Haymarket	29. 8.50	206
Accolade: Emlyn Williams	Aldwych	7. 9.50	180
Who Is Sylvia?: Terence Rattigan	Criterion	24.10.50	380
Point of Departure: Anouilh/Kitty Black	Duke of York's	26.12.50	149

1951

A Penny for a Song: John Whiting	Haymarket	1. 3.51	36
Waters of the Moon: N. C. Hunter	Haymarket	19. 4.51	234
Three Sisters: Chekhov	Aldwych	3. 5.51	140
The Winter's Tale: Shakespeare	Phoenix	27. 6.51	212
The Lyric Revue: Revue	Globe	26. 9.51	314
Figure of Fun: Roussin/Macrae	Aldwych	16.10.51	213
Relative Values: Noël Coward	Savoy	28.11.51	477
Indian Summer: Peter Watling	Criterion	12.12.51	21
Colombe: Anouilh/Denis Cannan	New	13.12.51	116

1952

Summer and Smoke: Tennessee Williams	Duchess	23. 1.52	44
Much Ado about Nothing: Shakespeare	Phoenix	11. 1.52	
Emlyn Williams as Charles Dickens	Duchess	19. 1.52	70
The Deep Blue Sea: Terence Rattigan	Duchess	6. 3.52	450
The Same Sky: Yvonne Mitchell	Duke of York's	18. 3.52	44
The Vortex: Noël Coward	Criterion	9. 4.52	44
Under the Sycamore Tree: Sam Spewack	Aldwych	23. 4.52	196
The Mortimer Touch: Eric Linklater	Duke of York's	30. 4.52	45
The Gay Dog: Joseph Cotton	Piccadilly	11. 6.52	274
The Millionairess: Bernard Shaw	New	27. 6.52	96
The Globe Revue: Revue	Globe	10. 7.52	235
Bleak House: Dickens/Emlyn Williams	Ambassadors	3. 9.52	69
Quadrille: Noël Coward	Phoenix	12. 9.52	327
Letter from Paris: Henry James/Dodie Smith	Aldwych	10.10.52	27
The River Line: Charles Morgan	Strand	28.10.52	150

1953

A Woman of No Importance: Oscar Wilde	Savoy	12. 2.53	178
The White Carnation: R. C. Sherriff	Globe	20. 3.53	89
The Apple Cart: Bernard Shaw	Haymarket	7. 5.53	100
The Seven Year Itch: George Axelrod	Aldwych	14. 5.53	331
The Private Life of Helen of Troy: Roussin/Macrae	Globe	11. 6.53	196
Aren't We All?: Frederick Lonsdale	Haymarket	6. 8.53	123
Someone Waiting: Emlyn Williams	Globe	25.11.53	157
A Day by the Sea: N. C. Hunter	Haymarket	26.11.53	388
A Question of Fact: Gerald Savory	Piccadilly	10.12.53	332
At the Lyric: Revue	Lyric	23.12.53	163

1954

Charley's Aunt: Brandon Thomas	New	10. 2.54	124
The Burning Glass: Charles Morgan	Apollo	12. 2.54	
Hippo Dancing: Roussin/Robert Morley	Lyric	7. 4.54	443
Marching Song: John Whiting	St. Martin's	8. 4.54	43
The Prisoner: Bridget Boland	Globe	14. 4.54	60
The Dark is Light Enough: Christopher Fry	Aldwych	30. 4.54	241
Going to Town (At The Lyric): Revue	St. Martin's	20. 5.54	68
The Cherry Orchard: Chekhov	Lyric, Hammersmith	21. 5.54	123
Both Ends Meet: Arthur Macrae	Apollo	9. 6.54	284
After The Ball: Noël Coward	Piccadilly	10. 6.54	181
Hedda Gabler: Ibsen/Ashmore	Lyric, Hammersmith & Westminster	8. 9.54	155
Bell Book & Candle: John van Druten	Phoenix	5.10.54	484
The Matchmaker: Thornton Wilder	Haymarket	4.11.54	274
An Evening with Beatrice Lillie	Globe	24.11.54	195
Simon and Laura: Alan Melville	Strand & Apollo	25.11.54	210
Time Remembered: Anouilh/Patricia Moyes	Lyric, Hammersmith & New	2.12.54	181

234

1955

Skupa Puppets	Lyric, Hammersmith	11. 4.55	64
The Bad Seed: Maxwell Anderson	Aldwych	14. 4.55	195
The Lark: Anouilh/Christopher Fry	Lyric, Hammersmith	11. 5.55	
My Three Angels: Sam & Bella Spewack	Apollo	12. 5.55	228
Into Thin Air: Chester Erskine	Globe	19. 5.55	4
Dylan Thomas Growing Up	Globe	31. 5.55	85
Mrs Willie: Alan Melville	Globe	17. 8.55	141
The Buccaneer: Sandy Wilson	Lyric, Hammersmith & Apollo	8. 9.55	201
A Life in the Sun: Thornton Wilder	Edinburgh Festival		
Anniversary Waltz: Jerome Chodorov	Lyric	30.11.55	86
Hamlet: Shakespeare	Phoenix	8.12.55	124
Charley's Aunt: Brandon Thomas	Globe	22.12.55	103

1956

Misalliance: Bernard Shaw	Lyric, Hammersmith	8. 2.56	53
A Likely Tale: Gerald Savory	Globe	22. 3.56	238
The Power and the Glory: Graham Greene	Phoenix	5. 4.56	68
The Chalk Garden: Enid Bagnold	Haymarket	11. 4.56	658
South Sea Bubble: Noël Coward	Lyric	25. 4.56	277
Hotel Paradiso: Feydeau/Peter Glenville	Winter Garden	2. 5.56	212
Family Reunion: T. S. Eliot	Phoenix	7. 6.56	100
Man Alive: John Deighton	Aldwych	14. 6.56	84
Love Affair: Dulcie Gray	Lyric, Hammersmith	1. 6.56	19
Anything May . . .	Lyric, Hammersmith	20. 6.56	20
Ruth Draper	St. James	2. 7.56	31
Under Milk Wood: Dylan Thomas	Tour	13. 8.56	
A River Breeze: Roland Culver	Phoenix	6. 9.56	68
Nude with Violin: Noël Coward	Globe	7.11.56	511
The Devil's Disciple: Bernard Shaw	Winter Garden	8.11.56	36
A Boy Growing Up/Charles Dickens: Emlyn Williams	Tour	3.12.56	8
The Diary of Anne Frank: Francis Goodrich & Albert Hackett	Phoenix	29.11.56	139

1957

The Glass Cage: J. B. Priestley	Piccadilly	26. 4.57	35
A Dead Secret: Rodney Ackland	Piccadilly	30. 5.57	193
Ride a Cock Horse: David Mercer	Tour	10. 6.57	
Flowering Cherry: Robert Bolt	Haymarket	21.11.57	441

1958

Cat on a Hot Tin Roof: Tennessee Williams	Comedy	30. 1.58	129
A Touch Of The Sun: N. C. Hunter	Saville & Princes	31. 1.58	202
Where's Charley?: Brandon Thomas/	Palace	20. 2.58	381
The Potting Shed: Graham Greene	Globe	5. 3.58	110
Duel of Angels: Giraudoux/Fry	Apollo	24. 4.58	252
My Fair Lady: Shaw/Lerner/Loewe	Drury Lane	30. 4.58	2,281
Variation on a Theme: Terence Rattigan	Globe	8. 5.58	132
The Big Tickle: Ronald Millar	Duke of York's	23. 5.58	27
Living for Pleasure: Arthur Macrae	Garrick	10. 7.58	379
Five Finger Exercise: Peter Shaffer	Comedy	16. 7.58	609
Irma la Douce: Alexandre Breffort (adapted by Julian More, David Henneker & Monty Norman; music by Marguerite Monnot)	Lyric	17. 8.58	1,025
A Boy Growing Up: Dylan Thomas/Emlyn Williams	Globe	2. 9.58	21
Long Day's Journey into Night: Eugene O'Neill	Globe	29. 9.58	103
Moon on a Rainbow Shawl: Errol John	Royal Court	4.12.58	35

West Side Story: Arthur Laurents, Stephen Sondheim & Leonard Bernstein	Her Majesty's	12.12.58	1,039
Two for the Seesaw: William Gibson	Haymarket	17.12.58	139

1959

Eighty in the Shade: Clemence Dane	Globe	8. 1.59	179
The Coast of Coromandel: J. M. Sadler	Tour	26. 1.59	
The Pleasure of His Company: Samuel Taylor	Haymarket	23. 4.59	403
The Complaisant Lover: Graham Greene	Globe	18. 6.59	402
Farewell, Farewell, Eugene: John Vari/Rodney Ackland	Garrick	5. 6.59	282
The Ages of Man: Shakespeare/Rylands	Queen's	8. 7.59	29

1960

Look on Tempests: Joan Henry	Comedy	22. 3.60	29
The Ages of Man (Revival): Shakespeare/Rylands	Haymarket	13. 4.60	28
The Most Happy Fella: Frank Loesser	Coliseum	21. 4.60	290
Ross: Terence Rattigan	Haymarket	12. 5.60	762
A Lovely Light: Howard Lindsay	Globe	9. 6.60	11
The Visit: Dürrenmatt/Valency	Royalty	23. 6.60	148
A Man For All Seasons: Robert Bolt	Globe	1. 7.60	320
Joie de Vivre: Coward musical	Queen's	14. 7.60	4
The Tiger and the Horse: Robert Bolt	Queen's	24. 8.60	229
The Last Joke: Enid Bagnold	Phoenix	28. 9.60	61

1961

The Lady from the Sea: Ibsen	Queen's	15. 3.61	83
The Rehearsal: Anouilh/Hansford Johnson/Black	Globe (then Queen's, Globe, Apollo)	6. 4.61	344
Dazzling Prospect: M. J. Farrell & John Perry	Globe	1. 6.61	20
On the Avenue: Revue	Globe	21. 6.61	14
Oh Dad, Poor Dad, Mama's Hung You in the Closet and I'm Feeling So Sad: Arthur Kopit	Lyric, Hammersmith	5. 7.61	13
Bye Bye Birdie: Michael Stuart/Charles Strouse	Her Majesty's	15. 6.61	268
Do Re Mi: Garson Kanin/Lee Adams & Julie Styne	Prince of Wales	12.10.61	170
Becket: Anouilh/Lucienne Hill	Globe (transferred from Aldwych after approx. 100 perfor- mances)	13.12.61	164

1962

H.M.S. Pinafore & The Pirates of Penzance: Gilbert & Sullivan	Her Majesty's	8. 2.62 15. 2.62	75 72
Joyce Grenfell	Haymarket	14. 3.62	20
Write Me a Murder: Frederick Knott	Lyric	28. 3.62	179
The School for Scandal: Sheridan	Haymarket	5. 4.62	258
The Private Ear and *The Public Eye*: Peter Shaffer	Globe	10. 5.62	547
Judith: Giraudoux	Her Majesty's	20. 6.62	29
A Touch of the Poet: Eugene O'Neill	Tour	24. 9.62	
The Tulip Tree: N. C. Hunter	Haymarket	29.11.62	136

1963

Carnival: Michael Stuart & Bob Merrill	Lyric	8. 2.63	35
Mary, Mary: Jean Kerr	Queen's, trans: Globe	27. 2.63 2. 9.63	422
Some Men and Women: Thorndike/Casson	Haymarket	8. 5.63	13
The Doctor's Dilemma: Bernard Shaw	Haymarket	23. 5.63	84
On the Town: Revue	Prince of Wales	30. 5.63	36
Virtue in Danger (Musical): Vanbrugh	(Transfer:) Strand	3. 6.63	32
Where Angels Fear to Tread: Elizabeth Hart	Arts (then: St. Martin's)	6. 6.63 9. 7.63	262
The Ides of March: Jerome Kilty	Haymarket	8. 8.63	60
Man and Boy: Terence Rattigan	Queen's	4. 9.63	69
At The Drop of Another Hat: Flanders & Swann	Haymarket	2.10.63	171
Gentle Jack: Robert Bolt	Queen's	28.11.63	75

1964

The Merchant of Venice } Shakespeare A Midsummer Night's Dream }	Latin America Tour	10. 1.64	
My Fair Lady: Shaw/Lerner & Loewe	Southern National Tour	30. 3.64	
I Love You, Mrs Patterson: John Bowen	St. Martin's	12. 5.64	38
The Photographer: Kenneth Jupp	Tour	25. 5.64	
The Tiger and The Typists: Murray Schisgal	Globe	30. 5.64	38
The Trigon: James Broome Lynne	Arts	27. 5.64	19
Season of Goodwill: Arthur Marshall/Dorothea Malm	Queen's	16. 9.64	21
Carving a Statue: Graham Greene	Haymarket	17. 9.64	52
Marlene Dietrich	Queen's	23.11.64	24

1965

Ring of Jackals: Edmund Ward	Queen's	10. 2.65	13
Joyce Grenfell	Queen's	23. 3.65	30
La Contessa: Maurice Druon/Moura Budberg	Tour only	6. 4.65	
Present Laughter: Noël Coward	Queen's	21. 4.65	364
The Elephant's Foot: William Trevor	Tour only	3. 5.65	
The Chinese Prime Minister: Enid Bagnold	Globe	20. 5.65	108
Marlene Dietrich	Tour		
Emlyn Williams as Charles Dickens	Globe	29. 9.65	
At The Drop of Another Hat: Flanders/Swann	Globe	29. 9.65	140
Ivanov: Chekhov	Phoenix	30. 9.65	122
Hello, Dolly: Thornton Wilder, Michael Stuart, Jerry Herman	Drury Lane	2.12.65	794
The Glass Menagerie: Tennessee Williams	Haymarket	1.12.65	43

1966

You Never Can Tell: Bernard Shaw	Haymarket	11. 1.66	284
Incident at Vichy: Arthur Miller	Phoenix	26. 1.66	91
Suite in Three Keys: Noël Coward	Queen's	14. 4.66	124
The Rivals: Sheridan	Haymarket	6.10.66	348
The Odd Couple: Neil Simon	Queen's	12.10.66	352
Lady Windermere's Fan: Oscar Wilde	Phoenix	13.10.66	167
Marlene Dietrich	Tour		

1967

Cactus Flower: Abe Burrows	Lyric	6. 3.67	169
Horizontal Hold: Stanley Price	Comedy	23. 5.67	32
Beware of the Dog: Adapted from Chekhov	St. Martin's	7. 6.67	37
The Merchant of Venice: Shakespeare	Haymarket	7. 9.67	72
The Cherry Orchard: Chekhov	Queen's	5.10.67	41
Heartbreak House: Bernard Shaw	Lyric	9.11.67	117
Halfway up the Tree: Peter Ustinov	Queen's	21.11.67	544

1968

The Importance of Being Earnest: Oscar Wilde	Haymarket	8. 2.68	283
The White Liars and Black Comedy: Peter Shaffer	Lyric	21. 2.68	93
I Do! I Do!: Ian Jones	Lyric	16. 5.68	102
You Know I Can't Hear You When the Water's Running: Robert Anderson	New	26. 6.68	37
Ring Round the Moon: Anouilh/Fry	Haymarket	30.10.68	101
The Cocktail Party: T. S. Eliot	Wyndham's (transferred to Haymarket)	6.11.68 3. 2 69	149

1969

Your Own Timing: Hal Hester/Danny Apolinar	Comedy	6. 2.69	58
What The Butler Saw: Joe Orton	Queen's	5. 3.69	102
Cat among the Pigeons: Feydeau/Mortimer	Prince of Wales	15. 4.69	117
Play It Again, Sam: Woody Allen	Globe	11. 9.69	363
The Magistrate: Pinero	Cambridge	18. 9.69	247
Promises, Promises: Neil Simon	Prince of Wales	2.10.69	570

237

1970

Play on Love: Françoise Dorin	St. Martin's	14. 1.70	29
The Battle of Shrivings: Peter Shaffer	Lyric	5. 2.70	72
Blithe Spirit: Noël Coward	Globe	23. 7.70	203
	Tour to Toronto	19. 1.72	
A Bequest to the Nation: Terence Rattigan	Haymarket	23. 9.70	124
Vivat, Vivat Regina: Robert Bolt	Piccadilly	8.10.70	442
Butterflies are Free: Leonard Gershe	Apollo	4.11.70	37
The Winslow Boy: Terence Rattigan	New	5.11.70	234

1971

Captain Brassbound's Conversion: Bernard Shaw	Cambridge	18. 2.71	187
The Patrick Pearse Motel: Feydeau/Hugh Leonard	Queen's	17. 6.71	76
West of Suez: John Osborne	Cambridge	6.10.71	130
Dear Antoine: Anouilh/Lucienne Hill	Piccadilly	3.11.71	47
Godspell: John Michael Tebelak & Steven Schwartz	Round House	17.11.71	
	(Transferred to Wyndham's after 76 perfs)	26. 1.72	1,192

1972

Reunion in Vienna: Robert E. Sherwood	Piccadilly	17. 2.72	44
Private Lives: Noël Coward	Queen's & Globe	21. 9.72	98

1973

A Private Matter: Ronald Mavor	Vaudeville	21. 2.73	128
Suzanna Andler: Françoise Sagan/	Aldwych	5. 3.73	21
The Constant Wife: Somerset Maugham	Albery	19. 9.73	264

b: Chronology of productions by Tennent Plays Ltd, subsequently Tennent Productions Ltd: 1942–1967

Play	Author	Theatre	Date of opening
Macbeth	Shakespeare	Piccadilly	8. 7.42
Love for Love	Congreve	Phoenix	9. 4.43
		Haymarket	8. 8.43
They Came to a City	J. B. Priestley	Globe	22. 4.43
A Month in the Country	Chekhov (adapted by Emlyn Williams)	St. James's	11. 2.43
Hamlet	Shakespeare ⎫	Haymarket	11.10.44
A Midsummer Night's Dream	Shakespeare ⎬	(in repertoire)	25. 1.45
The Duchess of Malfi	Webster ⎭		19. 4.45
Lady Windermere's Fan	Oscar Wilde	Haymarket	21. 8.45
The Rivals	Sheridan	Criterion	25. 9.45
Our Town	Thornton Wilder	New	30. 4.46
Crime and Punishment	Dostoievsky	New	26. 6.46
		Tr. Globe	9. 9.46
The Skin of Our Teeth	Thornton Wilder	Piccadilly	11. 9.46
Antony and Cleopatra	Shakespeare	Piccadilly	19.12.46
Othello	Shakespeare ⎫	Piccadilly	25. 3.47
Candida	Bernard Shaw ⎭		

Tennent Plays Ltd. wound up – Tennent Productions Ltd. formed

Play	Author	Theatre	Date of opening
Deep Are The Roots	Arnaud d'Usseau & James Gow	Wyndham's	2. 6.47
*Caste	T. W. Robertson	Duke of York's	4. 1.47
*The Eagle Has Two Heads	Cocteau (translated by Ronald Duncan)	Haymarket	12. 2.47
*Tuppence Coloured	Revue	Globe	15.10.47
*Dark Summer	Wynyard Browne	St. Martin's	15.12.47
Macbeth	Shakespeare	Aldwych	18.12.47
*The Relapse	Sir John Vanbrugh	Phoenix	28. 1.48
*All My Sons	Arthur Miller	Globe	15. 6.48
The Glass Menagerie	Tennessee Williams	Haymarket	28. 7.48
*Crime Passionnel	Sartre (translated by Kitty Black)	Garrick	4. 8.48
Medea	Euripides	Globe	29. 9.48
The Return of the Prodigal	St. John Hankin	Globe	24.11.48
September Tide	Daphne du Maurier	Aldwych	16.12.48
*Oranges and Lemons	Revue	Globe	26. 1.49
The Heiress	Henry James (adapted by Ruth & Augustus Goetz)	Haymarket	1. 2.49
The Lady's Not For Burning	Christopher Fry	Globe	11. 5.49
*Dark of The Moon	Howard Richardson & William Berney	Ambassadors	12. 4.49
Death of a Salesman	Arthur Miller	Phoenix	28. 7.49
*Love in Albania	Eric Linklater	St. James's	22. 7.49
Treasure Hunt	M. J. Farrell & John Perry	Apollo	14. 9.49
A Streetcar Named Desire	Tennessee Williams	Aldwych	12.10.49
*The Seagull	Chekhov	St. James's	16.11.49
Ring Round The Moon	Anouilh (translated by Christopher Fry)	Globe	26. 1.50
The Second Mrs Tanqueray	Pinero	Haymarket	29. 8.50
*The Holly and The Ivy	Wynyard Browne	Duchess	10. 5.50
*Point of Departure	Anouilh (translated by Kitty Black)	Duke of York's	26.12.50
A Penny for a Song	John Whiting	Haymarket	1. 3.51

239

Waters of The Moon	N. C. Hunter	Haymarket	19. 4.51
The Three Sisters	Chekhov	Aldwych	3. 5.51
The Winter's Tale	Shakespeare	Phoenix	27. 6.51
*The Lyric Revue	Revue	Globe	26. 9.51
Indian Summer	Peter Watling	Criterion	12.12.51
Colombe	Anouilh (translated by Denis Cannan)	New	13.12.51
Much Ado about Nothing	Shakespeare	Phoenix	11. 1.52
*Summer and Smoke	Tennessee Williams	Duchess	23. 1.52
*The Vortex	Noël Coward	Criterion	9. 4.52
The Same Sky	Yvonne Mitchell	Duke of York's	18. 3.52
Under the Sycamore Tree	Sam Spewack	Aldwych	23. 4.52
The Mortimer Touch	Eric Linklater	Duke of York's	30. 4.52
The Millionairess	Bernard Shaw	New	24. 6.52
The Globe Revue	(2nd edition)	Globe	10. 7.52
Bleak House	Charles Dickens & Emlyn Williams	Ambassadors	3. 9.52
Letter from Paris	Henry James (adapted by Dodie Smith)	Aldwych	10.10.52
*The River Line	Charles Morgan	Strand	28.10.52
A Woman of No Importance	Oscar Wilde	Savoy	12. 2.53
The Apple Cart	Bernard Shaw	Haymarket	7. 5.53
The Private Life of Helen	André Roussin & Madeleine Gray (adapted by Arthur Macrae)	Globe	11. 6.53
Aren't We All?	Frederick Lonsdale	Haymarket	6. 8.53
A Day by The Sea	N. C. Hunter	Haymarket	25.11.53
A Question of Fact	Wynyard Browne	Piccadilly	10.12.53
*At The Lyric (2nd edition) – Going To Town	Revue	St. Martin's	20. 3.53
The Burning Glass	Charles Morgan	Apollo	18. 2.54
Marching Song	John Whiting	St. Martin's	12. 2.54
The Dark Is Light Enough	Christopher Fry	Aldwych	30. 4.54
The Prisoner	Bridget Boland	Globe	14. 4.54
After the Ball	Wilde/Coward	Globe	10. 6.54
The Matchmaker	Thornton Wilder	Haymarket	4.11.54
Nina	André Roussin (translated by Arthur Macrae)	Haymarket	27. 7.55
Hamlet	Shakespeare	Phoenix	8.12.55
The Power and the Glory	Graham Greene	(Scofield	5. 4.56
Family Reunion	T. S. Eliot	Season)	6. 6.56
The Devil's Disciple	Bernard Shaw	Winter Garden	8.11.56
The Chalk Garden	Enid Bagnold	Haymarket	10. 4.56
A Dead Secret	Rodney Ackland	Piccadilly	30. 5.57
The Tempest (with RSC)	Shakespeare	Drury Lane	4.12.57
A Touch of The Sun	N. C. Hunter	Saville (then Princes	31. 1.58 21. 4.58
Living for Pleasure	Revue	Garrick	10. 7.58
A Boy Growing Up	Dylan Thomas/Emlyn Williams	Globe	1. 9.58
Moon on a Rainbow Shawl	Errol John	Royal Court	3.12.58
Eighty in the Shade	Clemence Dane	Globe	8. 1.59
Ages of Man (with John Gielgud)	George Rylands/Shakespeare	Queen's then Haymarket	5. 7.59 11. 4.60
A Passage To India	Santha Rama Rau (from E. M. Forster)	Comedy	20. 4.60
The Last Joke	Enid Bagnold	Phoenix	28. 9.60
Lady from the Sea	Ibsen	Queen's	15. 3.61
The Rehearsal	Anouilh (translated by Pamela Hansford Johnson & Kitty Black)	Globe (then Queen's, Globe, Apollo)	6. 4.61 6.61 7.61 12.61
Becket (with RSC)	Anouilh (translated by Lucienne Hill)	Globe	16.12.61
H.M.S. Pinafore	Gilbert & Sullivan	Her Majesty's	9. 2.62
The Pirates of Penzance			
The School for Scandal	Sheridan	Haymarket	4. 4.62
The Ages of Man	Shakespeare/Rylands	Tour	4.62
A Touch of The Poet	Eugene O'Neill	Dublin Festival & Venice	24. 9.62
Some Men and Women	Poetry recital: Sybil Thorndike & Lewis Casson	Haymarket	8. 5.63
The Doctor's Dilemma	Bernard Shaw	Haymarket	23. 5.63
Where Angels Fear to Tread	Elizabeth Hart (from E. M. Forster)	Arts Theatre (then St. Martin's)	6. 6.63 9. 7.63

240

Virtue in Danger (musical)	Paul Dehn & James Bernard (from *The Relapse*)	Mermaid (then Strand)	10. 4.63 3. 6.63
The Merchant of Venice	Shakespeare	Brighton & South America	10. 2.64
A Midsummer Night's Dream			
The Seagull (with English Stage Co.)	Chekhov	Queen's	12. 3.64
I Love You, Mrs. Patterson	John Bowen	St. Martin's	11. 5.64
Saint Joan of The Stockyards	Bertolt Brecht	Queen's	11. 6.64
The Elephant's Foot	William Trevor	Tour	19. 4.65
Ivanov	Chekhov (adapted by John Gielgud)	Phoenix & New York	30. 9.65
The Cavern	Anouilh (translated by Lucienne Hill)	Strand	11.11.65
The Glass Menagerie	Tennessee Williams	Haymarket	1.12.65
You Never Can Tell	Bernard Shaw	Haymarket	12. 1.66
Incident at Vichy	Arthur Miller	Phoenix	26. 1.66
The Rivals	Sheridan	Haymarket	5.10.66
Beware of The Dog	Gabriel Arout (from Chekhov)	St. Martin's	7. 6.67
The Merchant of Venice	Shakespeare	Haymarket	2.12.67

* Denotes a Company of Four production.

c: Chronology of productions by The Company of Four: 1945–1956

Play	Author	Date of opening at Lyric Theatre, Hammersmith
The Shouting Dies	Ronda Keane	5.10.45
The Trojan Women and	Euripides (translated by F. Kinchin-Smith)	9.11.45
The Happy Journey from Trenton to Camden	Thornton Wilder	
Spring 1600	Emlyn Williams	7.12.45
Death of a Rat	Jan de Hartog	15. 1.46
The Time of Your Life	William Saroyan	14. 2.46
Tomorrow's Child	John Coates	12. 3.46
Red Roses for Me	Sean O'Casey	9. 4.46
The Thracian Horses	Maurice J. Valency	7. 5.46
The Brothers Karamazov	Dostoievsky (adapted by Alec Guinness)	6. 7.46
Summer at Nohant	S. Iwaszkiewicz	9. 7.46
Fear No More	Walter Macken & Diana Hamilton	5. 8.46
The Eagle Has Two Heads	Cocteau (adapted by Ronald Duncan)	4. 9.46
(Transferred to Haymarket 12. 2.47)		
The Assassin	Peter Yates	14.10.46
The King Stag	Goldoni	Christmas season
(The Young Vic)		
Caste	T. W. Robertson	4. 1.47
(Transferred to Duke of York's)		
Galway Handicap	Walter Macken	4. 2.47
The Rossiters	Kenneth Hyde	4. 3.47
The Play's The Thing	Ferenc Molnar	14. 4.47
(Transferred to St. James's Theatre)		
Oak Leaves and Lavender	Sean O'Casey	12. 5.47
Pygmalion	Bernard Shaw	17. 6.47
Men Without Shadows and	Sartre (translated by Kitty Black)	22. 7.47
The Respectable Prostitute		
Tuppence Coloured	Revue	4. 9.47
(Transferred to Globe Theatre)		
Dark Summer	Wynyard Browne	29. 9.47
(Transferred to St. Martin's Theatre)		
The Little Dry Thorn	Gordon Daviot	11.11.47
The Relapse	Vanbrugh	16.12.47
(Transferred to Phoenix Theatre)		
Bred in The Bone	Michael Egan	27. 1.48
Castle Anna	Elizabeth Bowen & John Perry	24. 2.48
Dandy Dick	Pinero	23. 3.48
All My Sons	Arthur Miller	11. 5.48
(Transferred to Globe Theatre)		
Crime Passionnel	Sartre (translated by Kitty Black)	16. 6.48
(Transferred to Garrick Theatre)		
An English Summer	Ronald Adam	1. 9.48
Captain Brassbound's Conversion	Bernard Shaw	13.10.48
Oranges and Lemons	Revue	26.11.48
(Transferred to Globe Theatre)		
The Damask Cheek	John van Druten & Lloyd Morris	2. 2.49
Dark of The Moon	Howard Richardson & William Berney	8. 3.49
(Transferred to Ambassador's Theatre)		
Royal Highness	Margaret Webster	13. 4.49

242

Love in Albania	Eric Linklater	7. 6.49
(Transferred to St. James's Theatre)		
The King of Friday's Men	Michael Molloy	30. 8.49
The Seagull	Chekhov (adapted by George Calderon)	4.10.49
Let's Make an Opera	Benjamin Britten & Eric Crozier	15.11.49
The Boy with a Cart and	Christopher Fry	19. 1.50
Shall We Join The Ladies?	J. M. Barrie	
Man of The World	C. E. Webber	22. 2.50
The Holly and The Ivy	Wynyard Browne	28. 3.50
(Transferred to Duchess Theatre)		
If This Be Error	Rachel Grieve	24. 5.50
Tartuffe	Molière (adapted by Miles Malleson)	27. 6.50
(Bristol Old Vic)		
The Beggar's Opera	John Gay (realised by Benjamin Britten)	17. 7.50
View over The Park	C. P. Snow	30. 8.50
The Old Ladies	Rodney Ackland	2.10.50
Point of Departure	Anouilh (translated by Kitty Black)	1.11.50
(Transferred to Duke of York's Theatre)		
Let's Make an Opera	Benjamin Britten & Eric Crozier	9.12.50
The Silver Box	John Galsworthy	31. 1.51
Northern Ireland Festival Co:		
The Passing Day	George Shiels	20. 3.51
Danger Men Working	John D. Stewart	
The Sham Prince	Jack Loudon	
English Opera Group:		
The Beggar's Opera	Benjamin Britten	1. 5.51
Albert Herring		
Lyric Revue	Revue	26. 5.51
(Transferred to Globe Theatre)		
A Phoenix Too Frequent and	Christopher Fry	1.10.51
Thor with Angels		
Charles Dickens	(Adapted by Emlyn Williams)	29.10.51
(Transferred to Criterion Theatre)		
Summer and Smoke	Tennessee Williams	19.11.51
(Transferred to Duchess Theatre)		
Let's Make an Opera	Benjamin Britten & Eric Crozier	24.12.51
The Same Sky	Yvonne Mitchell	31. 1.52
(Transferred to Duke of York's Theatre)		
The Vortex	Noël Coward	4. 3.52
(Transferred to Criterion Theatre)		
Montserrat	Lillian Hellman	8. 4.52
Trelawney of The Wells	Pinero	12. 5.52
Libby Holman	Solo	22. 7.52
Théâtre de Mime Français	(Directed by Louis Ducreux)	29. 7.52
The River Line	Charles Morgan	2. 9.52
(Transferred to Strand Theatre)		
The Square Ring	Ralph Petersen	21.10.52
John Wright's Marionettes		24.11.52
Ballet Rambert		2.12.52
John Gielgud Season:		
Richard II	Shakespeare	24.12.52
The Way of The World	Congreve	18. 2.53
Venice Preserv'd	Otway	14. 5.53
The Belgian National Theatre:		
Ondine	Giraudoux	20. 7.53
Le Heros et le Soldat	Bernard Shaw	20. 7.53
A Doll's House	Ibsen (adapted by Peter Ashmore)	8. 9.53
Lanchester's Marionettes		1.12.53
At The Lyric	Revue	23.12.53
The Cherry Orchard	Chekhov (adapted by John Gielgud)	21. 5.54
Hedda Gabler	Ibsen (adapted by Max Faber)	6. 9.54
(Transferred to Westminster Theatre)		
Time Remembered	Anouilh (adapted by Patricia Moyes)	29.11.55
(Transferred to New Theatre)		
Skupa Puppets		11. 4.55
The Lark	Anouilh (adapted by Christopher Fry)	10. 4.55
The Buccaneer	Sandy Wilson	8. 9.55
(Transferred to Apollo Theatre)		
Misalliance	Bernard Shaw	8. 2.56

Envoi

from *The Times*,
29 March 1973

Enid Bagnold writes:

When Binkie winked at me out of the television on Thursday
night he was dead. "No use hoping", the wink said. "With all
my enormous power" (which he had never mentioned in his
life) "I can do no more for you, dear." It was the "you and I"
wink which so few men of power know how to give. He sat
on his throne (and at one time it *was* a throne) disguised as a
charming mouse. He was the romantic Mount Everest of my
theatrical struggles – its steepest face.

This secret, secret man, aged, one guessed, between 27 and
70, gave no detail of his life. He flashed, a six-sided glass object, this way and that. Except once, when about two years ago,
Lady Diana Cooper and he and I, during a long supper at the
Yvonne Arnaud Theatre, he suddenly talked of pain and drink
and death. Just as though he had never fenced himself in.

I was fond of him. I wish he had been fond of me. But this
one could never know. Playwrights, maybe, were not his
closest friends. The "word" was dim to him. What he knew
was whether the Whole would appeal (and not in a low sense),
how it should be worked, and when, and who should be its
ministers. One couldn't believe, when one gossiped with him,
that he would not seek one's company the next day, or allow
one to seek his. But so it was. He gossiped in fascinating
intimacy – and disappeared. Much, and with the same disappointed surprise, as he has disappeared now.

Paul Scofield read that tribute at the Memorial Service held at
St. Paul's, Covent Garden, the Actors Church, where all the
stars of the theatrical profession gathered to say their
farewells. The name of Hugh Beaumont is carved on one of
the oak panels near the entrance but like Christopher Wren's in
another place, Binkie's real monument can be seen on the
walls of the Globe Theatre where hang the framed posters of
the productions he created over an unparalleled career. "We
shall not look upon his like again."

Index